War Room

ALSO BY MICHAEL HOLLEY

Red Sox Rule

Patriot Reign

War Room

*The Legacy of Bill Belichick and
the Art of Building the Perfect Team*

Michael Holley

HARPER LUXE

An Imprint of HarperCollinsPublishers

WAR ROOM. Copyright © 2011 by Michael Holley. All rights reserved. Printed in the United States of America. No part of this book may be used or reproduced in any manner whatsoever without written permission except in the case of brief quotations embodied in critical articles and reviews. For information address HarperCollins Publishers, 10 East 53rd Street, New York, NY 10022.

HarperCollins books may be purchased for educational, business, or sales promotional use. For information please write: Special Markets Department, HarperCollins Publishers, 10 East 53rd Street, New York, NY 10022.

FIRST HARPERLUXE EDITION

HarperLuxe™ is a trademark of HarperCollins Publishers

Library of Congress Cataloging-in-Publication Data is available upon request.

ISBN: 978-0-06-208887-1

11 12 13 14 ID/OPM 10 9 8 7 6 5 4 3 2 1

For my sons, Robinson and Beckham

Contents

1.
The Incubator

Bill Belichick, the dark-haired and youthful head coach of the Cleveland Browns, was full of ideas. Some, such as how he planned to limit the access of the media, were shamelessly lifted from the New York Giants, where he had spent a dozen years as an assistant coach. Others were original, simply a new coach's vision of what he wanted his team to be. It was the Big Idea, though, that was most ironic for Belichick in 1991.

The perception in northeast Ohio was that the thirty-nine-year-old coach, the NFL's youngest, was not a strong communicator. People used his press conferences as all the proof they needed. The first-year coach would seem bored as he sat or stood before the media giving shrugs, eye rolls, and terse answers to lengthy questions. But behind the scenes, Belichick was making clear communication his top Browns priority. In fact, it was how he planned to reconstruct one of the NFL's worst teams.

He quickly noticed that the Browns' pro and college scouts were not speaking the same language. There was one grading scale for evaluating the pros and an entirely different one for analyzing collegians. Even worse, in his opinion, there was no organizational identity. After all the scouting, who were the Browns trying to be? It seemed to him that there wasn't a good systematic answer to the question, so that became one of his missions: Build one player-evaluation system, for pro and college players alike, that always provided an instant snapshot of who a player was and whether he was capable of helping the Cleveland Browns. When the system was perfected, the coach imagined, everyone in the organization would be able to glance at a couple of numbers and letters on a scouting report and know exactly what type of player was being discussed.

The easiest part of the plan was that the architect knew what he wanted. He told Mike Lombardi, his player personnel director, that he envisioned a big, strong, fast team that was capable of performing in any weather. He wanted a team that wouldn't be distracted by playing at least ten Rust Belt games each season: eight in Cleveland Stadium, which sat on the edge of the unpredictable shores of Lake Erie, and one game apiece in Cincinnati and Pittsburgh, both cold-weather cities with open-air stadiums that overlooked the Ohio River. He wanted a team that could answer the no-nonsense, gladiatorial style of the Steelers one week and then go to Houston, another divisional rival, a week later and not be confused by the unusual formations employed by the Oilers since they operated in a place, the Astrodome, where the temperature was always the same.

It was good that Belichick brought Lombardi specifics. But building and programming a unique system was going to require some after-hours work for both of them. While Belichick had been the defensive coordinator of two celebrated Super Bowl–winning defenses in New York, including one the previous season, he had no interest in copying the Giants' scouting manual. He liked parts of it, but at times he thought it was too rigid and unnecessarily eliminated good players from draft consideration. He admired the grading system that Gil Brandt, the longtime Cowboys personnel man, had instituted in Dallas. For Belichick, Brandt's scale made the Dallas system tangible, so even if the Browns were looking for different players from the Cowboys, they could use the Dallas scale as a sketch for where they were trying to go.

Lombardi was entering his fifth season working with the Browns when Belichick arrived, and he hadn't met him before. He soon learned that not every idea Belichick had was one that he wanted to see in place the next day. He was a thinker who liked to deliberately weigh information, listen to a variety of opinions, and then make decisions. Those personality traits alone would ensure that his overhaul of the Browns' infrastructure was going to take time. It would also be an extended process because the system he wanted was, in the words of Lombardi, "the equivalent of a race car that could be modified and become adaptable to any course you asked it to run."

There were also some generational dynamics that had to be taken into account with the restructuring. Belichick planned to rely on the smarts and experience of his veteran scouts, men who were evaluating players when he was still in junior high school. But there was also the reality that even with the best intentions, scouts in their midfifties and early sixties weren't going to totally embrace a new way of doing business. That new way was fluid, and it might change two or three times in the next couple years before Belichick and Lombardi were comfortable with it. Scouts such as Dom Anile, Ron Marciniak, and Ernie Plank *knew* that their way worked, so it wasn't realistic to ask them to buy into something that wasn't even finished.

What Belichick needed was the wisdom of the scouts he had, as well as an influx of young, bright employees who would be "raised" in the Cleveland system. It was yet another idea he had when he took the job. He believed in developing scouts and coaches by hiring them for entry-level positions and then seeing if they could graduate from unofficial apprenticeships. The thought was that true football intellect and hunger could be displayed even while doing grunt work. And if the young employees were good at one thing, they would keep taking on responsibilities until they found their rightful place in the organization.

After the three-win team Belichick inherited won six games in 1991, the coach reached out to one of those gifted youth. Scott Pioli was a twenty-seven-year-old defensive line coach at Murray State, and Belichick offered him a $16,000-per-year job as a scouting assistant. The Cleveland job was a pay cut from Murray, where Pioli had once been so cash-strapped that he sold parts of his prized childhood baseball card collection so he could pay his less than $200 monthly rent. Pioli was a friend of a friend, and the report that Belichick got years earlier was that all the kid wanted was a career in football. He was an all–New England defensive tackle at Central Connecticut and he looked the part: He stood six feet tall, and even at ease, he appeared to have just finished three sets of bench presses.

Pioli thought he wanted to be a coach toward the end of his college playing days, and when he first met Belichick, he soaked up whatever he could from the brain of the Giants' defense. When he told Belichick he was commuting 120 miles each day from his hometown of Washingtonville, New York, to watch the Giants in training camp, Belichick told him he was welcome to sleep on the spare couch in the dorm room that Belichick shared with Giants assistant Al Groh.

"He had absolutely nothing to gain by that relationship, or by that offer," Pioli says. "He offered me something that was truly no strings attached. I couldn't do anything for him. Nothing. Zero. Zilch. The defensive coordinator of the Giants offered some kid from Central Connecticut a place to stay so he didn't have to travel as much and could watch multiple days of practice and film? That told me something about the guy."

Five years after his first meeting with Belichick, Pioli now had a chance to work for him. He had the option of leaving tiny Murray in western Kentucky for the NFL stage, and there was a proposal from the 49ers, too. It really didn't matter what was going on in

San Francisco. He was already loyal to the head coach of the Browns and he was going to work for him.

He would fit right in with the culture that was developing in the organization, with a hyper-focus on the job and no regard for the accumulation of hours spent working at it or thinking about it. While at Murray, Pioli had been so locked on and lost in his assignments that he was unaware of world events. Once, he had been on the road for three days recruiting, staying in cheap hotels and driving hundreds of miles in a car that had just a gravelly AM radio, when someone finally told him what the rest of the country had been buzzing about: America was at war in the Persian Gulf. He had no idea.

Initially, Pioli brought the same singular intensity to his new job. But as driven as Belichick was about football and reshaping the Browns, he sometimes pulled Pioli, who was single, aside and offered advice on how to approach having a family in the uncertain NFL.

"You're going to get fired in this business," Belichick told him. "You're going to quit. You're going to get fired and run out of more jobs than you can count. This just isn't a business where you last. Sometimes it's in your control, but most of the time it's not. If you're going to have a family, make sure you have someplace that your family can always call home. They need that one stable place, a place that they know they can go back to every year and it will be there forever."

Even then, with Belichick just one season into a five-year contract, he had a sense that Cleveland was not going to be that forever place. For his wife and three young children, the place to establish roots was already Nantucket, the small island south of the Massachusetts cape.

Pioli tucked away the words. He was a long way from marriage and Nantucket, especially on that salary. Most of the time when he was at work, he had the echoes of a brief exchange with Belichick ringing in his head. He had tried to thank the head coach for the opportunity in Cleveland, and he was cut off before he could finish the thought.

"Just thank me by doing a good job," Belichick said, ending the conversation.

For Pioli, that meant learning to do a few tasks at once and making sure all of them were as detailed as Belichick and Lombardi demanded. When he was required to drive players to the Cleveland Clinic for extensive physicals, he knew that he could be at the hospital anywhere from ninety minutes to three hours. So he would bring stacks of paperwork with him, and while he waited, he would alphabetize files; highlight key information from SportScan, the league news feed that was faxed to teams daily; and pull statistics from media guides. In between, he usually did some unconventional scouting and took notes: He always paid attention to how players interacted with doctors, nurses, and any other non-football people they came across at the clinic.

He wasn't always in work mode, and when he wasn't you could hear it for five or ten minutes. He and one of the Browns' volunteers in scouting, twenty-year-old Jay Muraco, became buddies instantly. They both appreciated a wide range of music as well as the prankster humor of the Jerky Boys. Whenever they put on a bit called "Car Salesman," which makes a reference to an area close to Pioli's hometown, they would laugh and anyone walking by would laugh with them. Even though there wasn't a huge age difference between them, Muraco looked up to Pioli. Sometimes Pioli would give Muraco assignments and use the same guidelines that Belichick used on him: Do a good job, and there will be more to come. If not, well, we'll move on to something else.

"We had these sheet-metal tags for the draft board, and you had to manually put the names of the players on them with a sticker," says Muraco. "One time Scott asked me to work on it, and I thought I did a pretty good job. But I looked in the draft room later and he was straightening everything I had done. I guess they were crooked. He asked me to help him out with other things after that, but not the tags."

Pioli's job description was proving to be exactly what Belichick said it was: a little of this and a little of that. Sometimes he was the handyman who fixed the jammed fax machine; sometimes he watched film. He and other employees, some his age and some thirty years older, were so focused on turning around the Browns that there was no time to realize that the team's office was filling with future stars. The problem was that the stars weren't on the field. The coaching staff had Nick Saban and Kirk Ferentz. The scouting department had Terry McDonough, Jim Schwartz, and Lionel Vital. Ozzie Newsome, the former Browns tight end, was available to both groups as he tried to figure out which he loved more, coaching or personnel.

"I'll tell you what it was: It was a great football think tank," Lombardi says.

The Browns who played on Sundays were a different story, and there was some local disagreement over why the team had finished just 7-9 in Belichick's second season. In the eyes of Clevelanders, the Browns shouldn't have been so far away. They had played for the conference championship just two years before Belichick was hired, and they still had quarterback Bernie

Kosar, the city's most popular athlete. Kosar had a lifetime goodwill pass from the fans, as much for what he had said as how he played. He was a local boy, from just outside of Youngstown, who had gone big time. He played his college football at the other Miami, not the university three hundred miles from his hometown but the one fifteen hundred miles away in sunny Coral Gables. He led the Hurricanes to a national championship as a redshirt freshman and was a second-team All-American and fourth-place Heisman finisher as a sophomore.

He was also smart. After just three years of college, he was a few courses shy of graduating. That's when he got Cleveland's attention: He stood up and told the nation that he wanted to be a Brown. The city was forever defensive about the recurring Cleveland jokes that everyone in other cities seemed to tell, so Kosar's words made him a hero before he ever played a game. And when he fought the NFL and intentionally bypassed the regular draft so he could be eligible for the supplemental one, in which Cleveland had maneuvered for the first pick, he automatically gained a city full of protectors. Bernie was theirs. Any problems the Browns had would never be placed on Bernie's shoulders.

Except Belichick didn't quite see Kosar, or the team, the way the city saw them. He didn't think it was a fluke that the Browns had gone 3-13 the year before he got the job. He saw a roster that couldn't easily be shaped into the type of team he told Lombardi he wanted. In Kosar, he saw an intelligent leader who was becoming more and more physically limited, especially with an ankle that was broken twice in 1992. Belichick didn't say that publicly, at least not for a while, but it didn't matter: If the average Browns fan had to blame someone for the team losing, and the candidates were Kosar and Belichick, everyone knew that was a landslide.

But the task of restocking the Browns became a lot easier after the 1992 season. In September of '92, a federal judge in Minneapolis named David Doty ruled that the NFL's version of free agency was illegal. Before the ruling, the Browns and every other team in the league were allowed to designate thirty-seven of their forty-five players as protected. Even if a player's contract had expired, his original team maintained right of first refusal on any contract offers and was obligated to receive compensation if a player signed elsewhere. It was called Plan B free agency, and Doty ruled that it was restraint of trade and violated antitrust laws. The ruling meant that true free agency would exist the next season. It was good news for bad teams like the Browns, who struggled to find thirty-seven players whom they actually *wanted* to protect.

Through their first two drafts in Cleveland, Belichick and Lombardi had been spotty. They had selected Eric Turner, a physical safety who fit the blueprint for what they were looking for, with the second overall pick in '91. But their second-rounder, guard Ed King, was a bust. The next year was worse. The first four picks were Tommy Vardell, Patrick Rowe, Bill Johnson, and Gerald Dixon. Only one, Johnson, came close to being an impact player in Cleveland.

That's why free agency was so important for the Browns, and it's why they set their sights on the biggest prize available. Reggie White, a Hall of Fame–caliber defensive end in Philadelphia, was a free agent on tour for the best fit and the best contract. Cleveland had one of the early high bids, surprising since team owner Art Modell would soon complain of financial troubles. But ultimately White, an ordained minister, said God led him to Green Bay and greenbacks, and he signed a $17 million deal with the Packers. The Browns' major free-agent signing was more controversial and considerably cheaper: Vinny Testaverde, who lost a quarterback competition to Kosar when both were college kids in Miami, was coming to compete with him again. He said he was comfortable being Kosar's backup in Cleveland, but the Browns weren't thinking that way. They signed him to a one-year deal for $2.5 million, which was $1 million more than he made the previous season as a starter.

Pioli's first year in the NFL had been quite an education. He learned a lot about the constant tension between team executives and the media by following the way Belichick was covered. If it wasn't already an open secret, it would be during the 1993 season: The coach had dramatically reduced the media's access, so in turn he wasn't going to get any slack from the press. They would have to praise through clenched teeth if Belichick's Browns put together a winning season. Anything short of that would bring them back to the villain, for whom they already had scripts written.

There was also plenty to learn by watching the veteran scouts. Pioli adored them, and they reciprocated because he was eager to learn and willing to listen. One of his favorites was a local, born and raised just forty minutes away in industrial Barberton. He was fifty-eight, but he was in better shape than most people in the office due to his football genes and his obsession with playing racquetball. There were many ways to describe his personality, but his nickname said it all: Bulldog.

"A man's man," says Vital. "The kind of guy who wouldn't back down from anything. He'd invite you to his home for a meal and had a beautiful heart, but you just knew he wasn't going to let you handle him any kind of way."

"Old-school guy all the way," says Belichick. "Very focused, very tough, and a hard grader. If *he* said a player was tough, you could take that to the bank."

His given name was Thomas George Dimitroff, but most people used that appropriate nickname or just "Tom." Pioli called him "Mr. D." The stories about him were legendary. His parents, immigrants from Macedonia and Hungary, used to own a restaurant-bar in nearby Portage Lakes called Van's Blue Gill. Tom, with his short-sleeved white dress shirt, skinny black tie, and horn-rimmed glasses, was often behind the bar serving drinks and food. He was a shade under six feet tall and was two hundred pounds of muscle. He was a gentleman and a brawler: Any hint of trouble at last call would lead to the removal of his glasses, and magically, it would seem as if the rowdies were seeing him for the first time. They always knew to stop the nonsense when the glasses came off.

Some people in Barberton remembered him as Tommy George, from the days when his parents believed that Americanizing their last name would lead to less grief for the family. But he was such a good high school quarterback that it wasn't long before *Duh-mitt-troff* was rolling off local tongues. He got a scholarship to play at Miami University, the in-state one, and played for future Notre Dame coach Ara Parseghian. He was actually drafted by the Browns in 1957, the same year the team selected Jim Brown in the first round, but instead played professionally in Canada. He had a brief stay in the AFL with the expansion Boston Patriots and was retired by the time he was twenty-five.

His parents wanted him to be an electrician, something that would provide steady work. But he was too competitive, and after helping out at Van's for a while, he got into coaching. By 1974, he was an assistant coach in the CFL as the offensive coordinator for the Ottawa Rough Riders. Two years later, his team won the Super Bowl of Canada, the Grey Cup. Between pro coaching opportunities in Hamilton; a head coaching stint at the University of Guelph, about an hour away from Toronto; and the chance to scout and pick players in Ottawa, Tom Dimitroff and his family stayed in Canada for fourteen years. Anyone who played for him knew what a stickler he was for details and how he had no tolerance for players who put themselves above the team and didn't want to listen.

Anyone who lived with him could tell you that, too.

"If I was ever bringing any of my friends to the house, I'd warn them before we went in there," says his son Thomas. "I'd say, 'Don't just grunt something out there.' He was an old-school coach, a disciplinarian. If you didn't call him 'Coach Dimitroff' or 'Mr. Dimitroff,' it bothered him and there'd be a problem."

Not only did the youngest of Tom and Helen Dimitroff's three children share his father's name, he also wanted to be in the same profession. Young Thomas idolized his father and inherited his intensity. When his father brought home six oversized bags that are typically used for sharpening football techniques, Thomas spent the entire summer doing bag drills. He was fourteen. His brother, Randy, who was four years older and a better athlete, told him to relax and be a kid. He wasn't interested. What really excited him was sneaking out to night practices at Guelph, where Tom was the head coach and Randy was a quarterback. Tom would sometimes glare across the field and ask him what he was doing there, but he'd always let him stay, knowing the familiar look of someone smitten by a game.

By the time Thomas graduated from high school and went to play at Guelph as a cornerback-safety, his father had taken a scouting job with the Browns. Randy was still there, so they were able to play one season together. After that, Thomas was on his own and he emerged as a team captain. But despite all his drills, and despite meticulously watching the Dallas Cowboys on TV because he loved cornerback Everson Walls's ability to backpedal and anticipate, he knew what was coming. He didn't just inherit Tom's intensity; he had his honesty, too. He wasn't good enough to play in the NFL or CFL. His future was in coaching or evaluating players. He already knew it, and he'd overheard his parents, one of them the NFL scout in the family, confirm it.

"Let's face it, Helen," his father had said. "Tommy's smart and works his ass off, but he's an average athlete."

Average? It wasn't exactly the analysis he wanted to hear but he agreed it was the right one. When he graduated in 1990, he began scouting in Canada. Three years later, at the start of the 1993 NFL season, he was working side by side in Cleveland with his father. In theory, at least.

While the man known as Bulldog was continuing to scout for the toughest players in the country, his twenty-six-year-old son was a first-year member of the Browns' grounds crew. Thomas had gained scouting experience in Saskatchewan and in the NFL-backed World League of American Football. He wasn't above getting dirty for the job, so when the World League folded he leapt at the part-time opportunity in a city his parents called home. Four days a week, Thomas was like any other groundskeeper the Browns employed at the suburban practice facility: His sandy brown hair was usually filled with grass blades and paint; he limed the field; he sprayed fertilizer; he did his best to avoid swirling neurotoxins.

But he had a couple things going on that many of his landscaping coworkers weren't aware of, although Belichick was. The most impressive thing he could say was that he had access to the Browns' files on college players. That's because he had Belichick's blessing to look at the files, even though he was working part time for another team. Thomas was a part-time weekend scout for the Kansas City Chiefs. What it meant was that he scouted Ohio and Pennsylvania, all via car trips, from Friday through Sunday.

Belichick knew that Thomas was watching tape in the office, but he didn't mind because it didn't interfere with what the Browns were doing and he had great respect for his father. It's also why Thomas the Groundskeeper, full of funk and ambition, was allowed to pop into scouting and talk with his father, if he was in town. Sometimes he'd go in there, toting his vegan lunch, to talk with Pioli and Muraco.

"Oh, we all remember what it was like when he'd come in," says Muraco. "He'd have all this dust on him, he'd be wearing dirty shorts, and he'd have paint on his chin. If I was filing reports, he'd sit there and help me file them. Sometimes we'd order food from a place called Bucci's, an Italian restaurant in Berea, and we'd be eating chicken parm and rigatoni. He'd pull out a Tupperware container full of rice and tomatoes. It was always a good time when he was around."

As the Browns approached the midway point of the '93 season, it was hard for most people to complain.

The team had begun the season with its best start under Belichick, 3-0, and was 5-2 heading into its bye week after a satisfying win over its most hated rival, Pittsburgh. Cleveland and Pittsburgh were separated by just 130 miles, so while the rest of the NFL gave respectful nods from afar to the Steelers for the four Super Bowls they'd won in a six-year span, Cleveland was the empty-handed neighbor forced to stand by and watch the frequent celebrations. No one had to be reminded that the Steelers had basically lived at the Super Bowl while the Browns had never been. It was that void that made a loyal fan base even more manic, and it's why the recent mini-drought of losing seasons was so irritating.

While Belichick had named Bernie Kosar the starter for the 1993 season, his actions seemed to suggest that his heart was elsewhere. At the hint of any struggles from Kosar, Belichick would pull him and replace him with Vinny Testaverde. Objectively, Testaverde looked better on the job. His arm was stronger and he was more mobile, although he didn't have Kosar's ability to quickly diagnose what defenses were trying to do to him. After being pulled from three straight games, Kosar saw the inevitable happen. He lost his starting job to Testaverde. But the only negative to the Steelers win was that Testaverde was simultaneously crushed by two linebackers and separated his right shoulder. He was out for the season, so by default, the job was Kosar's again.

Temporarily.

On November 7, an unforgettable Monday in Cleveland, the Browns held a 5-3 record after coming out of their bye with a loss to Denver. They were in first place in their division. On that same day, they cut Kosar, a move that hurt many Clevelanders more than all the combined heartache the organization had suffered since 1964, when the Browns last won a title. This wasn't just painful in their eyes. This was a crime against the family. This was disrespectful. Bernie *was* Cleveland: big, sprawling, and unconventional at first sight, but after you looked around for a while, a lot better than you thought.

But nine seasons into Kosar's career, Belichick had announced that his skills had diminished. This was personal. Kosar had won division titles for them, gotten them to the cusp of the Super Bowl three times. They'd written songs about him, taking the melody of Richard Berry's classic "Louie Louie" and making a new song called "Bernie Bernie." *Bernie Bernie / Oh yeah / How you can throw* . . . It was as if everything Belichick said about Kosar he was saying to them, too. What do you mean *we're* diminished? What do you mean *we're* not good enough for this team? Who the hell are you?

Some fans dragged out their grills and set their season tickets on fire. A twenty-year-old student at Baldwin-Wallace College, just down the road from the Browns' practice facility, paced outside with a huge sign: CUT BELICHICK, NOT BERNIE. When she was asked to elaborate in an interview she said, "Bernie Kosar is the heart and soul of the Cleveland Browns. Bill Belichick bites the big one."

Belichick was right by saying Kosar's skills had diminished, but he was still the best quarterback he had, especially with Testaverde out. Many years later, he would be faced with another quarterback controversy and he would handle it much differently. But this was a public-relations nightmare from which he wouldn't recover.

Modell publicly backed his coach, for the second time in less than a month. The first sign of support came in late October when he extended Belichick's contract by two years, which meant he would theoretically have him coaching the Browns through 1997. But Modell was no real ally. Few people in Cleveland knew what a financial mess the owner had gotten himself into, and no one could have guessed what his solution was going to be. Modell not only was left out of the new downtown stadium/arena projects for the Indians and Cavaliers, he lost significant income when he was no longer the Indians' landlord. It wouldn't be long before he started having secret meetings with another city about the piles of yet-to-be-claimed cash it had earmarked for a pro football team, and those meetings would eventually lure him out of town, with the entire franchise in tow.

The Browns lost five of their next six games after releasing Kosar, practically guaranteeing Belichick's third consecutive losing season. The team needed help with everything: the stadium, ownership, players, dialogue with the public. The words that Belichick delivered to Pioli a year earlier seemed much sharper now. A long run in the NFL was hard enough and even harder if you were bold enough to make decisions that could turn an entire region against you.

Once again, the season ended without a trip to the playoffs. The Browns were 7-9 for the second year in a row. Belichick and Lombardi had agreed that their scouting system might go through some starts and stops before it finally flourished, and that was proving to be true through the 1994 draft. The issue was franchise-altering, impactful players. The Browns had drafted one, arguably, from 1991 to 1994, and that was Turner, Belichick's first Cleveland draft pick. They had six selections in the top thirty in that period without hitting on one who could be considered the best at his position in the league.

They had worked out some of the language issues, getting the pro and college scouting departments on the same page in terms of how a player was described. They all knew the alerts of the system, from the lowercase "a" (which meant there was some type of concern about a player's age) to the uppercase "Z" (which meant that a player lacked the required size or height according to the height/weight/speed organizational charts). The problem was swinging on draft day, when they didn't necessarily swing and miss but they came up with a lot of harmless singles.

The percentages were much better in free agency, where in back-to-back years Belichick had brought in two of his smartest defensive players from the Giants. Carl Banks and Pepper Johnson were everything Belichick wanted in linebackers: studious, instinctive, and big. Both were outliers to that old saw: Those who can do do; those who can't teach. They could do and teach, which gave them credibility with coaches and players.

There was a good feel to the beginning of the 1994 season. Testaverde was healthy again, so there was no quarterback drama to keep up with. Kosar had won a Super Bowl ring as a backup with the Cowboys after being cut by the Browns, and now he had returned to his college home to be a backup with the Dolphins. The issue was over for three hours every Sunday, but it would always be a regional talking point.

On game days, the only thing to discuss was the Browns' defense. Nick Saban, who was as close to being Belichick's coaching twin as anyone in sports, had the unit playing better than any in the league. It helped that Saban got a Pro Bowl season out of Turner, but he also coaxed one out of Johnson, just the second of the thirty-year-old inside linebacker's career. In November, after beating the Oilers by 24 points, the Browns had their ninth win, securing the first winning season of Belichick's career. Cleveland finished 11-5 and allowed 204 points, the fewest in the league. The last time a Browns defense had such sparkling numbers was the 1950s, when they were coached by Hall of Famer Paul Brown.

The 1994 season's high and low points came in consecutive weeks. On New Year's Day 1995, the Browns won their first play-off game since 1989 with a wild-card victory over the New England Patriots, who were coached by Belichick's former boss Bill Parcells. The next week, the Browns went to see their rivals, the Steelers, and were easily rubbed out, 29–9.

Thomas left the Browns to take a scouting job with the Lions, moving to Atlanta to become their Southeast scout in 1994. He got insight on the Browns' productive season from talks with his father and Pioli. He missed joking with Pioli at the office and seeing his father, and his extended family, so often when he lived in Ohio. The positive was that when his father was on the road scouting, he had a connection to the family, because sometimes they'd be scouting at the same schools. They'd talk about players, have dinner, and make fun of each other.

Tom always told his sons and his players about the importance of being on time. So Thomas loved it when he would arrive on campus forty-five minutes to an hour before his father did. "I see how it is," Thomas would say, pointing to his watch. "Slacking off a bit this morning, huh?" When Tom learned that his son was a vegan, he'd tease him about what he was, or wasn't, eating. "Berries and twigs today?" he'd ask. "Or 'too-fu'?" But then the ultimate meat-and-potatoes man, in a meat-and-potatoes business, would mention that he loved the fact that his son had principles and was sticking to them.

Tom liked that his son and Pioli took the time to truly listen to what they were told, sometimes to a fault. When Thomas moved to Atlanta, his father told him that any full-time scout in the league needed a reliable car. The obvious choice was his father's favorite, the Ford Taurus. Thomas got a cobalt-blue one, quickly became conscious of how uncool it was, and told the half-truth that it was a "company car" when he took women out on dates. Car tips aside, Tom gave his younger son business survival tips, often using his own mistakes as lesson plans.

"Keep doing what you're doing and you'll be fine," he told his son. "And know when to express yourself and when to bite your tongue. I probably could have done a few more things in this game if I had held my tongue more often."

On a few occasions he would tell Helen, "If you're lucky in this life, you can count your true friends on one hand . . . Thomas has got a true friend in Scott."

It was yet another example of superior advance scouting, because Tom couldn't have realized just how prophetic his words would turn out to be.

Although everyone could see Tom's toughness, and his nickname suggested that he didn't have much nuance, he could surprise you away from the office. His wife, whom he met in Barberton, was his best friend. They loved to spend hours in their garden or take road trips to flea markets and antique shops, where Helen could look at the Victorian furniture that she was partial to. None of the other scouts would have been able to grasp the image of the Bulldog in an antique shop. The man they knew was tireless in talking about football and playing racquetball. Whenever he talked to his older son, Randy, and he knew that a visit was coming, he'd always end the conversation with "Bring your racquet."

"He wouldn't stop at five games," Helen says. "If you'd let him, he'd go to seven or eight."

As the Browns headed into 1995, Belichick's fifth season, Tom felt refreshed. He was fifty-nine, still as active and athletic as ever. Early in the year, a couple months before the April draft, he was on the road and played a half dozen rigorous games of racquetball as usual. What wasn't normal was that, after the games, his body was telling him that he had to urinate yet he still couldn't go.

He told Helen about it when he got home, and she said it was something they definitely needed to monitor. Soon after, there was another problem. He was scheduled to leave town again for at least a week, but he was starting to wonder what was going on. He called Helen into the bathroom. "Oh my God," he said. "You've got to see this."

He had been able to go this time, but the toilet was filled with blood.

"Don't panic," he said to Helen.

"I'm not panicking," she replied, trying her hardest to be calm. "But you can't go on the road in the morning. We need to see a doctor."

What they learned was that Tom had a massive, ten-inch cancerous tumor, about the length of a football, around his kidneys. Doctors were able to remove the tumor and kept Tom in the hospital for a week. About six weeks later, he was playing racquetball again.

Tom and Helen Dimitroff, who had led a football life and raised a football family for more than thirty years, weren't thinking about the sport as much as usual at the start of the '95 season. Tom had been doing well since the scare in March. But the hardest thing for him to come to terms with at that time was the emotional separation he had been forced to make from the Browns.

They had fired him.

His mind was as sharp as ever and no one knew the game better. He was well liked by most and fairly paid, but by no means was his salary burdensome. Lombardi was in charge of the scouting department, and there were times when he and Tom didn't see things the same way. Everyone who had been around Tom knew that he was a passionate defender of his positions and was much more in favor of raw opinions than diplomatic filters. There were arguments with Lombardi, and often they'd become heated and personal. The dismissal of Tom led to some intense conversations when all of the Dimitroffs were together. There was considerable time spent trying to sort out some of the feelings they had toward Lombardi.

"I had a lot of respect for Tom, and I know I could have handled the situation a lot better," Lombardi says. "I made some mistakes. I take full responsibility for them."

It was a challenging time for the Dimitroffs because the family members were in different places. Randy was in Canada, Thomas was in Atlanta, and while their sister, Sharon, was in the Strongsville area, where Tom and Helen lived, she was there raising her own young family. Being away from his father was a source of guilt for Thomas, who went back and forth on whether he should leave his job with the Lions. Both Tom and Helen told him the thought was ridiculous and that they'd be fine. They also let him know that they were getting unsolicited visits from Pioli.

There were times when Pioli would make the short drive to Strongsville just to sit and talk football with a lifelong player, coach, and scout. Sometimes, that's all the Bulldog needed. Their talks could be profound or trivial, like the time Tom spent a few minutes trying to persuade Pioli to incorporate bison jerky into his diet. To make these visits, Pioli would take his multitasking to a higher level so he could get all his work done and still make time for people whom he considered family.

Tom wasn't working with the hometown team anymore, but there hadn't been anything alarming with his health for a few months. His follow-up visits and checkups were all clean, and he even found time to play a few racquetball games in September and October. After playing one day he said to Helen, "I don't feel good."

"Tom, you're not twenty-one anymore," she answered. "Maybe you should play fewer games."

"No, I don't think that's it. I just don't feel like myself."

Their wedding anniversary was October 28, and they were planning to celebrate out with some friends. But Helen noticed that Tom wasn't quite right, so she told him that they could cancel and stay in for the night.

"I think we should go," he said. "Something tells me this may be the last time we get the chance to do it."

They did go out that night, and everyone could see it. The Tom they knew was the guy who once had a taco-eating contest with a coach and was jubilant when he won, 14 to 13. He was someone who would go through three or four bottles of Tabasco sauce a year because he'd pour the blazing stuff all over his plate. He was the one who went crazy for his wife's Hungarian stuffed peppers, and he'd clean those medium-hot banana peppers himself because when Helen tried they brought tears to her eyes. His foods had spice, and so did he. He was a presence. He told great stories and enjoyed a muscular laugh as much as anyone. But none of it was there that night. He was quieter than his wife and friends had ever remembered, seemingly drifting elsewhere.

He went to see his doctor again, in November, and was given a CAT scan. When they got the news, they were speechless. The tumor had returned and spread throughout his abdomen. He had renal-cell carcinoma. It was too much for even a world-class hospital like the Cleveland Clinic to control.

"How long do I have?" Tom asked.

He was still a coach, a scout, a tough guy. He had a way of getting answers to questions that aren't normally answered. He wanted the truth or the best guess at it.

"It doesn't look good," he was told. "Maybe two months."

There wasn't a lot they could or wanted to say. Helen immediately thought of alternative therapies and made appointments with an acupuncturist. They told their children, and all of them tried to visit when they could, adjusting work and family schedules. Pioli heard the news and didn't wait for the family to ask for anything. He wanted to know when Tom needed to go to the clinic, and when he found out, he'd be the one to take him. When Tom was at home, covered in blankets in his den and simply in need of a football conversation, Pioli was there. No questions asked.

"My mom didn't like to drive down to the Cleveland Clinic, and my dad was in a really bad place," Thomas says. "And there's Scott, you know, in a very precarious situation, working at a place that had let go of my father but still taking time away from there and letting it be known to them that he was being a friend.

"His humanity was more important than a job. And I think he understood that if *this* was crossing the line, he could get a job somewhere else and still be able to look [at] himself in the mirror. Scott was taking my dad to chemotherapy. I know my mom will forever remember that."

There was a less important precariousness at the office but one that still had deflated the entire region. The news had finally broken about Modell and the Browns. They were moving to Baltimore. Modell was seduced by the reality of making twice as much in stadium revenue in Baltimore as he had in Cleveland. He had slyly met with Maryland politicians for months, once having an entire meeting on a private jet while never leaving the tarmac. After having their letters and phone calls unreturned, Ohio politicians began to sniff out what Modell was up to in late September. It was confirmed in November. He had gone to Maryland, signed the Browns over to that state, and naively thought that the story wouldn't get out until the Browns were safely out of town.

Headlines screamed, and fans and talk-radio hosts screamed louder. The Browns, fixtures on Sunday afternoons since 1946, were leaving. They were 4-4 when the news leaked. Afterward, they went 1-7. No one's job was safe, Belichick and Pioli included.

Tom Dimitroff had already lost his job, then his team, and now he was fighting for his life.

In his last days, he sometimes sounded like himself. That was if he could muster the strength and be lucid through all the drugs he took to dull his pain. On those days, he still had words for his family. He asked

Thomas and Randy to please find it in their hearts to forgive the Cleveland Browns. He loved all his children, and he was particularly moved that his sons were so protective of their father. But he had advice that was initially tough for them to hear.

"Forgive Mike Lombardi," Tom had whispered.

He learned that friends, former players, and prayer warriors whom he didn't know were praying for him. He was touched by their phone calls and letters. "You know what, Helen?" he said one day. "I'm sorry the Lord is taking me now because I have so much witnessing to do for Him."

After Christmas and New Year's, he got weaker. What he wanted at that point was to be comfortable and around his family. He knew he was going to die, and he didn't want to do it in hospice care. Thomas wrote a song for him, "Dad, My Hero," and sang it to him, strumming a guitar. Tom smiled and tears welled. He slept for long hours at home, and as he slept, a wooden cross was placed on his chest. It was a reference to one of his favorite gospel songs, "The Old Rugged Cross."

It wouldn't be long.

"I'll never forget when we were all gathered around him," Thomas says. "My mom had to deliver the message of what the doctors had told her. They didn't expect him to make it longer than a couple days. And my dad said, in the calmest voice, 'Helen, I'm going home. This is what I've been praying for.'"

Thomas pauses for several seconds as he recalls the story. He tries to continue the thought without becoming emotional but can't: "In that moment, you definitely feel God's presence . . . I don't know . . . I still tear up about it . . ."

Thomas George Dimitroff Sr. died on January 20, 1996. He was sixty.

His funeral was on a harsh, gray, and icy day in northeast Ohio. They were the kind of conditions he would have expected his players to execute in without excuses. Many of those players were there, as pallbearers carrying his casket to its final resting place. One of the pallbearers was Scott Pioli.

There had been a bit of a family stir earlier when Lombardi had arrived to pay his respects. But Thomas remembered the words of his father, and although he still had questions about how things ended with the Browns, he greeted Lombardi warmly.

At the grave site, five minutes from where Tom had gone to high school, a singer performed "Amazing Grace." As the casket was lowered into the ground, a man approached Helen Dimitroff. It was Bill Belichick. He knew then that he wasn't going to be a part of the Browns' future, but he felt compelled to apologize for their past. The Browns hadn't had a good 1995, from the dismissal of an ailing Tom Dimitroff to sneaking out of town. They were just a few weeks away from dismissing Belichick, too.

Belichick said he was sorry for the way things were handled with her husband and best friend, and apologized for some of the mistakes he made during that time. Then he and Helen embraced.

"Would you mind if I put a rose on your husband's casket?" he asked.

She thought it was a beautiful gesture and nodded. He placed the rose on the casket and then stepped back. Helen could sense his sincerity. She knew as well as anyone how unpredictable the business of pro sports was, and it was part of the reason she made a point of encouraging people she knew in the business. She had always done that with her husband and son, and she was known for writing cards with small notes of encouragement to their friends. Bill Belichick was going to be added to her list. There would be a time when Helen would send one of those cards to Belichick's office, and the address wouldn't be just his place of business; it would be Thomas's and Pioli's as well.

2.

The Patriot Way

In one of his first team meetings as head coach of the Patriots, Bill Belichick stood before a roomful of players and coaches and began speaking calmly. He planned to tell this group what he expected in the 2000 season, and he hadn't been talking for very long, maybe two minutes, when a player entered, walked past the coach, and tried to take an empty seat in the second row.

"Katzenmoyer!" Belichick snapped at the linebacker, one of the team's two first-round picks in 1999. "Who in the hell do you think you are? Get your ass outta here! I'll talk to you after the meeting."

A big man at six feet three inches and 260 pounds, Andy Katzenmoyer was made to feel small perhaps for the first time in his entitled, athletic life. While in college at Ohio State, he was the cliché star athlete who suspiciously slid through the academic system, having failing grades changed to passing ones and remaining eligible by taking intro-level golf, tennis, and music classes. When he was drafted by the Patriots, he joined a team that was often coddled by its head coach, Pete Carroll, and he took advantage of the relaxed working environment.

Being kicked out of a Belichick meeting for lateness was just a glimpse of what was to come for Katzenmoyer. He wasn't going to make it in New England. Not with this coach. He wasn't alone, because many people in the organization, from players to coaches to scouts, wouldn't be able to adjust to the cultural makeover, either. For many of them, the problem would be simple: They believed in things that Belichick didn't.

The players had gotten used to workdays in which pads were worn for half of practice, and the other half the pads would be taken off. Under the collegial and perpetually positive Carroll, special names were given to practice days, like "Turnover Thursday" and "No-Repeat Friday." Some players had found that they could glide into meetings a minute or two after they had begun without consequences from the coach or the captains, leading to an atmosphere that lacked tension. They knew that Carroll was the head coach but not the de facto general manager, so a few of them would take trips to the personnel department for an audience with Bobby Grier, who was the top personnel man at the time. All the while, the victory totals went from ten to nine to eight.

It took just a couple days to see that things were going to change under Belichick. His first press conference was in the evening on January 27, 2000. The next morning he fired a longtime strength coach who had four years left on his contract. When it came to one of his favorite topics, team-building, Belichick was likely to be unsentimental and blunt with his decision-making. It had been five years since his Cleveland dismissal, and he'd spent much of that time growing as a coach and football thinker.

He had weighed two intriguing job offers in February 1996, after being fired for the first time in his career. Jimmy Johnson, the former Cowboys coach, had taken over in Miami and wanted Belichick to be his defensive coordinator with the Dolphins. Belichick respected Johnson as a coach and collector of draft chips. In Dallas, before the era of true unrestricted free agency, Johnson took the one-win Cowboys and turned them into back-to-back Super Bowl champions in just five years. He did it exclusively through the draft. He was helped by one of the biggest trades in sports history, when in 1989 he cashed in his most valuable asset, running back Herschel Walker, in exchange for five Minnesota Vikings role players and six draft picks. The picks were always what excited Johnson, and he stacked them and dealt them more aggressively than anyone in the NFL. He approached picks like they were quarters for Vegas slot machines, continually feeding with the expectation that a big payoff would eventually come. While in Dallas, he drafted two Hall of Famers and five other players who all would make at least four Pro Bowls.

Belichick turned Johnson down, but the two maintained a good relationship, a relationship that would help Belichick sharpen his draft focus. Instead of Miami, Belichick decided to go to New England, a region where he'd spent a year in high school, four years in college, and several summers as a resident of Nantucket. It was also where Bill Parcells, his former boss, was the head coach of the Patriots. Parcells named Belichick as an assistant head coach, and in their lone New England season together, Parcells and Belichick watched the young Patriots advance to the Super Bowl before losing to the heavily favored Green Bay Packers.

A feud over personnel power between Parcells and Patriots owner Robert Kraft led to Parcells departing New England for one of the area's most despised sports and cultural rivals: New York. Kraft wanted Parcells to focus on coaching and have Grier pick the players; Parcells wanted the full control and the cash that the New York Jets would give him. While the Jets searched for loopholes that would allow Parcells to be their coach without compensating the Patriots, they named Parcells as a consultant and Belichick as their head coach. Everyone, including Belichick, knew it was a ruse, and it lasted ten days. Still, Belichick knew what to do with authority, even if it was temporary. He used that week and a half to call the old Cleveland Browns, the Baltimore Ravens, so he could get permission to hire away Scott Pioli and Eric Mangini, two of his former star employees who had made the transition from Cleveland to Baltimore.

The Jets didn't have a losing season when Parcells and Belichick were there, advancing as far as the conference championship game in 1998. But when Parcells said he was done with coaching, moving into the role of GM and trying to appoint Belichick as his Jets successor after the 1999 season, his longtime assistant bristled. Belichick knew he had made mistakes in Cleveland, from player evaluation to dealing with the media. But the five years there didn't make him doubt his ability to be his own man, away from Parcells. If he had taken the Jets job, he wouldn't have been able to fully steer the franchise the way he wanted because Parcells would still have final say over how things were done. He surprised Parcells and Jets upper management when he rejected the job in a press conference that had been arranged to announce his acceptance. The episode infuriated Parcells as well as New York fans and media, and it guaranteed that Belichick would never again be described as a dutiful Parcells follower. The head coaching job he wanted was in New England, where, despite Parcells's problems with ownership, Belichick had enjoyed his year of conversations with Kraft and his oldest son, Jonathan.

He may have wanted to go to New England, but the Jets weren't going to let it happen without a legal fight. After a staggering amount of billable hours, Belichick became the head coach of the Patriots and the Jets received multiple draft picks, including a first-rounder in 2000.

One early morning in New York, just as the conflict was coming to an end, Belichick talked with Pioli for twenty minutes. He was likely going to ask him to join him in New England so they could resume building the draft system that they had started in Cleveland. After a year of being in pro personnel in Baltimore and three in New York, Pioli was ready to assume the role that Mike Lombardi held for Belichick with the Browns.

But that wasn't the talk Belichick wanted to have at four A.M. Pioli had followed the coach to the Jets facility in Hempstead, where Belichick was going to drop off his team-issued car. Pioli would then drive him home since they lived in the same neighborhood.

During the drive, Belichick did most of the talking.

"There are highs and lows in this business," he said, "and this is one of those moments where you're reminded that we all in this business don't treat our families well enough. We don't give them what they deserve. You know, the only people who are going to support you unconditionally are your family."

The recently married Pioli drove and listened. Belichick had given him a similar talk eight years earlier in Cleveland. But that one had felt more speculative and far-off. This was more relevant and pointed, especially since Pioli was going to have to learn to expertly balance professional success with family connections.

His wife, Dallas, was Parcells's daughter. Parcells had been in the business long enough to understand how to compartmentalize. From one perspective, Pioli was someone who had known Belichick for more than a decade and was loyal to him for bringing him to the NFL. Looking at it that way, of course Parcells was going to allow him the opportunity to advance professionally under someone who guided him through the business. As for holidays and family dinners and birthdays, Pioli and Parcells would give those the attention they deserved and keep them separate from their shoptalk.

Belichick's arrival in Foxboro, Massachusetts, was layered with significance. He had disagreed with Parcells many times over the years, but this was the first time the public got any hint of a rift. As a result, whatever he did in New England would now be viewed without a Parcells prism, and that hadn't happened since he was in his early thirties, before Parcells became head coach of the Giants. There would be no assisting Parcells or cynical whispers that he was trying to be Parcells. His actions had said it all. The last person he wanted to pattern himself after was the man he had said, "No, thanks," to in New York.

He was certainly going to bring some of the Parcells familiarity back to the Patriots, with no tolerance for excuses and a disdain for employees with a sense of entitlement. But he would do it his way, and it would start with the clout given to him by Kraft. This was his team to build, in all aspects of football operations. He officially had the autonomy that Kraft hadn't given Parcells. The only thing missing from Belichick's return, four years after he had left, was a Welcome Home banner.

"When Belichick took over in New England, there was a sort of purging of the Pete Carroll mentality," says Tedy Bruschi, who had been coached by Parcells and Belichick in 1996, his rookie year. "You know, Pete had that 'Everything's going to be okay' type of attitude. No, everything's *not* going to be okay. It's not going to be okay if you don't do anything about it. And that's the attitude that I always wanted.

"I made the most of what Pete was trying to do. I felt like I was one of his guys, too, to tell you the truth. Because I would believe in the head man in charge and try to convey his message to the team. But a lot of guys weren't hearing it. I truly believe you have to put pressure on professional athletes to get the most out of them. You have to threaten them with their jobs. Especially certain guys who get contracts and get comfortable—and add to that a coach who enables them—and they forget to work.

"Pete never used pressure. He was a very positive-reinforcement type of guy. And that coming in after Parcells was a stark contrast."

At the end of 2000, a five-win season, the Patriots parted ways with twenty-eight players who had spent at least one game on the roster. Included in the cuts were popular left tackle Bruce Armstrong and four high draft picks from Grier's classes. As for Grier, he was gone, too.

Fortunately for Belichick, he had good instincts when it came to football guys. When he hired Pioli in Cleveland, he felt the best place for him was in scouting. Pioli quickly proved himself with his willingness to work at all hours, and by the time the Browns left for Baltimore, he was one of the best personnel men in the league. When he was with the Jets, he displayed an ability to recognize all talent, from the obviously great players to the ones who would be subtle pieces in the machine. He fully endorsed pursuing Seattle free agent Kevin Mawae and making him the highest-paid center in the league, but he also pushed for players in their late twenties and early thirties whom other teams had discarded. Those were the gritty players, such as Anthony Pleasant, Rick Lyle, and Bryan Cox, who had such impactful personalities that they could be team leaders whether they started or became specialists.

In Cleveland, there had been more of a traditional boss-employee relationship between Belichick and the young man he hired in 1992, the twenty-seven-year-old Pioli. But in early 2001, with Belichick still clearly in command in New England, the working relationship had evolved into more of a partnership. Pioli was thirty-six and on the very short list of people whom Belichick trusted as advisers and confidants. Those who didn't know Belichick well were occasionally intimidated by his curiosity. The coach would sometimes ask people around him what they thought, which could lead to nervous rambling from those who weren't sure what the "right" answer was. But Pioli always knew the right answer: There wasn't one. Belichick was just asking for opinions. He wasn't trying to set people up. He might challenge a position that didn't seem quite right, but overall he was generally interested in the football thoughts of people on his staff and how they saw certain situations.

"I think it's this way with a lot of leaders: There are certain people they'll allow to disagree with them and continue to seek their opinions, and there are others they won't," Pioli says. "Bill never discouraged me. Because even when we disagreed and got into it, he never discouraged me from having a different opinion.

"But there were a lot of times where, because of Bill's personality, he would just ask questions. A lot of times he would just get your position on things and never tell you his. Now, this is why Bill is so different than so many people I've encountered in life, period: When he's asking those questions, you know that every fiber in his body is about winning and doing what is best for the team, with no personal and/or selfish motive.

"I knew him so well and trusted him implicitly; I didn't even have to consider if there was a backroom game going on in his head. And that makes the work environment easy, man. You knew he was all about winning, doing the job well, doing it thoroughly, and being prepared."

There were times Belichick didn't have to share his opinion with Pioli because their ideas were so similar. Pioli had Belichick's trust, so when it was time to reshape the team in the spring of 2001, the head coach knew he had a man in personnel who had a sharp mind for free agency and the draft. He needed all the power and wit of the minds around him, because his team had finished last in the AFC East.

Pioli found one of those gritty players with leadership potential in Pittsburgh. He was twenty-five, 260 pounds, and projected as a starting outside linebacker in New England. Those were the positives. What took some faith was the fact that he had played in fifty-one games in his career, started none of them, and had just eleven tackles in 2000. His name was Mike Vrabel. He was one of many linebackers who signed with the Patriots in the off-season, joining Cox, Roman Phifer, and Larry Izzo.

Few people outside of football operations realized what was happening in Foxboro. The firm but flexible scouting system that Belichick had dreamed of a decade earlier was finally ready to be put into practice.

In the early 1990s, he had asked for a system that was specific but not oppressively so. He asked for a grading scale that was easy to understand yet complex enough to reflect, for example, the value of an average offensive lineman who could play two positions vs. an above-average lineman who could just play one. He wanted to assign letters, numbers, and words that would accurately describe every player in pro and college football. In turn, he and Pioli could approach each draft and free-agency period with the best chance of scientifically building the team they wanted: bigger and stronger than most; tough enough to practice and play in the unpredictable weather of the Northeast; fast; infused with football smarts and passion.

The system borrowed from other places, but overall it was original, so it truly was creating another language. It had a basic overall grading scale, from 1 to 9. But arriving at that grade could be quite a process because some positions, such as safety, required a scout to consider as many as twenty-four different factors (from the ability to quarterback the secondary to effectiveness in deep zone coverage to catching skills). The three general areas from which grades were derived were called Major Factors, Critical Factors, and Position Skills. Most players were graded on Major Factors, which measure seven specific areas from athletic ability to personal behavior and toughness. The specifics of the other two categories changed depending on what position is being analyzed.

What made such an exhaustive system fun was that it was built with football evolution in mind. It could be expanded or reduced to capture the changes and trends in the game. The emergence of pass-catching tight ends and slot receivers increased the value of those positions, while the opposite is true of fullbacks, since the position has been recently deemphasized. One of the things that made the system different was that it absolutely required a scout to know his college area or region of coverage in addition to each member of the Patriots' fifty-three-man roster. All reports, without exception, were comparative and were based on what a given prospect could do vs. any current Patriot playing his position.

In April 2001, the Patriots went into the draft knowing that they wanted to spend their first two picks improving the defensive and offensive lines. They had detailed descriptions for the type of players they wanted at defensive end and left tackle. Now all they had to do was hope they fell to them. Their first two selections were in slots 6 and 39, which is proof that they were a bad team, but Belichick was still able to find an advantage from those draft positions.

"When you're picking at number six, in terms of your draft preparation, I think that's a relatively easy position to be in," he says. "You've got five teams ahead of you, and you know who a couple of those players are going to be. So then, what's left? And maybe it's A or B, but you have a pretty good idea what you're going to do. And then once you solidify that first pick, you know a lot of players will be gone when you pick at thirty-nine, and you know who those players are. I mean, not all of them, but certainly a big portion of them. So if you know who your pick's going to be at six, and you're not going to trade it, well, in the process now you're way ahead of the game."

To Belichick's point, three picks in the top five were locks: Michael Vick, Leonard Davis, and LaDainian Tomlinson. That left the Patriots sure they'd get the number one player on their board, six-foot-six-inch Richard Seymour from Georgia, a three-hundred-plus-pound defensive end. The fans wanted a receiver, but the Patriots were certain Seymour had All-Pro abilities and that he'd have no problems fulfilling any part of the system ideally at his position; he matched the team's player description perfectly: "This player must have explosive strength and leverage to stuff an offensive lineman and win the battle for the neutral zone . . . He must be able to play with strong, fast hands . . . He must be able to knock the offensive line back and establish a new line of scrimmage . . . This is a disciplined position that requires discipline in technique and responsibility. Other defenders' ability and production is tied directly to this player's performance."

When Seymour came off the board and the draft unfolded, the Patriots realized they still had several players they liked when they got to 39. So they traded back in the draft, and when the tackle they wanted, Purdue University's Matt Light, appeared to be on the Jets' radar, they moved one slot ahead of them and picked him.

The first two picks alone made it a successful and smart day of drafting and had already put Belichick far ahead of where he was with the Browns. He and Pioli had just picked two immediate starters with Pro Bowl talents.

On September 23, 2001, the Patriots trailed the Jets by a touchdown, 10–3, in the fourth quarter. With five minutes to play, Drew Bledsoe rolled to his right and began to run upfield. He seemed to be indecisive. He couldn't figure out if he wanted to run out of bounds and come up short of the first-down marker or stay in play and take on linebacker Mo Lewis.

Bledsoe took on Lewis, and the rest is both sports and medical history. Lewis hit Bledsoe with such force that the collision led to a sheared blood vessel in the quarterback's chest cavity. No one was aware just how severe the injury was until Bledsoe got to Massachusetts General Hospital and had to have blood drained from the left side of his chest. One of the doctors who treated Bledsoe said he had never seen an injury like it in a professional athlete. The Patriots lost that game, fell to 0-2, and decided to play the rest of the season with Bledsoe's backup, Tom Brady.

When Bledsoe recovered and was ready to take his starting job back, he was told that such a thing didn't exist. He still had a job, just not one as a starter. He had signed a ten-year contract extension in the off-season that could be worth up to $103 million if he reached each roster bonus and incentive. He was a smart man, though, and whenever he asked Belichick about the job the answer was the same: The job was Brady's. Bledsoe was the first Patriots star who believed that Belichick had swindled him out of a position, but he would have had more perspective if he could have seen the future or even considered what had happened with Bernie Kosar in Belichick's past. Over the years, making tough decisions and replacing seemingly indispensable players would become the Patriots' way of doing business.

"I'll tell you this story, and it's mean and it's, you know, the brutality of the NFL," Bruschi says. "I didn't know how seriously Drew had been hurt after that hit by Mo Lewis. I was driving home after the game by myself, talking to my brother on the phone. I told him, 'It's no wonder Drew got the crap knocked out of him. He's been holding the ball too long all year.' That's the frustration I was having with Drew at the time, and we're talking about a guy who was one of my good friends on the team. That's just the way football is. It's either you're helping us win or you're not.

"Honestly, I saw Brady in there and thought, 'Man, it's time. It really is time.' I saw that we had good players and were getting a foundation. I thought we could take that step and get better."

Brady-Bledsoe was a local story that became national when the Patriots started to put together some wins under second-year quarterback Brady. He had been the best and luckiest pick of Belichick's first draft class in 2000, lasting until the sixth round and the 199th overall selection. He was a throwing and breathing reminder that sometimes karma and chance sneak into the scouting process, which is usually the realm of cold analysis and lots of cold cash.

Belichick had no problem with that. He had been around long enough to remember lucky and unlucky breaks. He still recalls a player he wanted in the third round and was just ten spots away from selecting. It was 1995, his last year in Cleveland and Parcells's next-to-last in New England.

"I called Bill and said, 'Look, we'll move up ten spots and give you a fourth.' It was a good deal. It was way more than what it should have been for that move," Belichick says. "And Bill was usually looking to accumulate picks. He said, 'It's pretty good. Yeah, I think we might be interested in doing that. Let me think about it.' So he called back and said he was going to stay and pick. He only saw one guy left who he really wanted. We saw one guy left, too. Once Bill turned down the deal, I knew he was going to pick him."

It was running back Curtis Martin, who played for the Patriots and Jets. He ended his career as the fourth-leading rusher in NFL history. Sometimes you just miss on Curtis Martin and land a quarterback named Eric Zeier instead. Sometimes you pick Adrian Klemm and Dave Stachelski before stumbling into Tom Brady.

With all the 2001 focus on Bledsoe and Brady and their leading dramatic roles in *The Franchise vs. the Near Freshman*, it was easy to forget that similar battles for starting jobs were happening on defense, too.

Bruschi had not begun the season as the starting inside linebacker. He was part of the rotation, but a lot of the reps had gone to Cox and Ted Johnson. When they both got hurt, Bruschi stepped in and never came out. He would go to work on Wednesday mornings, eager to see the game plans. That's where players found out everything they needed to know. If their numbers were listed on those pages in starting positions, they knew they'd be getting a heavy workload in the game. Each Wednesday, Bruschi saw a "54" in the space for starting inside linebacker. The coaches had continually told the players that they would go with whoever was playing best at the time, no matter what, and they were proving it by playing the best middle linebacker and the best quarterback.

While the Patriots on the field were gaining confidence, the same could be said for upstart Patriots in the front office. Since his Cleveland days, Belichick had been a believer in developing young coaching and scouting talent. In 2001, he brought in an entry-level employee who would be used as a helper for coaches and scouts. Josh McDaniels was twenty-five and grew up in the birthplace of pro football, Canton, Ohio. His father, Thom, was a high school football coach who once led Canton's McKinley High to an undefeated season and a national championship. That team was quarterbacked by Josh's brother, Ben. Josh McDaniels had worked at Michigan State for one of Belichick's best friends in coaching, Nick Saban. In New England, he was expected to do whatever Pioli asked in scouting, and he was also given an important and tedious coaching task that Belichick would carefully inspect.

"I used to do what were called pads, which were the game breakdowns," McDaniels says. "Everything you saw on film, you had to draw and put on those pads. It wasn't easy and they took forever to get done. I remember the first time I handed them in to Bill, he sent them back with what must have been sixty sticky notes on them. 'This is wrong . . . That guy wasn't there . . . This was the halfback, not the fullback.' On and on. And I thought, 'Okay, obviously I have some work to do.'

"The next one I did had twenty notes on them. The one after that came back with four. And then they weren't sent back anymore. It was simple: If I was given something to do, I was expected to do it absolutely perfectly, as best as I could, every time I did it. And if I did those things right, I'd get something else to do."

McDaniels also got a chance to see Pioli in action, whether it was managing the scouts, constructing contracts, speaking with agents, or looking for in-season ways to improve the roster. Pioli had tried to improve the '01 scouting staff as well by extending an offer to Thomas Dimitroff, trying to get one of his closest friends in football to scout for the Patriots.

Professionally, the move would make sense for everyone involved. Dimitroff would be a perfect fit for all aspects of the Patriots' culture. He was meticulous and efficient in writing his reports, just like his father had been. He believed in what he saw and didn't waste a lot of words trying to convince a director, or himself, that he was right. ("Some people want to write a portion of *The Iliad*," he liked to joke. "Let's stick with crisp, descriptive words and not get lost in the verbiage.") He trusted Belichick and Pioli more than anyone in the league, and he knew there was a better chance of sustained success in New England than with his organization, the new Cleveland Browns.

The NFL had granted Cleveland an expansion team after the original Browns left town in 1995. Dimitroff had been working with the Lions at that time and eventually began scouting the West. Scouts are typically based in the region that they cover, so Dimitroff settled in the utopia for lovers of the outdoors and clean living, Boulder, Colorado. He left the Lions for the Browns in 1998, a year before the new Browns took the field, and continued scouting the West.

It wasn't coincidental that he decided to work for the same team that his father proudly called an employer. He thought of his father's impassioned advice often, and he consciously thought of walking the same halls that the Bulldog had. He also knew that working for the Browns meant that, for job purposes, he would be in northeast Ohio for long stretches three different times during the season. He'd be in for two weeks during training camp and a week apiece for the December and February draft meetings. That would allow him to spend more time with his mother, Helen, who had decided that she didn't want to have another companion after losing her husband. It had been five years since Tom Dimitroff had passed, but he was still a presence.

Thomas Dimitroff told Pioli that the following season, 2002, would probably be a better time to work for the Patriots.

The story lines with the Patriots began to change in December and January. Only hard-core members of the Bledsoe Fan Club thought he should be the Patriots' starter. The offense, with 240-pound running back Antowain Smith as the hammer and receiver Troy Brown negotiating the slot and perimeter, clicked when Brady ran it. He also seemed to buy into the team mind-set that the starting quarterback was no different from a special-teamer who was clinging to the roster. He modestly deflected any suggestions that he was becoming an idol for teenage girls and their moms, too, due to his leading-man good looks. He parroted everything that the coaches and team captains said, repeatedly found nice words to share about Bledsoe, and tried to prove that he saw himself as just a piece of the operation.

But as much as he tried, it was hard to slow down Brady Mania. If Brady was willing, advertisers were there for him, and they knew they could have him pitching almost any product on the market. America would buy a likable kid with a simple name. America would buy cover-boy handsome with a tinge of aw-shucks sensibility. America would buy a winner.

Three days before Christmas, the Patriots played their last home game of the regular season. They had won four in a row, which made their record 9-5. They were facing the Dolphins, a team they hadn't beaten since Belichick became their coach. The Patriots won, 20–13, and jogged around Foxboro Stadium for ten minutes afterward. They were probably going to the play-offs, although it wasn't official. And even if they did, there was no guarantee that they would play at home. So as far as the fans and players knew, it was the last game in the stadium's history. A new facility, Gillette Stadium, was being constructed next door and would be ready for the 2002 season. But the demolition of Old Foxboro, with its aluminum seats and Division 2 luxuries, would have to wait.

"Our transformation was magical with the emergence of Brady," Bruschi says. "That's what happened. Before Brady got in there, did I think we were good? No. I didn't think we were upper-echelon. I thought if Drew had a Pro Bowl year, it would give us a chance of getting out of that so-so group and also give us a chance in the play-offs. But when Tom came in, boom, we took off."

But that was just part of it. For some reason, the real-life Patriots continued to encounter situations that seemed torn from the pages of fiction, and the fiction writer was always pro–New England. The fiction, either inspirational or horror, depending on where you lived, was tangible on January 19 in Foxboro. The Patriots had won their division and secured the number two seed in the play-offs. It truly *was* a dark and stormy night as they played their divisional game against Oakland in five inches of snow. If not for handheld snowblowers, no one would have been able to distinguish the yard lines.

The game appeared to be over with 1:47 remaining and the Patriots trailing 13–10. Brady hadn't recognized his college teammate, Charles Woodson, coming on a corner blitz. Woodson struck Brady, the ball fell to the ground, and Raiders linebacker Greg Biekert smothered the ball, recovering the apparent fumble. The Patriots were out of time-outs, so all the Raiders had to do was call a few plays and run out the clock.

Except one of the replay officials in the press box had called for a review of the play. On CBS, which televised the game, announcer Greg Gumbel said that the previous play had "pretty much sealed" the win for Oakland. As he looked at the replays during the review, which was unusually long, he didn't see anything that changed his mind. But his broadcast partner, Phil Simms, alluded to an obscure rule that he couldn't remember the name of and said it might give possession to the Patriots.

During the delay, an ecstatic Woodson pranced around the stadium with his helmet off, acknowledging the crowd. But the longer the review took, the more sixty-thousand-plus fans believed that they had a chance, even if many of them couldn't make a case for why they felt that way.

"We thought the same thing that everyone else in the stadium thought: It was a fumble," says Roland Williams, the Raiders' starting tight end. "Tom Brady thought it was a fumble, too. Watch the replay and you can see his head sink. He was dejected. And then came the review of infamy. It makes you wonder if it was a personal vendetta against [Raiders owner] Al Davis.

That review took so long that you had time to call your cousin, your auntie, *and* your girl."

The suspense built, almost in lockstep with the song that was playing at the time, Phil Collins's tense and trancelike "In the Air Tonight." Brady stayed on the field for most of the review, his helmet pulled low near his eyes, fresh snow accumulating on the crown.

Remarkably, the play was overturned by virtue of the rule Simms couldn't remember the name of: the Tuck Rule. In the view of the officials, Brady was initially attempting to pass, with his arm going forward. As he tried to pull the ball, or tuck it, back to his body, it was knocked free, resulting in an incomplete pass. When the Raiders heard the explanation from referee Walt Coleman, all of them had the look of bitter employees who had completed their jobs yet somehow found themselves still on the clock.

They must have known it wasn't going to end well for them, even though kicker Adam Vinatieri still had to make the most difficult kick of his career, a forty-five-yarder, to tie the game. He had certainly made kicks from that distance before, although all but one of the six kicks he missed during the regular season were in the forty- to forty-nine-yard range. The snow was the obvious hurdle, causing Vinatieri to alter his approach. His kick would have been perfect for Fenway

Park: a low line drive headed for the top of the manual scoreboard on the Green Monster. Vinatieri's low and powerful kick pierced the snow and then got lost in it, a football competing with a New England snowstorm. Those in the crowd who couldn't actually see it looked at the officials, and they signaled that the kick, which barely cleared the crossbar, was good.

The rest of the night, and season, would be in the hands of storytellers and dreamers. Eventually, Vinatieri would make another kick, much easier than his forty-five-yarder, and the Patriots were on their way to the conference championship game.

"I respect the hell out of Tom Brady for what he said after the game," Williams says. "He was shaking guys' hands and he said to a lot of us, 'Good game . . . I fumbled.' We got screwed. I don't know if the NFL was against us or not, but I want you to think about something: We played back-to-back play-off games, against the Jets and Patriots, and our opponents had a total of one penalty. One! Is that even possible?"

It was one of the topics the Raiders would debate on the way home. They called the back of their team plane "Club Taliban" for its collection of intimidating trash-talkers, card and dice players, and unofficial scouts who liked to tell you, through sips of alcohol, how you could have played better that day. Anyone who wanted to use the bathroom on the cross-country flight had to pass through that area. "It was a helluva ride," Williams says. "At least we can all say we catapulted Brady's and Vinatieri's careers."

For Belichick and Pioli, who arrived in New England with a vision for decades-long excellence, the unexpected success of the Patriots was going to require open minds and discipline. They had to be open-minded because they knew the team had flaws. Both of them had virtually grown up with the New York Giants, one of them as a coach and the other as a fan, and they knew how true greatness was supposed to look. The Patriots had elements of greatness, but through and through, they weren't there yet. The men in charge of building the roster knew that they would have to take second and third looks at free agents who were appearing to be more than stopgaps and veteran players who were playing far above what their capabilities were supposed to be.

They'd also need to be disciplined enough to avoid getting swept in the region's and, increasingly, nation's emotions about the team. The Patriots were embraceable because of how they were perceived. They were a starless group, the story went, that was powered by heart, luck, and Belichick's brain. If Belichick and Pioli made future personnel decisions based on local sentiment, they'd be tempted to keep the team as-is.

New England was deeply in love with the team, even before it arrived in Pittsburgh and upset the Steelers for the conference title, 24–17. In that game, the literary theme was redemption, with Brady spraining an ankle and turning the game over to his backup, Drew Bledsoe. Bledsoe was so excited to play, for the first time since he had gotten hurt, that he practically skipped on the field. He didn't throw passes as much as he launched them, the football coming out of his hand with such velocity that it seemed as if it were fired from a throwing machine. On one play, he even rolled to the sideline, in a Mo Lewis redux, and was popped as he went out of bounds. But this time he leapt up, smiling and clapping his hands. Usually buttoned-down and restrained, Bledsoe was more emotional than he'd ever been in his nine seasons in New England. He completed ten passes, one of them a touchdown to David Patten. After the game, he held the Lamar Hunt Trophy and wept.

When the Patriots arrived in New Orleans for the Super Bowl, they may have been the only ones in the city looking forward to the actual game. Their opponent would be the last team they had lost to, the Saint Louis Rams, and it wasn't supposed to be close. Leading up to the game, the general conversations were about the surreal New Orleans parties, the irresistible food at dozens of city restaurants, the approaching Mardi Gras season, and the fact that the Rams might be on their way to a dynasty with a second Super Bowl win in three seasons.

Most of the Patriots were too confident to listen to the consensus of Football America, and a couple of them weren't even in town to hear it. Because of the quick turnaround of traveling from Pittsburgh to Foxboro to New Orleans, Belichick came up with an idea. His coordinators, Charlie Weis and Romeo Crennel, would stay in New England an extra day and prepare their game plans. That way, Weis and Crennel could focus on a normal workday, travel after work, and not have to worry about disrupting their routine and losing time.

Belichick traveled with the team and then huddled with Ernie Adams, a man he had known since they were both teenage football players at Phillips Academy, a prestigious New England prep school. Adams had many roles for the Patriots. He sat in the coaches' box on game days and had frequent conversations with Belichick about what he saw from the sky. He sat in on scouting meetings. He was a football historian-savant who, off the top of his head, could connect a formation from the present to a similar one that someone used in 1955. He was a sounding board and adviser, just another smart voice that Belichick could go to for opinions.

With Belichick and Adams in one city and Weis and Crennel in the other, the group faxed ideas back and forth until they came up with a collaborative, Best of Our Ideas plan to upset the Rams. They had a blizzard of schemes and stats, but they would never present those to the team. Belichick, the son of a coach and a schoolteacher, knew how to make complex ideas simple. He was going to stress just a few things to the defense, with number one being stopping Marshall Faulk. They believed that he truly was the team's quarterback, even though Kurt Warner played the position. They could learn a lot about what the Rams' offense wanted to do by studying Faulk, so he was the key man for the week.

The nation wasn't buying it. As lovable as the Patriots were, Las Vegas saw a runaway coming. Oddsmakers installed the Rams as 14-point favorites. Many believed that it would be a mini-upset if the Patriots were still competitive by halftime. But the day before the game, Belichick sat in his work suite at the team's French Quarter hotel, the Fairmont, and coolly answered, "Sure," when asked if he saw a way of slowing the Rams down.

"Oh, they're definitely more talented than we are," he said, leaning back in his chair. "And they're fast.

But think of a fast-break team in basketball. They usually don't want to play a half-court game. They don't want to be pushed around. It makes them a different team."

True to what they had become during the season, the Patriots began Super Bowl XXXVI unlike anyone else. For years, Super Bowl tradition had been solo introductions of team members. It might be your only chance to play in such a big game, recognized by a worldwide audience, so why not at least take off your helmet and let the world hear your name and see your face? The previous year, Baltimore's Ray Lewis was introduced and took the opportunity to do an elaborate fraternity dance. But the Patriots, who had talked all year of the group being more powerful than the individual, chose to be introduced as a team.

"It was us making a statement that this was how we were going to win," Troy Brown says. "We had come together many times that season and become closer, from 9/11 to the death of [quarterbacks coach] Dick Rehbein. We didn't think it was the time to be taking off our helmets and celebrating ourselves. We thought, 'If you're going to beat us, you're going to have to beat us this way.' "

"I knew it was over as soon as I saw that," says Williams, the Raiders' tight end. "They just destroyed everybody's psyche with that move. Whoever came up with it was a freakin' genius."

In the second quarter, all aspects of teamwork got everyone's attention in the Superdome. Warner dropped back to pass and appeared to be surprised by Crennel's defensive call. The Patriots were in a 46 defense, popularized in the 1980s by Buddy Ryan, the father of Patriots linebackers coach Rob Ryan. The call was Turkey Zero, and it left Vrabel with a free shot at Warner. He hit him just as he threw, causing the ball to float. Cornerback Ty Law quickly read the play, caught the ball while he was in stride, and ran forty-seven yards down the sideline for a touchdown.

A couple of series later, the "half-court football" continued. Rams receiver Ricky Proehl was hit hard by the Patriots' Antwan Harris and fumbled. That led to another touchdown, Brady to Patten, and a 14–3 Patriots lead. Just as they had planned, the Patriots followed Faulk and pushed him whenever they could. Even when he didn't appear to be the primary option on passing plays, Faulk got a bump or shiver from a defensive lineman or linebacker. It seemed to disrupt the Rams until the fourth quarter.

The Patriots were on the verge of a blowout with ten minutes to play. The Rams had driven to the Patriots' three, but Warner fumbled the ball into the hands of safety Tebucky Jones. Jones sprinted ninety-seven yards for what was thought to be a touchdown and 24–3 lead. But the officials had noticed Willie McGinest bear-hugging the game's target, Faulk, and called holding. The Rams eventually scored to make it 17–10.

Brady and the offense were having a hard time moving against the quick and aggressive Rams defense. They were the third-best unit in the league, and they seemed to know exactly what the Patriots wanted to do. They kept giving Warner and the offense chances to produce, and the offense finally delivered with 1:37 to play to tie the score at 17.

By the time Brown returned the kickoff to the Patriots' seventeen-yard line, there was just 1:21 to play. Both teams were out of time-outs. John Madden, a Fox broadcaster and Hall of Fame coach, went on the air and outlined what the Patriots should do: "With this field position, you have to just run the clock out. You have to play for overtime now. I don't think you want to force anything here. You don't want to do anything stupid. Because you have no time-outs and you're backed up."

After a four-yard pass to J. R. Redmond, Madden continued.

"I don't agree with what the Patriots are doing right here," he said. He stuttered a bit over the next thought, seeming to slightly doubt himself as he said it: "I would play for overtime. If I had good field position I wouldn't. But in this field position I would play for overtime."

But Brady had been told the opposite on the sideline by Belichick and Weis. They trusted him, and they didn't trust leaving their fate to a coin flip and, perhaps, an escape from the box by Faulk. Who could chance it? And why would they, since they hadn't thought and played that way all season? Despite the effective game plan, the Rams still had gained significantly more yards. The Rams had an edge in time of possession. The Rams had momentum. Yet the Patriots, with no turnovers, had the ball and an opportunity to go for the win.

Robert Kraft; his wife, Myra; and his son Jonathan were paying no attention to John Madden. They weren't listening to an NFL official, either, who had come to their private box with six minutes to play and offered to escort them to the field. No chance. The official came back a few minutes later. Still, not interested. They'd watch the entire game and then worry about getting to the field later.

What they were able to see was confidence and precision from Brady. The one time he could have been flustered, on a Rams blitz, he stepped to his right and threw the ball out of bounds. On the next play, from the Patriots' forty-one, Brady and Weis displayed just how much they believed in what they were doing. They called a play, RT 64 MAX ALL IN XQ, that had gone for an incompletion earlier. So they called it again.

"When I saw how they lined up, I knew they weren't going to be in a man defense," Brown says. "I said, 'There's going to be a hole somewhere, I just have to find it.' Once I caught the ball and got close to the sideline, I knew I could have made a better move to make the defender miss. But I wanted to be sure we had enough time to run one more play and spike, so I ran out of bounds. But I know I could have had more."

What he gave them was good enough, a twenty-three-yard play that moved the ball to the Rams' thirty-six. Twenty-one seconds remained. The Patriots needed just a few more yards to be in comfortable field-goal range.

In a season of unintentional poetry, it was fitting that the next play would practically be a catch by all who had been with the Patriots since their local TV black-outs, one- and two-win seasons, and franchise coffers that had more singles than hundred-dollar bills. Jermaine Wiggins, a tight end from East Boston, was the only Patriots player who had been born and raised in the area. He understood what it would mean for the

THE PATRIOT WAY · 75

Patriots to win something. This was a team that almost moved to Saint Louis after the 1993 season. Of the Red Sox, Bruins, and Celtics, it was the only local franchise that couldn't claim a single championship. So it was perfect that the Boston kid, Wiggy, would represent the city and catch Brady's final pass of the day for six yards.

"What Tom Brady just did gives me goose bumps," the converted Madden told his TV audience as the Patriots prepared for the win.

With seven seconds left, Vinatieri took the field. No one had been steadier in the postseason. He had gotten the team here by kicking his way through snowflakes, and in the temperature-controlled dome, he knew that confetti would be the only thing that might be falling from above. As he walked to the field, white lights flashed around him. He heard chatter from his own team and the Rams, too, but he blocked them all out. This is what he had mapped out the night before as he sat in his hotel room, halfway paging through a few magazines, and what he thought of the next morning as he determinedly took the first team bus to the stadium. He was as confident in his abilities as Brady was in his, so there was nothing anyone could say or do in this moment to bother him.

The ball was snapped and Vinatieri stepped into it and kicked as if there was a chance someone would move the goalposts back ten yards. It was a wallop. It exploded off his right black shoe, purposefully one size smaller than normal so there wouldn't be slippage, and it required neither prayers nor body English. It was something everyone could understand: right down the middle and good from forty-eight yards. The Patriots were Super Bowl champions.

Belichick had won his first Super Bowl as a head coach, and he had done it standing near his father, Steve, the man who taught him the game. The eldest of his three children, daughter Amanda, was the first person to reach him and wrap him in a hug. Safety Lawyer Milloy was next. There were hugs in the owner's box, where the Krafts still were, before they were taken to the field in a rickety freight elevator. In the coaches' box, Scott Pioli had been so excited that he tumbled down the stairs and into a massive embrace with screaming colleagues. Brady found Drew Bledsoe and excitedly slapped his shoulder pads. Some players dropped to their knees and cried.

In the vision of Belichick and Pioli, this was just part of what they had in mind when they thought of the New England Patriots. This was the part of the story where they win the championship, but it's not where the story ends. The plan all along was to win and be in position to repeat the process, year after year. Some would call it the pursuit of the impossible in a salary-cap league, a league that is designed to make things even. But Belichick was passionate about who the Patriots were and who they could become.

As he sat in a nearly empty coaches' locker room, well after the game had ended, he was asked to describe what he had just seen. He shook his head in disbelief.

"This was miraculous," he said.

He then went on to say, with all respect, that the team that had just won the Super Bowl had a lot of work to do to reach the ideal of consistent championship contender. It meant that the team in the front office, coaches and scouts, were going to have to get back to work soon. And the team on the field shouldn't get too comfortable. He was asked how many players on the Super Bowl champs would have to be replaced before he could call them perennial championship threats. He didn't hesitate:

"About twenty."

3.

The Culture of Winners

The conference room, filled with coaches, was mostly dark. There was a giant screen on the wall farthest away from the door, and all eyes were on that screen. The coaches met like this daily, shuttling into the room to analyze what they had just seen in practice. They came armed with pens and notepads, bottled water, coffee, packs of gum or mints, and, in some cases, spitting cups for their tobacco.

There was always something to be found on the big screen that they hadn't seen live in practice. But on this fall afternoon in 2002, it didn't take the Patriots' coaching audience long to realize that this was not going to be a good day at the movies. Bill Belichick was in control of the clicker, and he continued to do the same thing for what seemed like twenty-five minutes:

He would let the practice images roll for a few seconds, stop, rewind, and shake his head.

"Not good," he would say after one sequence.

"This is bad," he'd say after another.

"This is terrible . . . what kind of technique is that? Are any of us teaching him to play like *that*?" he'd add to yet another replay.

On this October day, all of his commentary was reserved for one of the new guys, defensive tackle Steve Martin, who was signed to help stop the run. No one was happy with Martin's play, but he at least was a reminder of how blessed the Patriots had been in 2001. It had been one of those years that few people, in any profession, experience. It was a year when all negatives became positive. The starting quarterback got hurt and his backup turned out to be better. A game was won in Buffalo when it was determined that an *unconscious receiver*, sprawled near the sideline, had possession of the ball. A fumble that would have ended the season was ruled an incompletion, which opened the door for not one but two successful field goals in a blizzard. A two-touchdown underdog won the Super Bowl.

Even every free agent the Patriots touched had been golden. They were the I-can't-believe-it stars of a bargain-shopping commercial. They had found: a discarded running back in Antowain Smith who gave them 1,100 rushing yards and 12 touchdowns; a special-teams captain, Larry Izzo; a wide receiver in David Patten, unwanted by the 3-13 Browns, who became a starter and deep threat; a young, starting outside linebacker, Mike Vrabel, who was both good enough to play in their system and smart enough to teach it; and a versatile, starting guard in Mike Compton who could flip between playing center and guard within a series.

The Patriots had been good for most of 2001, and when the games were most important they had been great. It carried them to one of the most unlikely championships in the history of pro sports. But the truth was that they had been lucky, too. The phrases usually don't go together, but they were a defending Super Bowl champion that was in the middle of rebuilding. They knew that internally, although they forever lost the right to say it publicly as soon as the red, white, and blue confetti swirled among them on an unforgettable February night in the Superdome.

They were agitated in 2002. They weren't living up to their billing, and the shine from their luck was gone. At best, their signings could be described as marginal. The 320-pound Martin, a frequent target of the coaches, was supposed to add a dimension that the Super Bowl champs didn't have the previous year. He'd be their true, two-gapping nose tackle. It meant that he would have the discipline and strength to stay square at the point of attack. He'd be able to control the gaps to his left and right, be tough, and allow his teammates to get the glory for his dirty work. But Martin wanted media glory more than anything else, and as Belichick pointed out to the coaches in the film room, his technique was inconsistent and substandard.

It was an odd position for a champion to be in. There hadn't been a rush by Belichick and Scott Pioli to retain the team they had. On the contrary, at their end-of-season self-scouting meetings with the coaches, they pointed to several positions where they needed to improve.

They thought they could upgrade the safety spot, where Matt Stevens and Tebucky Jones had split time in '01. Stevens had an off-the-charts score on the Wonderlic, the predraft test used to see how quickly a player could process information, but the coaches didn't always feel he played smart. Jones was big and athletically gifted, but he had poor technique. So veteran safety Victor Green was signed away from the Jets, and despite his guile and want-to, the Patriots discovered Green's speed had fallen off dramatically and the team suddenly had a player at the end of his career. They had gone most of the previous season without a reliable third receiver, so they drafted Louisville's Deion

Branch late in the second round and took a chance in the seventh round on Notre Dame's David Givens. Those were hits. The big miss came in free agency, when they looked to Carolina and thought they had a found a young star, twenty-seven-year-old Donald Hayes, who was ready to break out. But the multiple route options in the Patriots' offense tripped up Hayes, and he became a nonfactor after admitting in an interview that he didn't know the plays.

It was a return to most teams' normal: one up, one down. They wanted to be better at tight end, even if East Boston's own Jermaine Wiggins had caught ten balls in the play-off win against the Raiders and had made the last catch against the Rams to set up Adam Vinatieri's Super Bowl–winning kick. (In fact, one of the coaches had derisively said that Wiggins was only able to create separation when the games were in the snow.) Wiggins left as a free agent and the Patriots moved up eleven spots in the first round for Colorado tight end Daniel Graham. He was a ferocious blocker, but he spent a lot of his rookie season watching as most of the catches went to free-agent signee Christian Fauria.

The Patriots would go through the entire month of October without a victory, and by the time they got to November a few realities were tough to ignore. Sure, they were like many other champions who had to endure a sixteen-game season-after tour in which they got every opponent's complete focus and best game. And they had to develop new chemistry, too, with Drew Bledsoe traded to Buffalo for a 2003 first-round pick and Tom Brady, in his first full season as a starter, expected to become one of the league's top quarterbacks. More than that, though, were the words of Belichick after winning the Super Bowl. He had said they were twenty players away from consistent greatness, and he was right. The Patriots had a solid core, but they could point to a couple of areas where players were starting and the team didn't think they should be. For example, the starting defensive ends from the Super Bowl season, Anthony Pleasant and Bobby Hamilton, were both smart players. Yet Pleasant was thirty-four and well past his prime, and Hamilton, despite his strong technique, was someone the coaches ultimately saw as a rotation guy. It was only a matter of time, maybe a draft or two, before both players would be replaced.

Belichick and Pioli knew all of this logically, but their competitiveness led them to expect more than what was possible during the games. Belichick had become so frustrated with Martin that at times he put Hamilton, forty pounds lighter than Martin, at nose tackle just to illustrate what technique he was looking for. It didn't matter. Martin's performance was unchanged. Pioli would watch games in the coaches' box, see a breakdown, and say to no one in particular, "Are you kidding me with that? Come on." Brilliant coaching and scouting and player leadership wouldn't be enough to fix some of the Patriots' issues during the season. It was a good thing for them that they officially had people in-house who could diagnose and correct the problems.

After trying for more than a year, Pioli, with a new vice president's title and salary bump, had finally been able to sell Thomas Dimitroff on joining the scouting staff in New England. Dimitroff would continue to live in Boulder, Colorado, one of the most liberal and laid-back cities in the country, while being a national scout for the Patriots. From afar, it seemed like a personality-balancing exercise: There was the clearly defined, militaristic hierarchy of the Patriots paired with the live-and-let-live spirit of the small city in the Rockies.

Dimitroff was planted in both worlds. He was an avid mountain biker and snowboarder who once thought of opening his own bike-outfitting shop if he didn't have a career in football. He was passionate about the environment, animal rights, and nutrition, and had been either a vegan or vegetarian for a decade. He was a Presbyterian but was also intrigued by Taoism and had educated himself on its teachings by reading numerous books. Once, while living in Saskatchewan, his primary mode of transportation was a bicycle. His friends nicknamed it "Steel Wind" because he would ride it in any conditions. He would pedal through the prairies, the unplowed side roads packed with snow, in minus-15-degree temperatures (he didn't own his first car until he was twenty-six). At the time, his living situation could have been the inspiration for a reality show on Canadian TV: He was a fledgling scout residing in the basement of a house, and his four housemates, all women, were members of the Canadian national volleyball team.

He may have looked, talked, and dressed differently from most scouts he came across, but he was as in tune with what the Patriots expected as anyone in the NFL. He considered Pioli a brother, and six years after the passing of his father, he was grateful that Belichick had continued to stay in touch with his mother. Dimitroff also had studied enough of Belichick's and Pioli's hiring practices to sense a trend: "Bill and Scott have a knack for hiring people who are their own worst critics. Those two send a clear message: Do your job as well as you can, do your part, play your role. They rarely have to come down hard on their employees, because they pick their employees so well. You never would see anyone with a sense of entitlement there. They wouldn't survive."

Dimitroff became one of those employees in 2002, and he could quickly sense what was at stake for the Patriots when he was in Foxboro for the December scouting meetings. The Patriots were 8-5 then, with a Monday-night game scheduled in Tennessee. The decent record hadn't fooled many careful observers of the team. The Patriots were at or near the bottom of the league in run defense the entire season. There were too many missed tackles in the secondary and not enough speed, a couple of facts that automatically put Belichick on edge and would lead him to challenge anyone who had something positive to say about any of the team's safeties.

All the scouts had an idea of what the Patriots needed going forward, and those needs played out twice before national TV audiences in less than a week. The Monday-night game against the Titans was the worst of everything: The Titans ran whenever they wanted, the Patriots couldn't do anything offensively, and Brady suffered a separated right shoulder—although the team wouldn't confirm that until the season was over. They were scheduled to play the Jets six days later in Foxboro, with an opportunity to take control of the AFC East. Belichick tried to emphasize how significant the week was by imploring the team to study and focus on

what was important. The next day, he awoke to headlines that pointed out that the ever-quotable Martin
had called Jets center Kevin Mawae a dirty player. Belichick had already seen enough from Martin, and now
he was hearing and reading it, too. Martin either had
misread the rising anger and frustration from the head
coach or he didn't care. He was cut, mostly because he
didn't do the job, but also as a message to the rest of
the team.

It didn't translate to a win against New York. The
Patriots lost, 30–17.

After the loss to the Jets, Jeannette Belichick showed
her mother's intuition. The coach's mom, an octoge-
narian, wasn't even privy to the team's true injury
report. But she had been around long enough to know
something was wrong with Brady. She stood near her
husband, Steve, and whispered that Brady wasn't okay.
A few minutes later she saw the quarterback as he was
leaving the stadium. He leaned over to make better eye
contact with the petite woman, and she gently placed
her right hand on his face, told him how concerned
she was about him, and kissed him on the cheek. The
Patriots were 8-7 and play-off outsiders, looking for
help in the final week of the season.

Pioli understood that no matter what happened at
the end of the week, his department was going to need

to do its best work for the 2003 season. There had been too many conversations, either in Belichick's office after home games or on buses and planes on the road, for Pioli to misunderstand what the head coach was thinking. He didn't always have to listen to Belichick to know what was on his mind. There was a brooding that the coach went through, well after the normal postgame venting period was over. Pioli had known him for years, so he could easily sense it, but it was so obvious in 2002 that all the coaches could, too. Many of the assistants would get to coaches' meetings five and ten minutes ahead of Belichick and trade stories about what college football games they'd seen or something they'd heard Howard Stern say. But as soon as Belichick walked into a room, it was almost a scramble to prove that no one had been joking or had even thought of it. They laughed when he did. But he was rarely happy. He was so unhappy that in a few areas, he wasn't just looking for a tweak, he wanted an overhaul.

The Patriots' 2002 season ended, unofficially, as Belichick was driving home following a 27–24 win over the Dolphins. It was an awful feeling: The Patriots were 9-7 and needed help or else the Jets were going to take the division in a tiebreaker. There was no help coming, and Belichick could see that as he watched the first half of the Jets-Packers game from his office. His family and friends were there, but as the game got out of hand, he announced he was leaving. They could stay if they wanted, but he would be more comfortable sitting in postgame traffic, thinking of how to improve the Patriots in 2003. Some reinforcements were going to come, naturally, through the draft. But he already had a few free agents in mind, and it was going to take a lot of the owner's money to get them.

Robert Kraft was more than a football fan who grew up in Brookline, Massachusetts. He was a lifelong football risk-taker. As a college student at Columbia, he would sneak out to play intramural football, keeping the news from his parents. Practicing their Jewish faith, Kraft's parents didn't answer their phone until after sundown on the Sabbath, and that's when they learned that their son in New York was up to something: They received a call from the school and were told that he had been hurt in a game and needed knee surgery.

When he was twenty-nine, in 1971, Kraft bought his family Patriots season tickets. At the time they lived in a charming brick house on Gralynn Road in Newton, and the family tradition was that the Kraft children would swarm their father at the door as he entered the front foyer after work. He was a hero that day with his oldest son, seven-year-old Jonathan, as he opened his briefcase and held up the tickets. But the woman of the house, wife Myra, thought season tickets for a young family building its wealth was a stretch. The stretch became an elaborate chess game in the 1980s and early 1990s, as Kraft systematically put himself in position to buy the Patriots. The climactic moment came after the 1993 season, when the financially unstable franchise appeared to be headed to Saint Louis until Kraft, who already owned Foxboro Stadium, purchased the team for a record sum at the time, nearly $200 million.

The owner was invested in the team, by any definition.

Like everyone else in his organization in February 2002, he had the time of his life during Super Bowl week in New Orleans. He was the prince of the French Quarter. People he didn't know treated him as if he was an old buddy from their hometown and they needed to buy a few rounds to catch up and toast the memories. They bought him drinks and called him "Bobby," thankful that he presided over a franchise that had taken them on such an unpredictable journey. But historically, the Patriots' 2002 season was as predictable as it was disappointing. Just three teams in the previous twenty years, the 49ers, Cowboys, and Broncos, had won back-to-back Super Bowls. Excluding the repeat champions, all of the Super Bowl winners in that period had combined to win nine play-off games the year after winning the championship.

Still, Kraft searched for answers in January 2003. During one of the coaches' self-scouting meetings, Kraft quietly entered the conference room and took a seat by the door. The idea of the exercise was to rigorously analyze the strengths and weaknesses of each Patriot so everyone could understand where they were and where they needed to go. What was the point of diving into free-agency and draft needs if they weren't tuned in to their own personnel? The coaches were talking about offensive linemen, and when they got to the young and talented Damien Woody, they had good things to say. Woody had been drafted as a center but often played guard, especially when the team was in the shotgun formation. They called him smart, tough, competitive, and durable.

Kraft was annoyed. He raised his hand, signaling that he wanted to speak.

"I have an issue with the analysis of Woody," he said. "How do we say all those things about him and not mention his problems with shotgun snapping? It's either something that he needs to work on or something he can't do, but I think it should be mentioned."

A couple coaches made eye contact with the owner but didn't respond. Really, did any of them want to pick *this* issue as their battle point? A couple weeks earlier, still jolted by the non-play-off season, Kraft had left late-night voice mails for Belichick and Pioli, requesting a meeting to talk about why they thought the season unfolded the way it did. This clearly was not a case of absentee ownership. Just as quietly as he entered the room, Kraft completed his statement and walked out the door.

There were a few stunned glances just after he left, and then business continued as usual. There wasn't an assistant coach in the room who was going to stand up and challenge the owner for questioning their reports. And the one man who could have done it, Belichick, understood Kraft's thinking. The owner routinely negotiated a complicated pass in professional sports. He was able to regularly check in on football operations without meddling. He asked questions and threw out topics that could be debated, but he never made suggestions to Belichick about players he wanted to see signed or drafted. If there was a message to his visit, it was simply that he was paying attention.

All the Patriots coaches and scouts were used to animated debates, especially when they were trying to trim the fat and get to a bottom line. It was that time of year for the scouts, who were trying to bring the draft board into focus, and it was like that for the coaches, who were making their cases for players who should stay or go. One of the loudest and most uncomfortable arguments contained a bit of foreshadowing. It pitted Belichick vs. Eric Mangini, a thirty-two-year-old coach who had aced all of the projects Belichick had given him in Cleveland, New York, and New England and therefore advanced through the system.

Mangini was in charge of the secondary, and a few times during the season he seemed to take it personally when Belichick picked apart players whom he had coached. He was close to safety Tebucky Jones, and Jones happened to be one of the players with whom Belichick had a problem. Belichick liked for his scouts and assistant coaches to have opinions and voice them, but this would go beyond that. It would be an argument that didn't have an easy, agree-to-disagree exit button. Belichick had been disgusted by his defense, which had given up just 10 fewer points than the Houston Texans, who were in their first year of existence. He was embarrassed by it. He was on edge. He almost dared someone to make a case that he didn't think could be made: that Victor Green was fast and that Jones could tackle. Mangini took the bait.

Belichick sat at the head of a conference table and Mangini sat three or four seats away to his right. Pioli was in the room, too, along with the coaches, and many of them followed the points and counterpoints with their heads. It was like watching a profane match of verbal tennis. While Mangini held his ground making the case for Green's production, citing his team-leading three fumble recoveries and one touchdown off an interception, Belichick's argument was unassailable when the film came on. Green seemed to take forever running from Point A to B. He was tough and determined, and both men agreed on that. But it was clear, no matter how much Mangini protested, that he wouldn't be coaching Green or Jones, and maybe not even fan favorite Lawyer Milloy, in 2003.

The argument wasn't going anywhere fast, so someone suggested that they should all take a break. During the break, a couple of people who witnessed the disagreement shook their heads, whispering that Mangini had been too aggressive and crossed the line. Perhaps he had, but it was nothing compared to what Belichick vs. Mangini would become in the future.

On the other hand, Kraft's input was pointed yet always measured. He was one of the richest men in America and had dominated the paper products industry, but he wasn't afraid to ask football people questions that he didn't know the answer to. He would sit in on squad meetings and take notes. He worked at truly learning the ins and outs of the game. He occasionally challenged and questioned his football operations people in January and February, and in March he did something else: He sprang open his checkbook.

In 2003, the top available free agent was twenty-five-year-old linebacker Rosevelt Colvin III. He had what every team in the league was looking for: size, speed, and the ability to rush the passer. He was smart, too, sounding very much like a young man who had been raised by educators. His father, Rosevelt II, was a long-time science teacher in the Indianapolis public schools. His mother, Bessie, was a music teacher whose piano playing could be heard anywhere from school plays to local commercials.

The Patriots saw Colvin as someone who could give them a pass-rushing threat off the edge. Pleasant had done that, for other teams, when he was younger. And although Willie McGinest had the talent to do it, he was thirty-one and the team had left him unprotected in the 2002 expansion draft. If Colvin came to town, he'd likely be taking McGinest's starting job. But Colvin didn't appear to be a financial match for the Patriots. They weren't known for setting the market on a player, and it looked as if that was what it was going to take to land a linebacker who had a gift—getting to the quarterback—coveted by the entire league. When Colvin visited New England, he began to understand why the Patriots were known more as football purists than entertainers. He was picked up from the airport in a dusty 1989 Taurus, and when he got to the stadium he was given a tour in darkness.

"I remember seeing the weight room, the locker room, the meeting rooms, all with the lights off," Colvin says, laughing. "When I finally sat down with Bill and Scott, they quizzed me on what I was doing in certain situations on the field. And after that, Bill put on some old Giants film and we watched L.T. [Lawrence Taylor] and Pepper Johnson. That impressed me, man. This was about lineage. Bill and Romeo Crennel had coached L.T., who pretty much trademarked the game. These guys knew what they were talking about."

The unadorned approach to football appealed to him. He signed for seven years and $30 million, a reasonable contract relative to the projections, which were millions of dollars higher. A little more than a month before the draft, the Patriots were starting to carry out the plans that had been shaped by meetings, both cool and tense; scouting; and thorough film study. Rodney Harrison, a former San Diego Chargers safety with the temperament of a middle linebacker, signed a day after Colvin. At the very least, Harrison would be the replacement for Jones and maybe Milloy if the Patriots couldn't get him to take a pay cut and make his salary more cap-friendly. That was unlikely to happen for the proud Milloy, especially since he would be asked to take less money as the Patriots were spending it on his position. Free-agent cornerback Tyrone Poole signed next, most likely to replace thirty-seven-year-old Otis Smith, and eventually the much-debated Tebucky Jones was traded to New Orleans for draft picks in 2003 and 2004.

The maneuvering continued the night before the draft. In the NFL's version of easy money, the Patriots traded one of the picks they had gotten from New Orleans, a 2003 third, to Miami for a 2004 second. On the morning of the draft, game day for the scouts, the team's cafeteria was abuzz over what might happen in a few hours. The Patriots had a minimalist approach when it came to access to the draft room, so the majority of the scouts wouldn't be in there when decisions were made. They had their own unofficial session over scrambled eggs, bacon, and toast, excitedly going over the best players they had interviewed and worked out over the course of the year. Through a combination of instincts, gossip, and knowing the men they worked for, a couple of scouts had correctly predicted who the Patriots would pick with the first of their two first-rounders: Ty Warren, a defensive lineman from Texas A&M. Warren had played in a scheme similar to New

England's, and he had excelled at tackle and end. He also had the profile the team was looking for: mature for his age and serious about football. When the team brought him in for a predraft visit, he wore a jacket and tie. The team had interviewed other players who didn't seem as prepared for the moment as Warren was.

For Belichick and Pioli, their weekend of drafting was full of shifting and computing. They'd field an offer from one team, quickly weigh its pros and cons, and then take a phone call from someone else and see how that deal matched up. They traded up one spot with Chicago to secure Warren. They traded away their second first-round pick, at number 19, to Baltimore in exchange for a second-round pick in 2003 and a first-rounder in '04. They then took the second they got from Baltimore and, concerned that corners were coming off the board too quickly, moved up five spots to take Illinois cornerback Eugene Wilson. After selecting Wilson, they moved up again in the second to take receiver Bethel Johnson, Warren's teammate at A&M.

They were excited to move up in the fourth, too. There was a kid from Central Florida, Asante Samuel, whom defensive assistant Josh McDaniels had loved while working him out. McDaniels said the kid, a cornerback, loved playing against the best competition in the country, a sign that he would perform better than usual in big games. In the fifth, Belichick reacted as if he had been promised crème brûlée and simply got vanilla ice cream instead. Pioli had been high on a center from Boston College, but Belichick sighed when he officially picked Dan Koppen. He'd be more excited in a few months, when he'd see Koppen in training camp and watch him emerge as a first-year starter. Finally, in the seventh, the team got lucky and drafted Tully Banta-Cain, a defensive end from Cal-Berkeley who probably should have gone in the fourth.

It wasn't just that the draft weekend had been as smooth as they had planned; the previous couple months had been exceptional. Since Belichick and Pioli were hyper-conscious of the budget, they knew they still had some negotiating to do with Lawyer Milloy. He hadn't been great at safety in 2002, and his cap number for 2003 was well over $4 million. There was no way the Patriots were going to pay that, especially since they had signed Harrison. They knew it, Milloy knew it, and so did the entire team.

"You know Lawyer," former Patriots receiver Troy Brown says. "He's going to say what's on his mind. He was pretty open about his situation. It came up a lot during training camp. We all knew the team wanted him to take a pay cut."

What no one knew was how far the team was willing to go.

Players who had been part of the 2001 championship team were starting to get that same Super Bowl feeling in the summer of 2003. The defense had been switched to the one Belichick preferred, a 3-4, and a fourth-round pick had been sent to Chicago for one of the best and surliest run stuffers in the game, nose tackle Ted Washington. He was exactly what the defense needed up front, a one-man mountain range who couldn't be budged and never could be blocked one on one. He was loved by his teammates, but he scowled when approached by reporters, grunting out reluctant answers to questions. He liked to hear jokes as much as anyone, yet he would shush the room when he believed the coaches were saying something that no one should miss.

With the new free agents and draft picks, the Patriots looked as strong as any team in the league at the start of the 2003 season. They just had to be strong without the vocal and emotional Milloy, one of their defensive captains. On the second day of September, a Tuesday morning, Belichick walked into a team meeting and said something that floored and then infuriated the Patriots: Milloy had been released. There was a wave of rustling and mumbling in the auditorium, while some players were too confused to say anything. The emotions ranged from *What?* to *Why now?* to *What are we doing?* to *Damn, they're cold.*

"I remember a lot of guys saying, 'How could they do this?' or 'I can't believe they'd do something like this.' Emotions were running high that day and that entire week," Brown says. "I was going into my eleventh season, so I kept saying and thinking, 'Man, this is the NFL. You just saw what happened to Drew Bledsoe, didn't you?' I'd remind guys, 'Eventually, this is going to happen to all of us.'"

It was an unusual week. There wasn't a lot of small talk before meetings or practice. For a few days, there was an unofficial line with coaches on one side and players on the other. This one stung, mostly because it was so out of place. For all the conversation about Bledsoe, players could understand that he was traded in the off-season. A couple years earlier, receiver Terry Glenn, a former top-ten pick, had been traded during the off-season. But this was no trade, it was in season, and it couldn't be viewed as another transaction.

A couple of defensive players organized a meeting in which they lectured the young players on saving their money and understanding exactly what type of short-term business they were in. After venting a bit more, they started to get back to their competitive selves and

think about how they were going to make the best of
the week and season. Their season opener was against
a divisional opponent, Buffalo, which had Drew Bledsoe at quarterback and a safety they had picked up in
midweek, Lawyer Milloy.

The game wasn't an accurate snapshot of what
either team was. The Patriots were a wreck, with Brady
throwing four interceptions. The Bills danced as much
as they played, with Milloy playing air guitar after
some of his stellar plays and a defensive tackle bigger
than Washington, Sam Adams, actually high-stepping
into the end zone with an interception and doing a duck
walk after a sack. The final score was 31–0.

On a Sunday afternoon when everyone in western
New York was a preacher with "Poetic Justice" as the
sermon, no one would have believed what was down
the road. Maybe even the Patriots wouldn't have believed that after their loss to Buffalo, on September 7,
and another loss in Washington three weeks later, they
wouldn't lose again.

They wouldn't lose in the fall, when New Englanders picked apples and pumpkins and saw beautiful red, orange, and brown leaves hover on trees before
blanketing the landscape. They wouldn't lose in winter,
when, as usual, local residents would be slammed
with ice and snow and be ever so grateful for a high

temperature in the 40s. They would be sun-splashed in the spring, wildly benefitting from the first-round pick they had gotten from Baltimore. Summer was for red carpet, live music, and the presentation of breathtaking diamond rings at Kraft's house in Brookline. There would be yet another September with new faces coming in and familiar ones gone, and it would take nearly an entire October before there was anything other than a "W" next to New England. Actually, the seasons would change more than the Patriots. They became a machine. They wouldn't lose again for a long, long time.

In corporate America, it's called "branding." Musicians and artists and writers call it "having a style" or "finding your voice." The Patriots didn't have a name for what they were developing. They just knew they had planted seeds for a system in which draft picks were "picks" in name only and always available to be traded; smart young employees would be schooled in the system and grow into coaches and scouts; players would be athletic and fast, of course, but smart and tough, too; and the unspoken trust, whether it was on the road with the scouts or in the locker room with the players, was that the job would be done at the highest level even when the boss wasn't looking.

"Man, we had the formula down," Tedy Bruschi says. "My locker was on the left, Willie McGinest's locker was on the right, and there was the door in the middle of us. And as early as we got there and as late as we stayed, we saw everyone who walked in and we saw everyone who walked out. And everyone who walked in late got a comment, everyone who walked out early got a comment about what they did that day. We held them accountable as soon as they walked in the door.

"Me and Willie, I mean, we policed that locker room as soon as you walked in. If we smelled you, you know, we wanted to know what was in your hand. 'What were you eating?' 'Did you bring in the McDonald's bag?' We wanted to know where you were going once you came in, did we have a meeting in one minute, or are you here to work out? Even if you were some veteran who had come in from another team, we didn't care where you were from because we were establishing ourselves as world champions, and we felt like, 'This is the way we do things around here. We're going to teach you how to do it.'"

The policy didn't go over well in the beginning for Harrison. Bruschi and McGinest were Patriots when Belichick was in New England the first time, in 1996, as an assistant coach. They remembered how things worked when Bill Parcells was the head coach and players, or anyone, had excuses for being late. Parcells would raise his eyebrows and say, "Oh, you have a *response*? Interesting." His point was unmistakable: Don't say anything.

It was clear that Harrison was going to be one of the Patriots' elite players in 2003, despite what happened in the Buffalo game, but Bruschi and McGinest felt he still had too much San Diego in him. The team had come a long way since Andy Katzenmoyer casually strolled into a team meeting two minutes late in 2000. By 2003, watching the door was something Belichick didn't have to do. The players would do it for him and turn it into a raucous yet lighthearted game when someone was even a hair late. Just by watching how Harrison carried himself, Bruschi and McGinest knew they could get under his skin, so they did it. But they did it because they saw something else in him and they planned to use it.

"Rodney was borderline arrogant when he first got to New England," Bruschi says. "He felt like he was established in the league and had gone to the Super Bowl as a rookie. He was a very confident person, you know. I remember him coming in just about twenty seconds late for a meeting. He came in and we gave it to him, and he had a little bit of an attitude. He used to try to spout off to us, like, 'You know, you're not going to do that to me,' or something like that, and we just kept giving it to him.

"And we had to do it with him over and over again until we said, 'Listen, man, we're trying to give you a message about how it's done. It's our way of giving you respect as a veteran but still letting you know this isn't San Diego.' He ended up falling in line, though, and being the same sort of enforcer that Willie and I were."

They were all enforcers on the field, especially on defense, even though they weren't getting the contribution they had expected. In just the second game of the season, Colvin reached down to recover a fumble and felt an awkward pain on his left side. He had a hip dislocation, a major injury that would end his season and threaten his career. The injury to Colvin meant that McGinest would be on the field more than anyone planned. But there wasn't a drop-off from Colvin to McGinest, just as there wasn't with the departed Milloy to the rookie second-rounder Wilson, who was drafted as a corner but was thriving at safety.

The theme of the 2003 Patriots seemed to be that someone, somehow, would find a way to win a game. Every other week, an oddity would contribute to the result. They won an October game in Miami, for example, because the Florida Marlins were preparing for the World Series. The Dolphins and Marlins shared the stadium, so the infield dirt was still intact amid the grass. Miami kicker Olindo Mare had two chances to win the game, but in both cases the dirt was a factor. He slipped on one and had the kick blocked by Richard Seymour. In overtime, he slipped again on the dirt and the ball sailed to the right. Brady then took the ball, on the dirt, and heaved a pass to Brown. He wasn't known for his deep speed, but Brown had managed to get behind the safety and score on an eighty-two-yard play.

The win gave them a record of 5-2. Two weeks later in Denver, they moved to 7-2 when the play of the game was an intentional safety. They were in poor field position and believed that punting would make things worse. So they conceded the 2 points, took advantage of a good free kick and a bad Broncos offensive series, and won on a perfect pass from Brady to David Givens.

They won their tenth game, in Indianapolis, by a single yard. The Patriots led 38–34 in the final minute, and the Colts had driven to the Patriots' one with twenty-four seconds remaining. On a second-down play, the Colts tried to execute a quick run to Edgerrin James to catch the Patriots out of position. But Mount Washington was occupying the guard-center gap. There was a mistimed fade route from Peyton Manning to Aaron Moorehead on third down. And on fourth down, McGinest bluffed as if he were going to do what he often did, jam a receiver at the line of scrimmage. Instead, he was blitzing and the Colts were running, so he met James in the backfield for a loss.

It was going to be that kind of season. They knew they would be in close, entertaining games. They also knew they would figure out a way to do the right thing. They studied along the way, and no matter where they were in the building, they had a lot of fun doing it.

Players loved to catch the Locker Room Police doing anything out of order so they could grill them for a change. McGinest was an easy target. He would doze off in defensive meetings, and if a player didn't elbow him, defensive coordinator Romeo Crennel had a method of getting his attention. He would go over coverages in a low, controlled voice and then suddenly shout, "*Boom!*" to startle the head-nodders and nappers.

Coaches didn't escape jokes, either. When Steve Belichick was in town from Annapolis, where he and his wife continued to live in the home where they raised Belichick, many of the assistants knew they had to be on their toes. The elder Belichick was a natural storyteller and jokester, so he would tease the staff about their fluctuating weight. He was eighty-four and still physically fit, so when he smirked and said, "I swear, this is the fattest coaching staff in the league. You get fatter every time I see you!" they had no comebacks. He was fun to be around, and the equipment staff liked to give him the latest Patriots gear they could find so he could add to his collection. At home, he had jackets from his son's stops with the Giants, Browns, Jets, and now Patriots. Jokes aside, he was all football, and he'd talk it with anyone who had a question and was willing to listen.

The Patriots on the second floor of the stadium, in scouting, were as in sync as the players and coaches below them. Belichick had the final say on draft day; Pioli reported to Belichick and had all the responsibilities of a general manager; and the new director of college scouting, Thomas Dimitroff, oversaw the scouts and helped Pioli relax, even though Dimitroff's primary residence was still two thousand miles away in Boulder.

Pioli and Dimitroff worked perfectly together. They understood each other and the type of scouting system Belichick was looking for. Their system was based on comparatives, Our Guys vs. the Guys in the Draft, so there were quizzical looks for any scout who described a player as a "first-round pick" or "backup safety." There was a numerical system in place, with alerts built into it so an evaluator could quickly see if a player was height deficient, went to a small school, had an injury history, was a character concern, or had problems picking up schemes. The idea was to find players in the country who had a realistic shot of being better than one of the fifty-three players on the Patriots' roster.

"I certainly took my lumps in New England, especially as a young scout," says Jim Nagy, who joined the Patriots' scouting staff in 2002 when he was twenty-seven. "It's not an easy system to learn in the beginning. It took me a while to grade players and I really struggled. Was I grading them too high? Was I grading them too low? I'd say it took me about two years before I started to feel comfortable."

Pioli and Dimitroff clearly had an advantage in professional experience and knowing what Belichick wanted, and so did Lionel Vital. Vital had scouted alongside Tom Dimitroff Sr. in Cleveland and Vital had been Belichick's coworker in New York with the Jets. By the time he was in New England with Pioli and Dimitroff, communicating in the system was second nature to all three of them. They'd go deep into their shared reservoir to say who a player was or wasn't, remembering obscure players like Romeo Bandison in Cleveland, how it was good value to get a starting nose tackle like Jason Ferguson in the seventh round in New York, and humbling one another by mentioning that a long-forgotten tight end named Dave Stachelski had been drafted before Tom Brady. It helped them get to that precise place they wanted to be: projecting what a player could be for them, not what he could be for the Colts or Bears. When Pioli and Dimitroff were together, their professional conversations ranged from players to the needs of the team to their different management styles.

Dimitroff was known for advocating on behalf of the scouts, so Pioli teased him and referred to him as the "union foreman." Pioli had incredibly high standards for the scouts, probably because he was a perfectionist himself. He was so organized that he had developed a habit of keeping detailed notes on everything he did and every conversation he had. He neatly wrote the notes by hand, and when he had time he'd turn them into Word documents. He once joked, "Magic Markers saved my life," so he always had dozens of them to help him maintain his color-coded system for notes and scouting reports:

- **A green highlight is for something good;**

- **Pink is not good;**

- **Yellow is simply information;**

- **Blue is an incompletion or inconsistency that needs to be checked on;**

- **Red and blue ink pens are for miscellaneous thoughts, not necessarily good or bad.**

A sloppy or incomplete report would irritate him to his core and was the quickest path to exasperating him. Dimitroff could approach him like no other, though, and in one of their frank conversations he told him that Pioli was missing an important color in his management stash: gray.

"When you're managing any level above someone, there are management things that you're dealing with, and pressure and responsibility, that no one who's working below you understands," says Pioli. "But Thomas did talk to me in a different way, and it forced me to change my style in certain situations. He's the only guy who could come to me and say, 'Scott, I think you need to back off these guys a little bit. Do you understand?' I changed my style in certain meetings and how I approached the guys. I think there were times I was too hard-lined, and yes, there was no gray.

"I found that with Thomas as the director, I didn't have to micromanage. On some things, I didn't even have to jump in until the tenth hour because it was being taken care of. It was the first time where I could genuinely have a piece of my head and my heart that I could delegate, and it was handled."

Pioli could call out Dimitroff, too. There were times when he told him that he was being too lenient with the scouts and wanted to see more pressure applied. It was a topic that they didn't always see the same way. Pioli wanted the reports to follow a certain formula, and if they didn't follow that script it got to him. One of the scouts who didn't always do it Pioli's way was Vital. He knew players as well as anyone, but he didn't enjoy writing long reports and preferred to get straight to the "Can he play or not?" stage, without all the window dressing. Dimitroff had known both Pioli and Vital for years, so he heard and understood both perspectives. He was able to be an advocate for Vital and his style while also making sure Pioli, his boss, got the essentials of what he wanted from reports. Sometimes, Pioli and Dimitroff were just like brothers, venting in front of each other but never for an audience. Once, Dimitroff tried the calm and thoughtful tack while talking with Pioli, but the boss wasn't having it.

"I hear you, Thomas, but it's not happening," he said. "Enough of your BS West Coast approach! I'm pulling back and doing things the way I know how to do them."

They were laughing about the West Coast shot a couple days later. And if they couldn't laugh about that, Jay Muraco usually knew how to get people smiling when he sensed that there was too much tension in the office. Muraco had worked with Pioli and Dimitroff in Cleveland as a volunteer in the scouting department.

He was working for the Eagles when Pioli got the New England job, and he joined his old friend shortly after he heard the news that Belichick, Pioli, and familiar faces like Vital were running a franchise again.

Muraco knew how to loosen up both guys. Making fun of Dimitroff's extensive, multisyllabic vocabulary, Muraco would go to Dictionary.com, find as many big words as he could, and send Dimitroff a lengthy e-mail that could basically be translated to "Please call the office." For Pioli, he could just peek at him and know if he was near a boiling point. When that happened, he would act out a skit that Pioli loved, a Will Ferrell–Christopher Walken classic from *Saturday Night Live*. Ferrell, wearing a shirt two sizes too small, was a fictional cowbell player on Blue Öyster Cult's "Don't Fear the Reaper." Walken was a legendary producer obsessed with the cowbell.

Muraco would rap on Pioli's office door as if he had something important to say and then go into the routine.

"Guess what?" Muraco would begin.

Pioli, not catching on yet, would answer, "What?"

"I've got a fever! And the *only* prescription is more cowbell."

It worked every time, and Pioli would roll.

They all had good reason for nonstop celebrations throughout 2003 and 2004. Anyone who entered the building was somehow feeding the machine, and the machine was producing historic results. The operation seemed glitch-proof. The players would come to work, get into energetic games of dominoes and backgammon in their downtime, and soak up whatever the coaches laid out for them in game plans.

They had a collection of diverse and charismatic personalities, which were usually hidden from the media because they all had been drilled that the agenda of the media was not necessarily the agenda of the Patriots. Brady may have been an idol outside of his office, but he was a one-liner target just like any other player or coach when he was at work. If Bruschi, McGinest, and Harrison were the enforcers, Mike Vrabel and Ty Law were the comedians. Vrabel turned the driest situation into laughing material and Law, as Colvin put it, "was Richard Pryor with a football player's body."

"It was just a great group of guys," Troy Brown says. "A lot of us had a little edge to us because we felt we never got the national credit for being the players we were. But we didn't make a lot of noise. Some guys would run from the media. We understood the game and we understood our roles. In the receiver meetings, do you know what we talked about? The importance of blocking. Yeah, we liked to make plays and have the ball in our hands, but we had a group of receivers who understood that it wasn't about who got the most catches and who was being featured in the game plan."

Brown had to make the distinction between receivers meetings and others because he had become a twenty-first-century rarity in pro football. He played extensively on offense and defense. Two-way players were from the era of grainy black-and-white film and leather helmets, yet when the modern Patriots had injuries at cornerback, Brown played in the secondary. He was coached there by Mangini, who, despite the heated argument with Belichick, still had the coach's trust and remained on the advancement track. Brown had the surest hands on special teams. And even though he didn't feel he was ever the same after chipping a bone in his knee in the third game of the 2002 season, he was Brady's default receiver.

The Patriots zipped through the 2003 regular season with a 14-2 record. After beating Tennessee and Indianapolis in the play-offs, they had a stunning fourteen-game winning streak going into their second Super Bowl in three years, this one in Houston against the Carolina Panthers.

In one of the quirkiest championship games ever played, with no scoring in the first and third quarters and binges in the second and fourth, the Patriots beat the Panthers, 32–29. Brady was the game's MVP, but he had help all around. Vrabel made plays on defense and offense, scoring a touchdown after lining up at tight end. Brown and a pair of second-year receivers, Deion Branch and David Givens, consistently got open against man coverage. It was a source of pride for them since receivers coach Brian Daboll had reminded them that the Panthers didn't think anybody could beat them in man.

After the game, there was the expected confetti raining from the top of the stadium, early-edition newspapers with SUPER BOWL CHAMPS in bold letters being displayed on the field, and all-night parties in the team hotel and elsewhere. It was a celebration, but the team-builders in the group were still thinking of what was next. It wasn't as if the scouts could go to the parade a couple of days later in Boston; they were going to be spread across the country, still trying to find players. And while Belichick and Pioli would go to the parade and wave to millions of happily frigid New Englanders, the vision, the big picture, always tugged.

"For whatever reason, what stood out more than the parties and parades was the reality of how far behind we were," Pioli says. "[Bill and I] missed the Senior Bowl, we missed the East-West game, the Combine's around the corner, and there's no time. And the thing is, it's just this obsession of wanting to have sustained success. One of the regrets is that we didn't celebrate enough."

How do you celebrate and still find time to make unemotional decisions? The Patriots didn't. The process began immediately, with Antowain Smith being released a week after the win over the Panthers. Smith had timed much slower in 2002 drills than he had in 2001, and he was slower in 2003 than he had been in '02. His regular-season production slipped so much that by the time he left, he had given the Patriots roughly half of what he had in '01, when he ran with power and passion. Damien Woody, their best offensive lineman, was a free agent and left to sign a huge deal with Detroit. Big Ted Washington, who was thirty-six, got a four-year contract with $5.5 million in year one from the Raiders. Some coaches left as well. Rob Ryan became the Raiders' defensive coordinator, and in the subsequent coaching reshuffle in New England, Josh McDaniels was promoted to a plum job. He was the new quarterbacks coach, replacing John Hufnagel, who became the Giants' offensive coordinator. McDaniels was twenty-seven, twenty-five years younger than Hufnagel and just sixteen months older than two-time Super Bowl MVP Brady.

The Patriots gave their idealistic machine its first major test a week before the 2004 draft by throwing the equivalent of limestone into the gears. They took the freebie second-round pick they had gotten from Miami and sent it to Cincinnati for the lead running back who would replace Smith, Corey Dillon. He was everything they said they weren't: high-profile, high-maintenance, high-risk. Dillon was one of the most talented backs in football, but he had ended his Bengals career by throwing his jersey and cleats into the stands, signaling to all how he felt about his future in the city. He also had been questioned by police in a domestic violence incident with his wife, but upon investigation, both of them said it had been a misunderstanding.

In New England, it may have been an early sign that the Patriots believed they could bring anyone into their system and have him be transformed. They believed that their structure and their players would keep Dillon in line. Technically, the running back was part of their 2004 draft class. They would indoctrinate him as to how things are supposed to be, just as they would for the two rookies they took in the first round. One of them, Vince Wilfork, was a shock. He had been projected to go in the top fifteen, but some teams were nervous that the University of Miami nose tackle wouldn't be able to control his weight and that guaranteed millions would relax rather than inspire him. But the Patriots were happy to take him at number 21, the pick they had gotten from Baltimore, and eventually watch him take over the role that Washington had held for a memorable season. Sometimes talk of sustained success is all about philosophy and theory. Sometimes it becomes even easier to understand, and it's as simple as watching a young star who shouldn't be available fall into your lap.

The Patriots had experienced mere good fortune during the run to their first championship, winning nine consecutive games to close out the regular season and play-offs. But as impressive as that streak was, it wasn't as mind-bending as what they had put together during the 2003 and 2004 seasons.

Going into a Halloween game in Pittsburgh in 2004, they had won twenty-one games in a row, an NFL record. They hadn't lost in 419 days, or since the shut-out in Buffalo. They were 6-0 and looking like early favorites to win their third championship in four years. The Steelers temporarily stalled the championship talk with an overwhelming performance. Dillon, who was having a great season, was unavailable for the game, so that allowed the Steelers to hold the Patriots to just five yards rushing. The Steelers were ahead 31–10 in the third quarter and won easily, 34–20. Not only was the streak over for the Patriots, but if both 6-1 teams continued to plow through their schedules, the Patriots would eventually have to return to Pittsburgh for the play-offs.

If the Patriots' theme for 2003 had been "Find a Way," 2004 had an undercurrent of "Last Run." They were like a successful band, producing hit after hit but reaching a creative point where guys felt it might be time to venture out on their own. Really, the coaching staff and front office were full of stars, and it was only a matter of time before Charlie Weis and Romeo Crennel would be head coaches. Pioli had already turned down offers from other teams, and more teams would come knocking. Even the relative kid coaches, Mangini and McDaniels, had the skills to be coordinators, either in New England or elsewhere.

There was no question that this would be the last time that the giant and selfless collective, from players to coaches to scouts, would be together for a championship run. Belichick already had begun to think of contingency plans just in case he lost Weis and Crennel at the same time. There were always things you planned for, like coaches taking new jobs, players departing for other places, and fresh-faced rookies coming in to learn the culture. But this was football and it was real life, too. Surprises happen. Minds change. Health fails. The urgency of 2004 was tangible yet unspoken, so through November and December it felt like normal business. After the loss to the Steelers, the Patriots went on another streak, six straight, before having a lapse in Miami. For the second year in a row, they finished the regular season 14-2, meaning they had won thirty-one of their previous thirty-five games.

Playing right into a self-motivating, popular, and hyperbolic Patriots refrain—"Nobody believes in us"—the nation was infatuated with Peyton Manning and the 2004 Colts before they played the Patriots in the divisional play-offs. The Colts had scored at will during the regular season, finishing first in the league, and had scored 49 points in their wild-card game against Denver. Manning was league MVP for the second consecutive year and had thrown a league-record forty-nine touchdown passes. He had a lot working in his favor when he looked at a battered Patriots secondary that was missing his nemesis, the injured Law. Instead he saw players with which he and a country were unfamiliar: second-year corner Asante Samuel; rookie Randall Gay; a wide receiver dressed up as a cornerback, Troy Brown; and a corner whose name was a constant tribute to the artistry and show-manship of 1970s R&B, Earthwind Moreland.

Several minutes before the game started, January in New England took over. Snow began to fall, making the subfreezing atmosphere even more miserable. The

Colts were at their best indoors in their domed stadium, where they could set the temperature. But as the wind made the snow swirl in Foxboro, a security guard approached Tedy Bruschi before kickoff and suggested something else was at work.

"Bob Kraft must have a pipeline to the Man Upstairs," he said, pointing to the heavens.

The Patriots had snow, defense, and Dillon on their side. The Colts were bothered by the weather, and it truly seemed to freeze their offense. It was slower and more robotic than usual. Manning seemed to be thinking constantly about the secondary. It had those no-names and Harrison back there, so it was worth taking a shot. But then again, was it? Their technique was sound and they were protecting the deep part of the field. Why throw into coverage?

Meanwhile, there was Dillon. He may have been limestone in April, but he was January's locomotive. He punished the Colts when he ran, initiating contact and then lowering his shoulder into the chest of defenders. He was a big man with the ability to make people miss. But on this day, he didn't seem to want to; crashing into linebackers in the cold was more fun. He rushed for 144 yards, allowing the Patriots to control the clock and increase the pressure on Manning each time he had the ball. But with their three turnovers and the discipline of the Patriots' defense, the Colts had their lowest offensive output in two years.

The final was 20–3. Bruschi was emotional in a TV interview immediately after the game. "We play," he said over the din of the postgame crowd. "We don't talk; we play. You want to change the rules? Change them. We still play. And we win. That's what we do."

He was referring to the previous year, in the conference championship game, when the Colts said that the Patriots were holding rather than defending against them. Before the 2004 season began, the league's competition committee announced that illegal-contact penalties would become more of a "point of emphasis" during the season. It was a warning that the officials would be calling the game more closely to eliminate aggressive defense after receivers were five yards from the line of scrimmage. It didn't escape the Patriots that Colts president Bill Polian, as smart as he was fiery, was influential in shaping policy. Polian was a brilliant team-builder and an opinionated football man, and could often be heard in press boxes before he was seen. It was hardly a coincidence that his head coach, Tony Dungy, was a member of a subcommittee that endorsed the new focus on and monitoring of defenses.

There was at least a culture clash between the Colts and Patriots and likely a silent disdain, too. They both won a staggering amount of games, but they couldn't have been more different doing it.

They scouted different players, with the Colts going faster and smaller to the Patriots' stronger and bigger. They played different defenses. The Colts relied on the consistency of the Tampa 2, a zone that was designed to both stop big passing plays, with the "2" representing the safeties protecting the deep part of the field, and encourage a fleet of players to get to the football at warp speed. The Patriots used multiple defenses, often changing their defensive fronts and going from zone to man. They liked hulking linebackers, ideally in the 255 to 265 range, fast enough to catch you and big enough to wear you down, physically and mentally. The quarterbacks, Manning and Brady, were their generation's great sports debate, following in the tradition of Mantle-Mays, Wilt-Russell, Bird-Magic, and Marino-Montana. As for the contrasts between their head coaches, Dungy and Belichick, the list could fill a psychologist's legal pad.

They were different, sure, and they'd be seeing a lot of each other in the next few years. But in January 2005, all that mattered to the Colts was that they were once again going home because of the Patriots, while their biggest rival had yet another chance to win a Super Bowl.

For all the big plays that had happened in the season's previous eighteen games, from forcing red-zone turnovers against the Colts in game one, to Adam Vinatieri throwing a touchdown pass to Brown in game seven against the Rams, to Harrison, in the conference championship game in Pittsburgh, intercepting a pass and returning it eighty-seven yards for a touchdown during a 41–27 win over the Steelers, big plays were not the definitive, mind's-eye snapshot from the Super Bowl in Jacksonville. The unforgettable photo was of a thirty-one-year-old father at peace on the field, back-pedaling and then falling backward onto the natural grass of Alltel Stadium, letting two of his sons playfully tackle and pin him.

Bruschi's pregame moment hours before the Patriots played the Philadelphia Eagles was appropriate, for reasons obvious and unseen. In February 2005, the linebacker was similar to several of his coworkers. Many of them had changed since the first Super Bowl. They were still in love with the game, but they loved their young families more. They still got their work in, but when possible, they manipulated their schedules so they could find space to be family men. For others, there was step-back awe and appreciation of what had been accomplished since New Orleans in 2002 and thankfulness for being able to share those moments with people they loved. As expected, some of them would be moving on. Weis had taken a head-coaching job at his alma mater, Notre Dame, and would go into full-time recruiting mode after the Super Bowl. As soon as the game was over, Crennel would be introduced as the new head coach of the Cleveland Browns.

Belichick was there with the man who taught him the fundamentals of the game, his father, Steve, still passionate about football at the age of eighty-six. Pioli was there with his wife, Dallas, and the couple now had a daughter, Mia, who was one and a half years old. Years earlier Dimitroff, true to his character, had been in a Boulder bike shop when a friend of a friend introduced him to a strikingly beautiful young woman named Angeline Bautista. She was smart, too, working for an educational publishing company. Initially, she wasn't interested in dating him. But now, he was five months away from marrying her.

So much had changed in just three years. Who could know where they'd all be in the next three and if they'd ever get back here again? As easy as it was to do so, you could never take it for granted.

Belichick had grown so comfortable with his team leaders that there wasn't much on the field he didn't trust them to do. "He'd listen to our suggestions,"

Rosevelt Colvin says. "I can't imagine that anyone could make adjustments as quickly as Bill, but sometimes he would overthink it. We'd say, 'Why don't we just go to our base stuff and beat them that way?' and sometimes he'd say, 'Okay.'"

"Belichick taught us a lot," Bruschi says, "but I also think we taught him some things. He was grateful learning from us, too. I'd share with him how I liked to see things done from a player's perspective, and he'd listen to us and see the way we worked. I think he developed along with me and with Brady. There are incredible examples of players developing and coaches developing as we got better. I think I'm one, Brady's one, and Bill's one as the head coach."

They knew they had a good plan against the Eagles, and despite how much they protested the role of favorite, they knew they were the better team. A couple days before the game, Belichick went to Bruschi and Vrabel and put in a defensive wrinkle that they hadn't practiced much all year. The play was called "Dolphin," and the plan was for Bruschi and Vrabel to alternate shooting the gaps. Belichick gave them the freedom to decide which one would shoot from series to series, with his thought being that the scheme would give Eagles quarterback Donovan McNabb a moment of pause. The two linebackers shrugged. That was Bill.

Besides, they liked the mental challenge of handling any last-minute twists he threw their way.

Philadelphia scored the game's first touchdown, but it was clear there was going to be a problem for the Eagles all evening. They were going to need to pass their way to a championship, because like they had done with Faulk, the Patriots identified a running back, Brian Westbrook, as the key to the Eagles' offense. He was a dynamic receiver as well, but they were determined to take him away as a runner. The Patriots didn't think McNabb was accurate enough as a passer to be able to dissect their defense enough to win.

The Eagles weren't as good as the Patriots, but they weren't pushovers. It was 14 apiece in the third quarter, and the game wasn't officially in control until the fourth, when Vinatieri made a short field goal for a 24–14 lead with more than eight minutes remaining. Strangely, McNabb and the Eagles seemed to lack what the 2004 Patriots had all season: urgency. They were deliberate as they marched to the line of scrimmage. They huddled rather than run an upbeat, two-minute offense. They seemed to carefully examine and parse each play before they ran it. The crowd of seventy-eight-thousand-plus was decidedly pro-Eagle green, and the curses and catcalls grew louder by the play.

When the Eagles finally scored a touchdown, with 1:48 left, it was too late.

For the third time in four years, the Patriots had a 3-point victory in their final game of the year and were champions. Receiver Deion Branch, in just his third season, tied a Super Bowl record with eleven receptions and was the game's MVP. The win allowed Belichick to capture his ninth consecutive postseason game, tying the great Vince Lombardi's record.

As Belichick was hugging his father, with Steve proudly wearing his blue Patriots cap, Bruschi doused them with water and embraced them both. Alert photographers caught the moment, and it became one of the priceless photos of the week in Jacksonville. There had also been a small huddle with three men who had crisscrossed the Northeast, working together for both New York teams and New England. Belichick, Weis, and Crennel had grown together as coaches, teaching some of the NFL's best players and producing flawless game plans when the lights were brightest and they had to be at their best. This was the sixth Super Bowl for Belichick and Crennel, the fifth for Weis.

They locked arms and hugged.

"Hey," Belichick said to them. "It's over."

It would never be as good as this again.

4.

Losing the Core

On February 15, 2005, nine days after the Super Bowl, Tedy Bruschi was in his home, about forty minutes south of Boston, when he awoke from a football dream. He had fallen asleep around one A.M., watching a replay of the Patriots' conference-championship win over the Steelers. In the dream, he was attempting to tackle Steelers running back Jerome Bettis. But as he lay awake at four, his arms were in the air and his muscles were contracting. He got out of bed to go to the bathroom, but his legs were wobbly and he nearly crashed into the windows that were to his right.

He didn't realize it until several hours later, but he was having a stroke.

Later in the morning, just after ten, his wife, Heidi, made a calm 911 call. When EMTs arrived at the house, they sat one of the stars of the three-time Super Bowl champs on the stairs; gave him a quick vision test, which he failed; and then strapped him to a stretcher and carried him to an ambulance. He was crying when he left the house, unsure of what was happening to him and confused about the lack of vision in his left eye. A few seconds later he heard the pitter-patter of small feet on pavement, running toward him. Soon he saw his two oldest sons, Tedy Jr. and Rex, eager to give him hugs. He told them he loved them, and they, too young to understand what was happening, told him to "have fun" wherever he was going.

He was going to Massachusetts General Hospital and would be introduced to a new team that would be with him for life, a team of cardiologists and neurologists. He learned that he had a hole in his heart, and a clot had traveled through his bloodstream and to his brain. He would spend three days in the hospital and then get ready for weeks of rehab. He had lost vision and balance, and when local TV stations showed his release from the hospital, it was obvious that he was fragile and incapable of walking alone. He and his fans had the same thought: His football career was over.

It was going to be a year of transition for Bruschi and the Patriots. The team had officially promoted Eric Mangini to replace Romeo Crennel, and unofficially,

Josh McDaniels was the coordinator who would take over for Charlie Weis. Those were football moves, and as nervous as some players were with them, they knew they were coming. Mangini certainly had the intellect for the job. The question was whether he could command the attention and respect of a room the same way Crennel, the son of a military man, could. As for McDaniels, he was taking over for one of the most deft play-callers in the league. Belichick tried to lessen the scrutiny on McDaniels by easing him into the position without making a public announcement. But it wasn't just the public he had to worry about. Receivers coach Brian Daboll was a year older than McDaniels and had recommended him when the Patriots were looking for an entry-level employee in 2001. The fact that McDaniels was promoted ahead of him would eventually lead to problems.

The biggest issue, clearly, was trying to find someone who could step in and approximate what the team's productive and popular middle linebacker had given. You can't just replace Tedy Bruschi, on a whim, in a matter of weeks. The Patriots signed a career backup linebacker, Monty Beisel, in April and drafted a long shot, Ryan Claridge, in the fifth round. They signed thirty-four-year-old Chad Brown, who was more of a natural outside linebacker than a middle one, in May.

By that time, Bruschi had been through a range of emotions. He initially came to terms with retirement and had tearful good-bye conversations with Belichick and Robert Kraft. The Patriots were prepared to give him a job as an "organizational trainee." After completing his rehab and feeling more like himself, he started thinking about playing again, which caused a month-long dispute with Heidi. She couldn't believe that a stroke survivor would even dream of returning to work when work entailed knocking heads with 300-pound guards and 260-pound fullbacks. His counter was that he had easily cleared all the medical hurdles that were before him, and if that was the case, why couldn't he do what no one else had even tried? The dispute dissolved in the summer and gave way to more stroke information and education, and by training camp in July, a hopeful Bruschi made sure the team knew that there was a chance he'd be ready to play sometime in 2005.

Bruschi still hadn't spoken to the public, so the assumption was that he couldn't, and wouldn't want to, play. He finally talked in September and said he was going to sit out a year before making a decision, but he quickly changed his mind a couple days later when he had an echocardiogram and the results were stellar. That morning, he and Heidi had breakfast and he said, "Let's go for it this year." She agreed. He was nearly two months away from one of the greatest comebacks in sports history.

But he would return to a Patriots team that wasn't the same. In the first six games of 2005, the Patriots were average, with a 3-3 record. Their biggest problems were on defense. Rodney Harrison had been injured in week three and was out for the season. Ty Law had been released for salary cap reasons and Tyrone Poole, whose signing in 2003 had led to hallway high-fives between Belichick and Scott Pioli, was hurt and developing an unflattering locker room reputation. Many players questioned his toughness and his ability to play through the slightest bit of pain. He had played at a near–Pro Bowl level in '03, but early in 2005 there was a feeling among team leaders that his heart wasn't in it.

Poole's absence led to Asante Samuel, a developing star, being paired with another cornerback who stood out for all the wrong reasons. The Patriots had sent a third-round pick to Arizona for Duane Starks, who had once been a top-ten pick of the Ravens. But that was in the late 1990s. When the Patriots got him, he performed as if he were determined to prove that he could do the exact opposite of all the things they valued. He was noncompetitive, temperamental, and slow to react to the ball. His low point came when he literally gave up before a game was over, walking back to the locker room and refusing to return. The team placed him on injured reserve, which ended his season and brief New England career.

After all the early-season mediocrity and frustration, it was refreshing to see an inspiring human-interest story occur on October 30. That's when Bruschi came running out of the Gillette Stadium tunnel to play in a game against Buffalo. It had been unthinkable in February and even in the spring, but Bruschi vowed to use his experience to raise stroke awareness. Bruschi would become an ambassador for stroke survivors and eventually go across America on speaking tours.

But ambassadors are not saviors, and even the uplifting Bruschi tale couldn't reverse the negative energy of the fall. When the Colts came to town in November, Peyton Manning passed for more than three hundred yards and led the offense to a 40-point performance on *Monday Night Football*. A couple weeks later, things got worse.

On November 19, eighty-six-year-old Steve Belichick died of heart failure. He not only had given his son a love of football, he and his wife had given him a love of books as well. The elder Belichick had written an industry book for scouts, *Football Scouting Methods*, in 1960, when Bill was eight. It was edited, appropriately, by his wife, who loved good writing so much that she had a hard time throwing it away. She had dozens of copies of the *New Yorker* in the family basement, probably because there was no room upstairs, where bookshelves and ledges were lined with hundreds of books.

Steve Belichick had been a football man all his life, but that's not what stood out to his only child. The man himself was so influential that his son once said, "It just so happened that he was a football coach, but I would have chosen any career that he had. If he had been a fireman, I probably would have been a fireman, too." His father's eye for detail was exacting, and Steve's thoroughness as an assistant coach at the Naval Academy rubbed off on him. Steve had been amazed by how his son's mind worked, even when Bill was a preteen. "Any time I asked him why he did something, he always had a good answer and a good reason," he said. "There was always a method to his thinking."

He learned how to break down film from his father. He also learned fiscal responsibility from the veteran of World War II. Steve Belichick was proud that he had paid for his modest house up front, because he didn't believe in borrowing or deferring payments. He continued to live there until the Saturday evening he died, after a full day of watching college football.

The Patriots had a game against the Saints on the twentieth, and Belichick didn't plan to inform the team about his father. "He wanted to coach his way through it and not tell anyone," Pioli says. "A couple of us knew. He didn't even want people to know before the game because he didn't want the distraction of pity." Pioli believed that was taking selflessness too far and pulled aside Tom Brady and a few others and told them what was going on. The team responded with a 24–17 win, pushing their record to 6-4, and presented Belichick with a game ball.

Afterward, everyone understood when Belichick announced that he wouldn't be with the team in the beginning of the week as they prepared for their next game, in Kansas City. Instead he was going to be in his hometown of Annapolis, saying good-bye at the Naval Academy Chapel. Steve Belichick had met and coached many people over the years, so it wasn't surprising that his funeral was attended by people from a wide range of fields, from the secretary of the navy to Joe Bellino, who won the Heisman Trophy at Navy in 1960, and several of Belichick's colleagues, such as Pioli, Kraft, Charlie Weis, and Al Groh.

During Belichick's eulogy, he addressed his mother, Jeannette: "You were the real strength behind two coaches in this family, and I love you." He marveled at his father's ability as a scout, how in the era before instant replay, he could see a play one time and recall what happened. He also put his father's career as a coach and teacher into perspective.

"Almost seventy-five years of football gave him a vast knowledge and reverence historically for the game that very few could match," he said. "He coached everything, and his ability to teach and interact with people has really come back to me in my lifetime and in the last few days."

As Belichick looked down at the casket in front of him, draped with the American flag, he said, "Dad, may you rest in peace."

When he returned to Foxboro, Belichick showed no outward signs of emotion to the media or his team. He was asked how he was doing in a press conference and his reply was a respectful and quick, "Good." He was back to focusing on football and the Chiefs. But the game wasn't much to see, as Brady threw an uncharacteristic four interceptions in a 26–16 loss. A four-game winning streak would follow, but it didn't feel like a championship season. In January, there was a play-off win over the Jaguars and then a grisly loss in Denver in which the team turned the ball over five times. Late in the game, Deion Branch was on the sideline with tears streaming down his cheeks. Maybe he knew it was his last game as a Patriot and that it would be the toughest, most dysfunctional off-season of them all.

Depending on who's telling the story, the problems began the week of the Denver game. Mangini knew that whenever the Patriots' postseason run ended, he was going to become the next head coach of the New York Jets. While some claim that he was trying to recruit players and coaches to join him in New York, during a play-off week, he swears it never happened. The speculation combined with the fact that he was going to a divisional opponent led to an awkward parting.

Other threads of the dynasty began to come apart, stitch by stitch, in the spring. In the middle of March, the wise enforcer from Long Beach, McGinest, signed a free-agent deal with Crennel's Browns. A week later, the region was in a rage. Adam Vinatieri was New England royalty, hailed as the best clutch kicker in history. The first championship was possible because of his right foot. So when he signed with the reviled Colts, there was very little anger toward him. The bulk of it was reserved for Belichick and Pioli. Fans never imagined that Vinatieri—the locals knowingly called him "Adam"—was ever going to leave.

The Colts knew the only way to secure the thirty-three-year-old free agent was to set the market, and they did, giving him a $3.5 million signing bonus as well as annual salaries that averaged $2.5 million a year. The Patriots' offer was in the $2 million range, and they weren't willing to go as high as the Colts were for the signing bonus. They also believed that Vinatieri was losing leg strength and, as a result, his kickoffs weren't as effective as they had been a couple years earlier.

It was all so analytical, and for followers of the team, Vinatieri was all about romanticism and nostalgia. It's not often that people had pictures of kickers, but everyone knew the significance when they went into New England bars and stores and saw the photo of a Patriot in the snow, getting a low kick over the outstretched arms of Raiders and through the uprights. They also found significance anytime Vinatieri attempted a field goal from forty-eight yards, because forty-eight was the magic number in New Orleans for the game-winner against the Rams. There were other kickers in the league with stronger legs and better numbers, but there was such a trust in Adam that most Patriots fans wouldn't have let him leave. Ever.

In April, the public didn't realize it, but another stitch loosened and fell out. As the Patriots made their final draft preparations, they began to focus on a couple players. This process was usually smooth since the staff saw so many prospects the same way. The Patriots had won three championships, aided by several key players the team had selected in the draft or acquired via their extra draft picks.

Belichick and Pioli had completed six drafts together, and there was at least one major building block from each one. Brady had been first. Next were Richard Seymour and Matt Light. The following year brought a Super Bowl MVP, Deion Branch. In 2003, a starting cornerback, Asante Samuel, was there in the fourth round, followed by one of Brady's favorite linemen, center Dan Koppen, in the fifth. The 2004 draft produced a nose tackle, Vince Wilfork, whom the Patriots didn't expect to see at number 21. In 2005, there was a pick that confused all the experts. No one saw Logan Mankins, a guard from Fresno State, as a first-rounder. But the Patriots liked his athleticism and toughness, took him at number 32, and noticed early that he was their best offensive lineman.

Weeks and now days before the 2006 draft, Belichick, Pioli, and Dimitroff had all asked their scouts for decisive, clear opinions on players. When they were asked about Minnesota running back Laurence Maroney and Florida receiver Chad Jackson, they couldn't have been clearer: Most scouts didn't want them to be Patriots. But something was happening during the process that hadn't taken place before. Outside opinions were considered, as usual, but they seemed to be more weighted than they had in the past. For example, the internal report on Maroney was that he had great ability, but his work ethic was poor and he was immature. However, McDaniels, the man who would be his offensive coordinator, liked him, and there was probably a good reason for it: His brother, Ben, was a member of the Minnesota coaching staff and gave a breakdown that seemed to contradict the Patriots' scouts.

Even with the support of the two McDanielses, the numbers didn't match up. Maroney didn't have enough of an in-house consensus to be ranked as high as he was on the Patriots' board, yet he remained there. Whether or not it was intended to be this way, the message to the scouts was that their exhaustive reports were not being considered as carefully as the opinions of the offensive coordinator, who understandably jumped into the draft process well after they did.

As for Jackson, the team had brought him in for several visits and couldn't agree on what his value was. Belichick had begun to develop a relationship with Florida coach Urban Meyer, who thought Jackson's skills would translate to the pros. Receivers coach Brian Daboll, who had good instincts when it came to potential divas, disagreed. He said he didn't want to coach him. Before his first season as receivers coach,

Daboll had interviewed University of Pittsburgh receiver Antonio Bryant and had basically sprinted back to Belichick to say that he was not the Patriots' type of guy. He had that same feeling about Jackson.

The scouts agreed with Daboll. They said Jackson had a bad attitude, was a bad route runner, had excellent straight-line speed, and was a "me" guy. Belichick and Pioli had an understanding that they would never select a player whom they didn't agree on, and certainly not two, but this was going to be a challenge for them. Pioli was leaning toward the scouts on the Maroney/ Jackson debate and Belichick wasn't. Draft debate was normal in Foxboro and everyone believed that it was healthy, but the Patriots rarely found themselves in such philosophical tangles as they got close to making a decision.

They all weren't on the same page, and those voting no on Maroney/Jackson could sense something bad was about to happen as draft day arrived. Those two players hovered on the board. When you're a scout, and you're not allowed in the room on draft day, all you can do is hope that someone else takes the player you don't want your team to have. Or you hope that there's a sudden change of heart with Belichick and that he sees something he doesn't like at the last minute.

One thing everyone did agree on was that the running back and receiver positions needed to be restocked. Corey Dillon had run for a team-record 1,635 yards in 2004, on 4.7 yards per carry. He looked just as powerful in 2005 but slower. He lost more than a yard off his per-carry average, down to 3.5. Meanwhile, the Patriots' top receivers, Deion Branch and David Givens, had both been good in 2005 and both were in their midtwenties. Unfortunately, they both were contract concerns. Givens was an unrestricted free agent and had already left for Tennessee. Branch was under contract and felt he deserved a new deal, so he planned to hold out.

If not Maroney and Jackson, some back-receiver tandem would be Patriots. On draft day, the scouts were sick when Maroney was New England's choice at number 21, ahead of DeAngelo Williams and Joseph Addai. In the second round, the Patriots not only picked Jackson, they moved up to get him. There had never been this much disagreement over players drafted so high. The scouts, truly on the outside of the room looking in, were left to wonder: Did Belichick really value the analyses of two college coaches more than theirs? Or, as he had many years earlier with Branch, had he seen something overwhelmingly positive that they hadn't? Even so, no one ever questioned Branch's attitude and work ethic, just his size, because he was barely five-nine. If Belichick saw Jackson's skills, that was fine, but there was no mistaking that the receiver who was bigger and faster than Branch didn't have an ounce of his game smarts or game want-to.

It had been an odd start to the draft. It didn't feel like the old Foxboro anymore.

Troy Brown knew the team was in trouble on a few counts in September 2006. First, he had been unimpressed by the attitude of the rookie Jackson. "Guys would try to pull him into meetings, and he'd be at his locker lying down," Brown says. "Or a group of receivers would be watching film and we'd try to get him to come with us, but he wouldn't. And he'd get an attitude when you'd ask. I'm not one to argue with anybody. If I ask you a few times and you don't do it, forget it. Some guys would ask seven or eight times.

"He was an athletic kid. Strong. He just wasn't willing to put in the work."

To their credit, the Patriots often didn't rely on draft choices to immediately save them. They liked to develop them on their terms and wait for them to naturally grow into their talent. But they had issues with a veteran, too. Branch was looking for that new deal and the Patriots weren't willing to meet his number. After going back and forth and granting him permission to speak with other teams, the Patriots traded Branch to the Seahawks for a 2007 first-round pick. As a sidebar, they also filed tampering charges against Eric Mangini's Jets. In the world of stocks, the Patriots believed the Jets would have been guilty of insider trading. The claim was that the Jets gave Branch knowledge that weakened the Patriots' position to make the best deal. The league reviewed the Patriots' claims and cleared the Jets of any wrongdoing five months later.

For the players, the reality was that they didn't have their best receiver.

"I wasn't expecting to play a role as a starting receiver," Brown says. He was the ultimate gamer but he was thirty-five, coming to the end of a career in which he had been a receiver, cornerback, and punt returner. "I remember telling Daboll, 'I don't know if I can play sixty to seventy plays a game . . . I was thinking thirty to forty.' Plus my knee wasn't the same after that 2002 season. I never felt quite right after that."

Since the Patriots had also lost Givens to free agency, Brady was throwing to the likes of Reche Caldwell, Doug Gabriel, and a few games into the season, Jabar Gaffney. Given the circumstances, it was probably the finest collaborative work of Brady and McDaniels, now officially the offensive coordinator. Brady threw for over thirty-five hundred yards and had twenty-four touchdown passes. His leading receiver was Caldwell, who, at best, was a number three receiver for most NFL teams.

The team finished with a 12-4 record, which gave Brady a winning percentage of .737 since becoming the full-time starter in 2002. He guided the team past the Jets at home in a wild-card game. The only drama in that one was how Belichick would address Mangini, who had once been one of his favorite pupils but now was on the enemies list. They upset the Chargers, the conference's number one seed, in San Diego. Big plays were made by Brown, who used his defensive-back training to force a fumble on a potentially game-ending Brady interception, and Caldwell, who recovered the fumble and also had a huge reception to set up the winning kick.

Of course, that set up another play-off game with the Colts, this one for the conference championship. The outcome of the game would affect the way the Patriots did business and, by extension, force all of America to pay attention, week after historic week.

5.

The Desert

On a gray and drizzly Sunday morning, typical of late April in New England, Randy Moss waited near a curb at Boston's Logan Airport, looking for his ride. The hood of his sweatshirt was pulled over his head but Moss, who stood six feet four inches, was easy for Josh McDaniels to recognize.

"What up, homie?" Moss said as he jumped into the passenger seat of the offensive coordinator's SUV.

For most people in America, it was simply April 29, 2007. For Football America, it was the second day of the NFL draft, and Moss was officially a member of the Patriots. He had just been acquired from Oakland for a fourth-round pick, a bargain in itself considering that Moss had recently turned thirty and had talent to burn. The risk for the Patriots was that the wide receiver *had* burned some of that talent the previous year in Northern California, pouting and going half speed during a season in which the Raiders were the Patriots in reverse, losing nine consecutive games and finishing with two wins.

McDaniels didn't normally make airport runs to meet his players, but Bill Belichick had made a special request the night before. He and Scott Pioli already had a chance to interview Moss to see what he was thinking, and he wanted McDaniels to be able to do the same thing. He thought the forty-minute drive to the stadium would be a good chance for McDaniels and Moss to set the tone for their relationship. They hadn't been driving long before Moss did a double take at something McDaniels said.

"You're the offensive coordinator?" Moss said in disbelief and admiration. All along, he thought he had been riding with one of the Patriots' college-age interns. "Damn."

McDaniels was thirty-one and could have passed for much younger. His brown hair was often cut to a buzz and he didn't have a trace of facial hair. He had a quick and bright smile, a sure candidate for class president. He and Moss talked for a bit longer and then Moss tried to catch a nap. Instead, his cell phone rang and a player from another team was on the line. Moss explained that he had just arrived in Boston and was a Patriot, and the player told him that New England was on their 2007 schedule.

"Dawg," Moss said in his thick West Virginia accent, "we could play y'all in a parking lot and we'd still tear y'all's hearts out."

McDaniels kept his eyes locked on the road, but it was difficult for him to contain his excitement. Moss had just answered several of his questions with that exchange. Now he didn't need to ask how much fire he had or what his mentality was as he prepared for the season. It was the same as theirs. Moss and the Patriots both had something to prove in 2007. Moss, forever scrutinized over his desire to win, would have to answer the unspoken yet implied Patriots question: Is football important to you? He was known for doing what he wanted, when he wanted, whether it was playing the game, leaving the field, celebrating a touchdown, or giving an interview. He was a notorious freestyler, at times a renegade, and he was always a sound bite away from scorching a franchise's reputation or, worse, his own. In New England, for the first time in Moss's nine-season career, an organization was literally going to take the money out of his pocket—he had agreed to waive the final $21 million remaining on his contract and sign a $3 million deal instead—and force him to be his dynamic self within a greater team structure. If not, they'd let him go.

As for the Patriots, they would have to prove that they could bounce back after the latest episode in their play-off trilogy with the Colts. It had been crushing three months earlier and the outcome continued to sting in April. For the first time, the Patriots had to travel to Indianapolis in January for a postseason game. They had dominated the Colts in the first half, holding them to 6 points. It appeared to be over in the second quarter when Asante Samuel read Marvin Harrison's route better than he did, snatched the Peyton Manning pass out of the air, and returned it thirty-nine yards for a touchdown. Samuel's score made it 21–3. When Samuel stood in the end zone and pounded his chest twice to celebrate what he'd done, you could hear the *thump thump* along with the Patriots' shouts in the quiet building.

The second half was a game-changer, short- and long-term. Not only did the result of it, being outscored 28–13, prevent the Patriots from matching the 1970s Steelers and winning four Super Bowls in six years. Not only did it expose weaknesses they had at receiver and linebacker, weaknesses that couldn't be disguised by scheme. It altered their outlook on when to strike in free agency, how much money they were willing to spend, and the type of weapons they were going to put around Tom Brady.

They weren't planning to match their rivals, step by step, in an arms race, but what they were designing on offense wasn't all that dissimilar from what the Colts had done over the years. It would no longer be accurate to claim that the Patriots didn't have a number one receiver. By the time the off-season was over, they'd have two contenders for that spot. Maybe January in Indianapolis didn't change them as much as it brought out a side that few had ever seen. The loss had taken them around the emotional globe. They were hurt and angered and embarrassed by it, and thus the off-season started to take on the feel of a movie trailer from one of those revenge thrillers, including the baritone of an overly dramatic narrator: *The Patriots had something taken away from them, and now they're on a mission to reclaim what's rightfully theirs* . . . They were bolder, edgier, more uncompromising than usual, and anyone who watched or came across them could feel just how piercing their vision for the 2007 season was. Within a couple weeks of the Colts' loss, all aspects of business were already in motion.

In late January and early February, receivers coach Brian Daboll tried to persuade Belichick to also make him the quarterbacks coach. Daboll, thirty-one, thought he had a case. He had been Belichick's first rise-through-the-system coaching assistant in New England. He had worked well with the receivers in his first five years as full-time assistant coach, getting the maximum out of Deion Branch, David Givens, Jabar Gaffney, and even Reche Caldwell, and he had tried to save the team from drafting Chad Jackson, who was already a bust. Yet McDaniels had gained more responsibilities and ultimately earned a higher-profile job. This was one of the drawbacks of putting young, bright, and highly motivated coaches through the system at the same time. Once in a while, one will hold a position that the other one wants, and it could create a super-intense environment of job climbers and job cannibals.

The Patriots had been fortunate that they rarely came across those situations. The young coaches and scouts usually got along and were too occupied with satisfying the demands of Belichick to think of anything else. Belichick respected Daboll but he had no intention of making him the quarterbacks coach and taking the job from McDaniels, who was doing double duty as coach and offensive coordinator. There had to be a good enough reason to make a move that would disrupt the trust and chemistry that Brady had with McDaniels. Adding the title would have been good for

Daboll and brought him closer to being an offensive coordinator, but it wasn't best for the Patriots.

They were going to remain as they were, and that realization had sunk in when the entire Patriots' coaching staff was in Hawaii for the Pro Bowl in February. A couple assistant coaches noticed that Daboll seemed more defiant than usual during meetings, once even putting his feet on the table when no one else was, and one coach pulled him aside and told him that he was being disrespectful. They wouldn't be able to pull him aside for long: In Foxboro, he'd already had someone clean out his office for him, and when the staff returned from the tropics they learned that Daboll was no longer one of them. He had gotten the quarterbacks job he was looking for. It was in New York, with Eric Mangini and the Jets.

Patriots-Jets stories and *The Godfather* analogies would be abundant in the fall, but no one was thinking that way in March. Belichick and Pioli were on deal-making sprees. Not even two full days into free agency, they had gone against form and jumped in early for linebacker Adalius Thomas. Usually, the Patriots waited for the market to reveal itself before they went in with an offer. But Thomas was their guy and they hooked him with a proposal that would pay $24 million in the first three years of a seven-year contract. He was their type, from being one of the largest linebackers in the league at 270 pounds, to his ability to play multiple positions on defense, to his 11½-sack, 106-tackle season in 2006. Legend was that he could even play corner and safety if you needed him to, and the Patriots, whose lack of speed at linebacker had been exploited in the loss to the Colts, needed his athleticism. He even sounded like a Patriot when speaking to reporters: "I'm a football player. I don't play a position. Whatever is needed for me to do here, I'm going to do." After Thomas, the Patriots picked up two receivers. They signed speedy free agent Donté Stallworth to a creatively structured deal that could be as long as six years or as short as one. Belichick and Pioli both loved the Dolphins' Wes Welker, so they cajoled, sweet-talked, and seduced their divisional rival to trade their top pass-catcher for second- and seventh-round picks.

It got even better just over a month later during the two days of the draft. On day one, the Patriots entered with two first-round picks and were open to trading whatever they had in any round. They didn't think the draft was particularly rich, so they were more interested in watching the phones than watching the board. They eventually used their higher first-rounder, number 24, on Miami safety Brandon Meriweather. They rejoiced when they got a phone call about the other one, number 28. San Francisco wanted back in the first round to take tackle Joe Staley, so the 49ers were offering the Patriots their first-round pick for the next season, when the prospects were projected to be much better. It was exactly what Belichick and Pioli wanted. They thought the draft was weak, and they didn't see many players on the board who could definitively fit into a spot currently held by one of their top fifty-three players. The 49ers, who had won seven games in 2006, believed they were close to being a winning team. But the trade was a gamble for the 49ers, and if they had even a hint of slippage, they risked handing a top-ten selection to one of the best teams in the league.

As much as they wanted to, the Patriots couldn't trade out of the entire draft. One of the issues was that they had a handful of compensatory picks, which were essentially refund picks from the NFL offices and couldn't be traded. Compensatory picks are awarded based on what happened in free agency the previous year. If you lose more free agents than you gain, based on the quality of player you lost, a compensatory (or consolation) pick is given somewhere between rounds three and seven. An even bigger issue was that league coaches and general managers saw the same thin talent pool that they did, so it was inevitable: Before the draft was over, the Patriots would be forced to select several players whom they had graded as wholly undraftable.

Late on day one, April 28, Belichick made the phone call to his offensive coordinator.

"What do you have going on tomorrow morning?" he asked. When McDaniels replied that he was available, Belichick confirmed the deal that McDaniels knew he had been working on but wasn't sure when or if he could close it. "We got Moss. I need you to pick him up from the airport."

And so it was. Randy Moss, who sometimes made plays that seemed possible only in the world of special effects, was going to be catching passes from Tom Brady, who had won well over 70 percent of his starts with receivers far less skilled than Moss. McDaniels was busy as soon as he dropped Moss off at the stadium on that Sunday morning. He had intense closed-door meetings with his offensive coaches every day for a week, repeatedly telling them, and himself, that it was time to think differently. When McDaniels and his staff finished working, they had conceived an offense that would become the best the league had ever seen.

One of the Patriots' most basic plays in 2007 was called Zero Out Slot 66 D Prick Snow. It was a play everyone on offense could recite without much thought, and they knew exactly what every letter, number, and word meant. The "Zero Out Slot" represented the formation, which would have its strength to the right and require the slot receiver to always line up away from the tight end. The "66" told everyone about the protection. In this case, six players would be protecting Brady. "D Prick Snow" was the route manual for all the potential receivers on the play: The tight end and slot would both run diagonal routes, the wide receiver would run an outside curl, and the halfback, after satisfying any blitz-pickup responsibilities, would leak out and be available for a short pass.

With the new Patriots being added to the offense, even the basic plays weren't quite so basic.

"All of a sudden it was, 'Okay, we're not dealing with the same menu of people that we were just a few months ago,'" McDaniels says. "I remember thinking about certain concepts when we got Stallworth and then Welker. We started thinking about what Welker could do inside and the flexibility Stallworth gave us on the perimeter. And there was a certain way of thinking about the new toys we had and tinkering with them a bit. Then, wow, Moss gets put into the mix.

"Now we've got to figure out what we're going to do to use him. It's like you've got something wonderful and you're not going to waste it. And it would have been a waste to just make him conform to things we had planned for other guys who didn't have his skill set. There were plays we created, and there were plays that we copied and stole from other teams with the thought being, 'Okay, these are things that this guy has done before. He's good at them. We haven't done them before. We need to get good at them.' So that spring was, I would say, a rather large undertaking in terms of where we were trying to be by the time we rolled the ball out there in June and July."

One thing everyone seemed comfortable with was the thought of Moss as a teammate. He was a bit of a contradiction, and it was a contradiction that the Patriots could embrace: Although Moss always seemed to be in the spotlight, he didn't seek it. He felt that he had been burned by reporters in the past, reporters unwilling to be fair and thorough, so he shut most of them down. It was different with his teammates and coaches. They loved his stories, his accent, his hilariously profane outbursts in the locker room, and, of course, his talent.

Even before minicamp in early June, he proved he could fit in with the biggest Patriot of them all. The team had a charity golf tournament a week before minicamp, and it was as much a family reunion as it was a tournament. Players greeted one another excitedly in the relaxed clubhouse atmosphere; proudly carried their modest swag bags; razzed each other during a spirited long-drive contest, which was won by Brady; and finally separated into small groups so they could actually play golf. Belichick had a blast in his group, often listening to and laughing at the tales of Moss, who was his golfing partner for the day.

Not much had changed a week later in Foxboro, nor in the weeks that followed going into training camp. Moss quickly grasped the offense—"One of the most intelligent players I've ever coached," says McDaniels—and proved to the coaches that he understood his role on each play they presented to him. But mastering the offense during drills and practices with your teammates isn't always the biggest challenge. What about the games? The problem for Moss in late July and all of August was that he had a slight pull in his left hamstring. The Patriots didn't want to take any chances so they took the most conservative tack possible. They held him out of the entire preseason. So despite all of McDaniels's work to integrate Moss into the offense, no one knew how it looked on the field against actual competition.

It would remain a mystery until the afternoon of September 9, the Patriots' first game of the regular season, against Mangini's Jets. That game in New Jersey would be full of events that would lead to broken records and broken relationships; it would spark year-long debates about integrity, excess, and authenticity from all directions—Internet posters, current and former NFL players and coaches, TV talking heads, and even a persistent U.S. senator; it would become sporting America's most passionate numbers game, with forty-four states on the offensive, six New England states playing defense, and fifty-three players believing, correctly, that 90 percent of the country was rooting for them to fail.

But before the NFL's reality TV show began in Jersey, the Patriots and their fans were dealt a humiliating sucker punch on the last day of August. One of their leaders, safety Rodney Harrison, admitted that he had purchased human growth hormone online. He got the NFL-banned drug by using an illegal prescription from a doctor he'd never met. He had been caught because the district attorney's office in Albany, New York, had been orchestrating a sting operation, trying to nab manufacturers and suppliers of illegal drugs. Harrison had given his real name and home address to a wellness center from which he placed orders in Florida, and when a doctor from that center was caught in the web, so was the Patriots' safety. Harrison met with commissioner Roger Goodell in New York and was suspended for the first four games of the season.

The suspension was tough to comprehend in New England. While Harrison was routinely called one of the dirtiest players in the league, the Patriots and their fans often substituted "dirtiest" for "toughest." Teammates raved about his overall leadership and the way he commandeered young defensive backs. More than that, he had been quietly generous in the community. When a Boston church needed a new floor for its gymnasium, Harrison paid for it and insisted to one of the ministers that he didn't have to share the news with the media. And when that same minister told Harrison that he was thinking of going back to school for an additional degree, Harrison offered to pay his tuition. But the Samaritan work got lost in the smallest print when the suspension came down.

The sentiment began in September and lasted through the fall and winter: The Patriots, once known as everyone's cuddly underdogs, were now viewed as frothing pit bulls.

On a couple of awkward occasions since leaving the Patriots for the Jets, Mangini had initiated telephone conversations with Belichick. Mangini lamented how sour the relationship had become and told his former boss, "It doesn't have to be this way." Belichick listened but remained skeptical, and the glowing United Nations photo op never happened. The two coaches were in a tough spot. It wasn't just because of the Patriots' staffers and players who flat-out told Belichick that Mangini was recruiting them to New York as they all prepared for a play-off game in Denver. Mangini dismissed the charge and pointed to the Patriots' five turnovers as the reason for the team's first postseason loss under Belichick. It wasn't because of New England's tampering charges against the Jets, either. The dilemma was that their families were close, even after the exit to New York. There were times when Mangini's wife, Julie, hosted Belichick's children at the Manginis' home and had them in her private suite at Giants Stadium. When they were together, the families tried their best to separate AFC East blood sport from the real world. But there was no sidestepping reality: Mangini knew the Patriots, inside and out.

In a sense, even if he hadn't left on questionable terms, he had to be kept at a distance. He knew too much. He was a divisional competitor who knew how the Patriots schemed, how they scouted, how they thought. Belichick was the one who had given Mangini NFL life when he was in his early twenties. He brought him to the Jets from Baltimore and brought him to New England from the Jets. Four years earlier, they had argued in a coaches' meeting until they were both red in the face, but that did nothing to stop Mangini's advancement, and two years after the intense argument, naturally, Mangini became defensive coordinator Romeo Crennel's replacement when Crennel left for Cleveland.

Mangini was different from most, if not all, of the young people Belichick hired. Most of them were grateful for the opportunity and wouldn't dream of crossing him, in any circumstance. Mangini was grateful, too, but he seemed to hold an "All is fair . . ." attitude when it came to debating Belichick in a meeting or competing against him on the field. There didn't seem to be many boundaries or places he wouldn't go in a competitive situation with Belichick. He may have been the only Belichick disciple who felt that way.

So it wasn't a surprise when the men found themselves at an impasse during one of their last clipped conversations. Each of their organizations thought that the other had been guilty of stationing a cameraman in a forbidden area of their stadium, with the purpose of videotaping coaches' signals. The Jets believed it happened to them in September 2006; the Patriots felt it happened to them during a play-off game between the teams in January 2007. With the constant back-and-forth and mistrust, it didn't seem that the relationship between Mangini and Belichick could get any worse. But it did.

In the Northeast, one of the best things about the start of the NFL season is that you can simultaneously experience summer and fall. All the sports schedules say that fall is just a few weeks away, with the arrival of play-off baseball and NHL and NBA training camps, yet the weather is still made for T-shirts, flip-flops, and the beach. It was a thought that everyone in the New York metropolitan area could relate to on September 9.

A crowd of nearly eighty thousand filed into Giants Stadium on a day that you wished you could order on demand: plentiful sun, 80 degrees, and just enough wind to keep anyone from complaining that it was too hot. The Patriots and Jets were minutes away from kicking off their season and continuing a rivalry that was rare for pro sports; while some rivalries are made-for-TV only, this one was just as nasty, if not nastier, when no one was looking. As usual, Mangini and Belichick strolled the sidelines without glancing at each other, while their families laughed and talked together in a suite high above the field. The stadium had a familiar first-game hum, a combination of excitement and the nerves of not knowing what to expect. Fans had it, and so did Josh McDaniels.

"I didn't know if I felt great. I didn't know if I was scared to death; I wasn't quite sure," he says. "I just thought, 'We've got a chance to do some good things.

I'm just not sure how this is all going to unfold.' With Randy missing the entire preseason, we still hadn't played together."

It was Patriots-Jets, so most eyes in the stadium were fixed on the field in the first quarter. Tom Brady had already connected with one of his new receivers, Wes Welker, for an eleven-yard scoring play and a quick 7–0 lead. There was no need for anyone to be looking at the sideline, unless it was someone on the lookout for a camera. Early in the game, Jets security had noticed a Patriots videographer, Matt Estrella, on the New England sideline. He was focusing on the New York defensive coaches and their hand signals. Within seconds, Estrella was escorted off the field, his camera was confiscated, and he was held in one of the stadium's private rooms.

Suddenly there were two events happening at the stadium that would have the nation talking for the rest of the year. The one that could be seen by both live and national audiences was impressive. The Patriots' Ellis Hobbs returned the third-quarter kickoff an NFL-record 108 yards for a touchdown and a 21–7 lead. Later in the third, Moss ran toward rookie cornerback Darrelle Revis as if he wanted to go down the right sideline. But he noticed the way he was being covered so he made an abrupt left turn; ran across the entire field while being hopelessly pursued by a linebacker, cornerback, and safety; and looked in the sky to find a heave from Brady descending into his arms. The only thing that kept it from being the typical, improvised backyard touchdown play was that most backyards don't stretch fifty-one yards. It was a dazzling play from a pitch-and-catch standpoint, but more telling was the amount of time Brady had to throw the football. He and the Patriots were almost impossible to beat if there was that much time for decision-making.

"You know what that day was? To me, that day changed football," McDaniels says. "That changed the way I perceived what we could do offensively in the NFL. I had never been a part of a game that things like that happened, and you're going, 'Man, we called a simple play and all of a sudden we scored a touchdown or we gained forty yards.' It didn't happen the previous year. We worked harder because we didn't have those kind of explosive players. And it opened up a whole new world for me."

Unfortunately for the Patriots, the day wasn't solely about their 38–14 win and their exciting offensive aesthetics. By the time most Patriots went to work on Monday morning, a new term was pushing its way into pop culture. People were calling it "Spygate." The news of what happened in the first quarter was initially reported by a Jets website. According to the report, the camera and its contents were turned over to the NFL and the league was investigating the matter. It didn't take long for the mainstream media to pick up the torch, and what a torch it was. The story went viral at warp speed, and soon it was the hottest topic in America.

The hours between Monday afternoon, when most football fans had heard about the story, and Thursday night, when the commissioner announced his ruling, could best be described as a verbal takedown of everything the Patriots had accomplished. They were officially accused of taping an opponent's defensive signals, but the Patriots were put on trial for dozens of other claims and slights. The composite national view was, "If they would videotape coaches' signals, what wouldn't they do to win? I'll believe almost anything."

Breaking news was mixed in with anecdotes and speculation, and it created a torrent of acid rain for the Patriots. There was a report that they had rigged the headsets and phones in their stadium so other teams couldn't communicate. There were reports that they taped mikes to their defensive players' jerseys so they could record the quarterback's verbiage and cadences. There was a story from Pittsburgh receiver Hines Ward, a member of two teams that lost conference championships to the Patriots, who focused on how suspicious it was that New England defenders were able to call out some of their plays. LaDainian Tomlinson, whose San Diego team was scheduled to play the Patriots in week two, said, "I think the Patriots actually live by the saying, 'If you're not cheating, you're not trying.' They live off that statement. Nothing surprises me, really. You keep hearing the different stories about the stuff that they do."

And that was just the buildup to the ruling. The commissioner didn't give credence to any of the wild reports; his focus was the tapes and what to do about them. The bad news for the Patriots came on Thursday night when Goodell announced that he was fining Belichick the maximum allowed, $500,000, as well as fining the organization $250,000, taking away a 2008 first-round pick—or a second and a third in the unlikely event that they didn't make the play-offs—and seizing all signal-related tapes and notes in the Patriots' possession. It was an unprecedented punishment. Belichick said in a statement that his misinterpretation of a league bylaw on cameras was a mistake. He was referring to a phrase that stated it was illegal to use electronic equipment "that might aid the team during the playing of a game." In the statement, Belichick said, "We have never used sideline video to obtain a competitive advantage while a game was in progress." The assumption, then, was that the Patriots were using the tapes for what former offensive coordinator Charlie Weis would call "research and development." But Belichick never specified in the statement why the team was taping, and he wouldn't comment on the matter for the rest of the season.

Seemingly a few seconds after Goodell's ruling, the talking heads were out with more criticism.

Don Shula, the NFL's all-time leader in coaching wins, said there should be an asterisk next to Belichick's record. Fox analyst and four-time Super Bowl champion Terry Bradshaw, in an open letter on TV, told Belichick, "You are now known as a cheater," and added that he hurt the team and the New England fans "all because of [his] arrogance." On NBC, former player Cris Collinsworth said the penalty handed down by Goodell wasn't enough. He said he wanted to see Belichick suspended for the next meeting with the Jets as well as a play-off game.

Belichick was aware of all that was being said, and he had a thought: "We've got to be ready to play on Sunday." He knew he could spend every minute of his time at the office talking about staying focused, but those players were going to be confronted with Spygate, everywhere, as soon as they left the building. On the afternoon of September 15, the day before the Patriots' second game of the season, Belichick had an idea.

A few years earlier, he had been on a cross-country flight to Los Angeles and was seated next to a man wearing a Patriots golf shirt. "Are you the new coach?" Belichick joked, and the man, a comedian named Lenny Clarke, replied, "Yes, I am." Clarke had been born and raised in Cambridge, Massachusetts, and once worked as a janitor in Cambridge's city hall. He and some colleagues went out to a bar one night and saw a few comedians, and one of Clarke's janitor friends said, "You're funnier than he is. You should be up there." Thus, a comedy and film career was born. As he sat next to Clarke on the flight, Belichick worked on studying draft prospects and Clarke worked on a movie script. When they landed, they exchanged numbers and promised to stay in touch.

By September 2007, they had talked and been to dinner many times. So Clarke wasn't surprised on the fifteenth when he was sitting in the owners' box at Fenway Park and a call came in from Belichick. Clarke was enjoying himself, not just because it was a Red Sox–Yankees game, but because he was hanging out with another comedian, Steve Martin.

"Lenny, I need a favor," Belichick said.

"You name it, Bill. Whatever you need."

"Lenny, I need you to come speak to the team tonight. It's been a rough week. Just come in and tell some jokes. You can rip me, whatever you need to do."

"But I'm at Fenway right now," Clarke said, realizing that the Patriots were meeting at least a half hour away in suburban Norwood.

"I know," Belichick said. "There's a car waiting for you behind home plate."

Clarke left the park, went over some ideas as he was driven to the hotel where the Patriots were meeting, and eventually walked into a room full of players and coaches. He delivered twenty-five minutes of risqué material. He got ahold of a minirecorder and made fun of Belichick. He made fun of players who even thought of being listed on the injury report. "This poor bastard has a hole in his heart and comes back from a stroke," he said, pointing to Tedy Bruschi, "and some of you still haven't recovered from sprained ankles." He went down the line: Belichick, Bruschi, Brady, Moss. No one was safe. The players were in tears from laughing, and dozens of them came up to him afterward to tell him how great he had been.

The message was clear. There was no need to tiptoe around what happened and have an internal pall over it. It was still football. That was their internal philosophy; they were far less carefree when challenged and questioned by fans, former and current players and coaches, and the media.

In New York, Mangini told his close friends that he never wanted Spygate to go as far as it did. He said he thought the matter could be worked out between the Patriots and Jets, and if it were up to him, he wouldn't have advised Jets security and upper management to be so aggressive in their handling of the situation. His feeling was that as he was coaching, his own organization was taking things further than he would have been willing to go; for example, he never wanted the league involved. His front office did, though. It was Patriots-Jets. It was always bitter, and the feeling was that the Patriots would have done the same thing if they had caught the Jets red-handed. That was an organizational view, but because of Mangini's history with Belichick, this became his story and his dime-dropping. By the time he walked off the field on September 9, wearing his charcoal Jets shirt, he really was the villain in black as far as the Patriots were concerned.

It no longer mattered to them how Mangini felt. They didn't care that he actually saw things the way they did and that he believed the taping in no way undermined what they had accomplished as champions. They didn't care that it bothered Mangini to see their dynasty, *his* dynasty, too, questioned and mocked. It didn't matter. Some Patriots coaches with whom he had remained close stopped taking his calls. Others, for obvious political reasons, were sure to keep him at a public distance. Some players in New England would soon refer to him as Fredo, the resentful Corleone who betrayed his brother Michael in *The Godfather*. Unlike Mario Puzo's characters, there was no acting involved between the coaches. The relationship was over.

The Harrison suspension, the Spygate penalties, the wild rumors of what they'd done, and the critics all simplified things for the team. They could have been stars of a new documentary, *America Hates the Patriots*, and as a result they became protective of their championships and defensive when anyone questioned their achievements. They had to send a message, and winning games wasn't going to be enough. They played with an attitude and a sneer, and if they didn't roll teams, especially those who had publicly doubted them, they were disappointed.

"Yeah, man. I was angry as hell," Bruschi says. "It was a lot of things. First, it had become open season, kind of an onslaught, on Bill Belichick. Then I felt anger that the media or our fans would think that any type of videotaping we did would help us win a football game . . . sometimes from film work, I'd recognize all the plays before they happened. I'd know formations, techniques, where the ball's going. But the other team would still get the first down, because their players are good, too. Or I'd get blocked. That's football.

"But the whole situation made me want to beat everyone by more than we did. I wanted to indirectly respond to the Spygate criticism. I wanted to say, 'All right, look at the players that we have and what we're able to do. We'll beat your team by fifty, forty, thirty, or whatever it takes. We'll still win. That's how good we are.' I used it as motivation. I had been using things that people had said about me ever since I was in high school. And now you're trying to stomp on the essence of why I play the game, which is to win world championships? You want us to prove that we're great? Well, all right. Here you go, Jets fans. There's Moss for fifty yards."

The mission could be seen in the season's first five games. The Patriots scored at least 34 points in each game, had at least four hundred total yards of offense in each, and barely allowed Brady to be touched as he was sacked a total of three times. They appeared to be a team constructed in one of John Madden's video games, a team in real life imitating electronic art. The only difference was that in the video games, there was no button you could push on the controller to give your team a grudge.

Every week, there was a new Spygate quote or column to add to the smoldering logs. If it wasn't the words of a former coach, it was the words of a current one. Colts coach Tony Dungy, one of the most respected voices in sports and a Patriots adversary, checked in to say that Spygate was sad for the league. He then wondered how Belichick would be perceived historically and made a reference to Barry Bonds. The insinuation was that Belichick and the use of a camera was comparable to Bonds's alleged performance-enhancing drug use on his way to seven MVPs and the all-time home-run record. Every week there was something the Patriots did on the field that would incite bloggers and talk-show callers.

In weeks six through eight, they were accused of running up the score. They started with a 48–27 win in Dallas, followed by a 49–28 victory in Miami. After what everyone else thought was a cruise over the Dolphins, Belichick tore into his defense and told them they were playing like the worst defense in the league. The whole team responded with a shutdown of Washington, 52–7. The Patriots had scoring drives in that game of sixty-seven, seventy-three, eighty-five, eighty-eight, and ninety yards. They were 8-0 and Brady had already set his career high in touchdown passes with thirty. Eleven of those TD passes had gone to Moss. On the flip side, Mangini's Jets were 1-7.

Halfway through their season, the Patriots were still tethered to week one in Jersey. Gregg Easterbrook, an intellectual who contributed to the *Atlantic Monthly* and the *New Republic,* wrote about the difference between the Patriots and Colts in his weekly column on ESPN.com. While the Colts and Dungy represented all that is good, the Patriots and Belichick were evil and "scoundrels in the service of that which is baleful: Dishonesty, cheating, arrogance, hubris, endless complaining, even in success." The writer went on to question Tom Brady's work with charity and compared his "smirk" to vice president Dick Cheney's. "People who smirk," Easterbrook wrote, "are fairly broadcasting the message: 'I'm hiding something.'"

The atmosphere created by Spygate, combined with the all-around force of what was happening on the field, brought out the strongest emotions from the unlikeliest Patriots.

Rosevelt Colvin had suffered a career-threatening hip injury in 2003, was back on the field in 2004, and had fully recovered by 2005. In 2007, he was part of a strong starting linebacker group that included Bruschi, Mike Vrabel, and Adalius Thomas. Colvin was one of the most devout Christians on the team. He didn't drink alcohol or curse, and as part of his faith, he gave 10 percent of his $4.6 million annual salary to his church. He was a big believer in humility because, as they say in Baptist churches like Colvin's, he had a testimony.

When he was a senior in high school, he wasn't just thinking about wearing a big-time school's hat on national signing day. He also had to think of his parents, who were being evicted from their home. They were forced to live in a place owned by friends of theirs until they regained their financial footing. Several years later, Colvin says he was headed down a bleak financial path himself. He was a young NFL player who wasn't saving his money and instead wasting it on cars and clothes that he didn't really want. The turnaround came when he renewed his faith and actually started saving more money than he ever had, even with the tithing to his church.

Colvin wasn't the type to take things for granted. Yet in 2007 he also thirsted for the Patriots' big plays and high scores, driven to prove that, unlike in Bonds's case, records could be broken without artificial help.

"Honestly, I loved it when we scored as much as we did," he says. "I think it was an 'F-you' to the league. What's funny is that some teams that were commenting about stealing signals, like the Colts, were some of the teams that were stealing signals. I know for a fact that the Colts were stealing; we'd talk about it before we played them. But it never offended me because it's football. People have to understand that it's not like a class where you get the answers to the test and do well. You can steal all you want in football, but you still have to play and figure out how to get around that three-hundred-pounder.

"I knew I wasn't giving my rings back. We played the way we did because we were good. Not because of film."

The issue Colvin raised was at the heart of dozens of Spygate-inspired conversations around the country. How much was too much? Everyone knew that stealing signs was fairly common in the history of football. One of Belichick's boyhood memories was going to scout college games with his father, Steve, and watching his dad decipher the hand signals of both teams by the second quarter. That was in the late 1950s and early 1960s. In modern pro football, most teams had someone giving "dummy signals" and someone communicating the real thing. The disagreement was over the act of taping the signals and studying them. The unspoken message, then, seemed to be that it's okay to steal what all of the public can see, as long as you do it without the use of a camera. Once the camera was introduced, the conversation changed, and most people couldn't explain why. But the consensus was that stealing and studying with the naked eye was acceptable, but stealing and studying on tape was not.

On November 4, Colvin had a chance to show his hometown just how good his team was. He grew up in Indianapolis and attended Broad Ripple High, fewer than ten miles from where the Patriots and Colts would play the most hyped game of the half season. Both teams were undefeated, with the Patriots at eight wins and the Colts at seven, and even if they hadn't been, there was always the inimitable Patriots-Colts backdrop. While the game was sloppy at times and didn't live up to the billing, it was the first real scare the Patriots had gotten all season.

With just under ten minutes to play, Peyton Manning scored on a sneak and the Patriots trailed 20–10. As had been the case the entire season, the biggest play occurred when Brady found Moss. The six-four receiver noticed that he was in a mismatch against five-eleven defensive back Antoine Bethea, and like a basketball player, Moss positioned himself so he could complete his end of a fifty-five-yard pass play. That set up a short touchdown pass from Brady to Wes Welker. The entire series had taken less than two minutes.

When the Colts got the ball back, still ahead 20–17, they didn't do much with it. Colvin was disruptive on a key third-down play, sacking Manning and forcing a fumble. The Colts recovered but were forced to punt, and when they did Welker put together a twenty-three-yard return. Another big play, this one from Brady to Donté Stallworth for thirty-three yards, set up another touchdown. Brady saw an open Kevin Faulk in the middle of the field and hit him for an easy thirteen-yard score. In about four minutes, Brady had thrown two TD passes. Appropriately, the 24–20 win was secured when Colvin, a graduate of the Indianapolis public schools as well as Purdue University, smothered a Manning fumble and allowed the Patriots to run out the clock.

The win over the Colts allowed the Patriots to go into their bye week a confident 9-0. They came out of it, on November 18, roaring. They were in Buffalo, playing for the first time all season in weather that was going to be similar to that of the play-offs. It was western New York in the fall, so of course it was freezing. Playing as if they heard whispers that they would crack in temperatures below 40, the Patriots offense produced a 35-point first half against the Bills. Brady threw four touchdown passes in the half, all to Moss. After just thirty minutes and a 35–7 lead, it was obvious that the Patriots and Bills were not playing the same game. But everyone associated with New England wanted more, even if the scoreboard showed that it was late and the eyes of their opponents were closed. More. Everyone wanted more. Not just on a cold November Sunday in Buffalo, where they'd go on to win 56–10, but every week.

"I remember every game that I watched, hoping, even though it was not the right way to think, that we'd win by at least twenty-something points," says Thomas Dimitroff. "I wanted sixty points or forty-five points, just as a member of that organization, to show: This is utter dominance. And I remember every game that came along, there was such a drive, it was this fueled desire to do *something*. And I didn't care if people thought, 'Oh, they're a bunch of bullies.' I wanted to be a bully one time in my life, where it was like, 'Let's just do something outrageous and be a part of history that way as well.' It was amazing, because that's not normally my makeup."

It was tough to define what normal was for Dimitroff, because things were beginning to change in his personal and professional life. He and wife, Angeline, had recently welcomed a son, Mason, to the world. Raising a child is challenging enough, and even more so when one of the parents is on the road for 225 days a year. That was Dimitroff's schedule as he hotel-hopped around the country, scouting, interviewing, and watching film at dozens of colleges. Even when he was in familiar Foxboro he was on the road, staying in a nearby Sheraton that acted as the team's Saturday-night headquarters before home games. He and other Patriot scouts had a job tougher than most of their peers since their college reports were directly tied to their knowledge of pro players. Dimitroff didn't complain about the schedule and the constant mint on the pillow and neither did Angeline, but the frenzy was going to change if he was able to take the next step for which he and Pioli had been planning.

No one in the organization was aware of it, but after Dimitroff and Pioli had completed their necessary work, they often had long talks about what Dimitroff needed to do to become a general manager. Pioli gave him a taste for what the job was like by making sure he was in the loop on contract talks and free-agent conversations, allowing him to speak at certain marketing functions in which Pioli would normally be the keynote speaker and giving him some media experience by permitting him to speak, off the record, with a handful of local and national beat writers and football columnists.

The depth of their relationship was apparent on several levels, including an ironic one: Pioli was preparing Dimitroff for a job that he technically didn't have himself. Everyone knew that Pioli was the Patriots'

GM in action and responsibilities, but he was officially the team's vice president of player personnel. He didn't have the GM title because the Patriots liked how there was already an understanding of the team's hierarchy and believed naming Pioli as a GM would have confused things. By helping a friend, Pioli was also potentially weakening his department, but he couldn't deny that Dimitroff was ready to lead his own personnel group. While Dimitroff's scouting was greatly influenced by his father, who marveled over tough players, his area of focus was different. He was most intrigued by athleticism and movement, along with the ability to compete and be tough. He also had the benefit of his father's hindsight.

"My dad always said that if he had gone back to coaching, he would have evaluated more and coached less. He said he would have backed off and let the athleticism of some of his players take over."

Tom Dimitroff also had words about being a GM. He told his son that if he ever secured one of those jobs, he hoped he'd stay true to who he is. "Don't become one of those big shots," his father had said, "who thinks they're better than everybody else."

In 2007, Pioli had such trust in Dimitroff's judgment and intelligence that he realized that he could ease up a bit, which allowed his staff to see the boss's other dimensions. Once a week, his wife and four-and-a-half-year-old daughter would come to the office and his demeanor would change instantly. His daughter, Mia, could get him to do things that no one else could.

"He started wearing nail polish on his toes," says a laughing Jay Muraco, who became the Patriots' college coordinator in 2000. "Mia would paint his toes and he wouldn't dare remove the paint. Everything started to revolve around his family. When he could, he was spending time with her. And if that meant something as simple as driving her to school, or getting out of the building a little earlier on Fridays than he had in the past, he was going to do it."

Now that they were both fathers, Pioli and Dimitroff could relate to the pursuit of excellence at work and at home. Their appetite for scouting and winning football games, as the 10-0 Patriots were doing in historic fashion, didn't change; what changed was a bigger appetite for things away from football. What they both hoped for was success in the business they loved, along with a sliver of stability, although stability was not what the NFL was known for.

Pioli knew what it had been like for his wife, Dallas, growing up as Bill Parcells's daughter. Before Parcells was a popular and witty pro head coach, he moved between several jobs in the college game, and his family moved with him. Dallas attended three different high schools, in three states, over four years. Pioli hoped that Mia wouldn't have to go through the same thing, but if the job did force him to relocate, he was certain that a couple things would never be affected by new cities and new friends.

Number one, of course, was the relationship with Mia. He had listened to enough family advice from people in his profession, and heard too many tales of regret, not to learn his lesson. He'd heard from men who were away so much, and so distracted by the game, that their kids became young adults in a flash, and they truly didn't know the people who held their last name. Pioli didn't need to be convinced. His daughter, with her deep blue eyes, seemed to see his thoughts before he said them, so sometimes as the two of them sat together quietly, driving on a father-daughter date, they'd glance at each other and just giggle.

The second thing went back fifteen years, to Cleveland. As a single and low-paid employee of the Browns, Pioli was told by Belichick to make sure there was always someplace in the country that the family could call home. One day you're a Cleveland Brown, for example, and with the stroke of a pen you become a Baltimore Raven. As the job changes, the family needs an anchor. It wasn't relevant news to Pioli's life at the time, but as he advanced in the league, married, became a father, and commanded a generous salary, the advice resonated. Like Belichick, Pioli also found that permanent family place on Nantucket. Many people on the island followed an unofficial tradition and put quarterboards on their homes, displaying a name. The Piolis did as well. Their quarterboard reads CASA MIA.

As the Patriots moved toward the 2007 holidays, they were scheduled to take on two mediocre teams, the Eagles and Ravens. They were drawing record TV numbers each time they played, with the audience still having a distaste for who they were yet not wanting to miss what they might do from game to game or series to series. In terms of the offensive standard they'd set in the first ten games, weeks eleven and twelve were a disappointment.

Three days after Thanksgiving, they couldn't shake the Eagles, playing without injured quarterback Donovan McNabb, at home. They were able to escape with a 31–28 win when Asante Samuel came up with an interception, his second of the game, with four minutes to play. They came out of the game with two news items, one each for the present and near future. The item that needed to be responded to immediately was the health of Colvin. He'd broken a bone in the middle of his right foot and would be out for the rest of the year. The other news involved the Eagles and their defensive approach.

Belichick had a lot of respect for Eagles coordinator Jim Johnson, and the men talked strategy several times during the season. He had been with the Eagles for nine seasons and was given complete control of their defense. He was one of the best coaches in the league at disguising his blitzes, and it's why the Eagles had accumulated more sacks than most teams in football over an eight-year period. Belichick enjoyed talking with Johnson because when Johnson was looking at football, he had a knack for seeing beyond the obvious.

Johnson had the right idea in the game against the Patriots, but he didn't have the right team with which to pull off the plan. If the Patriots ran into a play-off team with a Jim Johnson disciple leading the defense, it might be a problem. Johnson's defenses blitzed more than they brawled. The defensive ends and outside linebackers were built like ripped sprinters and small forwards, zipping past you before you could line them up and knock them down. They ran you to exhaustion when they were going well and then, when you were unsteady in the fourth quarter, they'd finally throw a jab. And knock you out.

After the 3-point win over the Eagles, the Patriots did the same thing against the Ravens on the road, although the win had twice as many theatrical moments as the Philadelphia game. It started with ESPN's *Monday*

Night Football booth, which included Don Shula for a quarter and a half as a guest commentator. As the last coach of an undefeated team in the NFL, his presence made a lot of sense. At times, the legendary coach could be heard celebrating with analyst Tony Kornheiser when it appeared that the Patriots were going to lose.

That was a strong possibility with the Patriots trailing 24–20 with 1:48 to play and facing a fourth-and-one. Brady went for a sneak and appeared to be stopped. The Ravens, led by emotional players such as Bart Scott, Ray Lewis, Ed Reed, and Terrell Suggs, briefly danced on the field. But the players became angry when they learned that the play was dead because Rex Ryan, their defensive coordinator, had called a time-out. When the Patriots eventually scored to win, 27–24, the Ravens went crazy.

Penalty flags were picked up and fired into the crowd. Helmets were thrown. Accusations of special treatment, as well as demeaning treatment, were tossed in all directions. Before all that happened, there was a bizarre sideline exchange between Rodney Harrison and Ravens head coach Brian Billick. After a Patriots interception, Harrison ran by Billick and made a comment about Baltimore quarterback Kyle Boller. Billick responded by blowing two kisses at Harrison. After the game, Ravens cornerback Samari Rolle claimed that an official dismissively called him "boy" because he was upset with Rolle's questioning of his calls. All of the Ravens seemed to suggest that America had more love than hate toward the Patriots, because the Patriots, in their eyes, were the people's choice. "It's hard to go out there and play the Patriots and the refs at the same time," Baltimore cornerback Chris McAlister told reporters afterward. "They put the crown on top and they want them to win."

Whatever the reason, the Patriots had a nation's full attention as they stood four games away from an undefeated regular season. They smashed Pittsburgh, 34–13, after a young Steelers safety, Anthony Smith, guaranteed that the Steelers would win. In a nondescript rematch of the season's first game, where the story of the year originated, the Jets became the first team to hold the Patriots to fewer than three hundred yards of total offense. Mangini knew what it took to slow down players he had practiced against and coaches with whom he had practically lived for six years. But New England and its 265 yards still moved to 14-0, and pushed the Jets to 3-11, with a 20–10 victory. The Patriots weren't sharp against the Dolphins and had four turnovers, but their record bulged to 15-0 in a runaway, 28–7.

One regular-season game remained, in Giants Stadium, and it was accessorized with two controversies.

The NFL Network was supposed to have exclusive broadcasting rights to the Saturday-night matchup between the Patriots and New York Giants. That had been the plan for the entire season, although as the Patriots piled up wins the broadcast schedule drew more attention.

The problem was that the network reached just forty-three million TV households, fewer than half of what was available in the country. There was a chance that the biggest season finale since 1972 would be missed by the majority of the nation, including fans in Boston and New York. The issue was becoming heated and political, until Roger Goodell made a political move: The commissioner announced that the game would be seen on three networks, NBC, CBS, and the NFL Network. That usually happened for breaking news and presidential debates, but the commissioner understood what was at stake.

As for the game itself, the debate around New York was whether the coach everyone wanted to fire the year before, Tom Coughlin, should go all-out in the final game of the year. The 10-5 Giants already knew they would be in the play-offs, win or lose, and would be going to Tampa to play the Buccaneers. Should they go for the knockout punch against the perfect Patriots and risk injury? What if they got into a competitive game against the Patriots and showed too much of what they could do to the Bucs, who had already started scouting them?

Coughlin weighed all the possibilities and decided to go for it. New York may have wanted him out after the Giants' average 2006 season, in which they finished 8-8 and lost in the first round of the play-offs, but the call he made against the Patriots was a sound one. And in the third quarter, it looked like a brilliant one. The Giants were ahead 28–16, and Eli Manning had already thrown three touchdown passes. Before the game, Eli had talked with his big brother, Peyton, who built him up by demythologizing the Patriots and explaining just how beatable he thought they were. Eli looked comfortable for most of the game, but the Patriots owned the final nineteen minutes. Laurence Maroney scored on a short run with four minutes left in the third quarter. It was a big moment for Maroney, but it was deceptive for what was happening in the game. The Giants were shutting the Patriots down on the ground but getting sliced by the pass. It was 28–23 after Maroney's score, and 31–28 after Tom Brady and Randy Moss had cosigned a piece of history with eleven minutes to play.

Brady entered the game with forty-nine touchdown passes and Moss had twenty-two touchdown receptions, both tied for the best marks in history. They set individual records on the same play, when Moss perfected the most universal pickup play of all time, *Go long!* and caught a Brady spiral that resulted in a sixty-five-yard scoring play. For the flourish, Moss caught the 2-point conversion from Brady as well. It was close to over about seven minutes later when Maroney scored again, on another short run, to make it 38–28. The final was 38–35.

Sixteen wins without a loss was never the goal, and as the Patriots liked to say, sixteen wins in the regular season doesn't buy you anything. But the Buckingham Palace guards of the NFL, usually stoic and quick to underplay their achievements in a game, had to celebrate this one. They hugged each other and laughed on the sideline, and they celebrated even more in the locker room and on the short plane ride back to New England. On December 29 in metropolitan New York, they had gotten a forty-eight-hour head start on Dick Clark and the revelers in Times Square. That's when a ball would drop and millions of people would resolve to be perfect at something. The Patriots had already done it. They had scored 589 points, entered the end zone seventy-five times, and converted 74 extra points, all league records. There had been warts, but they played the schedule presented to them perfectly.

Their final game was one the entire nation had seen, on three TV networks. It was the first time in forty years an NFL game had been shown by three distinct broadcasting companies. Which meant, on the Patriots' second trip of the season to Giants Stadium, cameras were a part of the story. But this time, the more cameras they saw the better they felt.

While parts of the Patriots' 2007 regular season had been described as controversial, with Spygate, all it took was a glimpse to the south to see just how minuscule their problems were. Sure, the Patriots had been fined and scrutinized and had even lost a first-round pick. But they weren't part of an organization in which the star player had been charged with and convicted of dogfighting and interstate gambling, resulting in a twenty-three-month prison sentence. Nor did they have to worry about a head coach, hired in January 2007, spending exactly eleven months on the job before deciding he had to get the hell out of there, even if there were three games left on the 2007 schedule.

The Atlanta Falcons were one of the few NFL teams that didn't give a damn about Spygate. With Michael Vick's imprisonment and Bobby Petrino's in-season departure for the University of Arkansas, they had their version of hell on earth to worry about. When the 16-0 Patriots were enjoying their bye week prior to the divisional play-offs in January 2008, the Falcons were looking for an identity. General manager Rich McKay was going to become the team's president, meaning that the Falcons were absent a head coach and GM. They were interested in, teased by, and down the aisle with some of the biggest names in the NFL. They thought they had an agreement with Bill Parcells, but he went to Miami instead. Bill Cowher was rumored to be a target, but he chose to stay with his lucrative, once-a-week TV gig. Pete Carroll had established a dominant program at Southern Cal, where McKay's dad, John, had won four national titles in the 1960s and '70s. Carroll was said to be interested if he could coach and pick the players, but that plan never materialized.

On and on the search went for the large Falcons search committee, with name after name being thrown into the mix. Finally, the Falcons decided that they'd go with an up-and-coming GM. The name most mentioned was Tom Heckert, a highly regarded GM in Philadelphia. Thomas Dimitroff was also a candidate, but he had a few things working against him. The perception in the scouting world was that he would never make it as a guy who had to go to the office every week. He was too Boulder, too snowboard and mountain bike, too free-spirited and work-at-your-own-pace. But that was perception. The bigger issue was reality: The Falcons were having a hard time getting permission to interview Dimitroff.

There was a small window in which the Falcons could interview candidates involved with play-off teams. They were making little progress with the Patriots, mostly because Bill Belichick was not convinced that a legitimate GM's job was available. He wondered if Dimitroff would have final say over personnel, or would he be working under McKay? Plus, he didn't want to lose one of his top personnel employees only to see him go to the Falcons and be swallowed up in office politics. After nearly a week of being blocked by Belichick, there was a conversation between the owners, the Falcons' Arthur Blank and the Patriots' Robert Kraft, and permission was finally granted. It was clear that the job was one where the GM would pick the players, but when that had been established, there wasn't much time for the Falcons to interview Dimitroff face-to-face.

On January 4, a Friday, Dimitroff got some bad news from Nick Polk, one of the Falcons' search committee members. They had simply run out of time. An interview, logistically, was impossible because members of the organization were spread across the country.

Dimitroff got off the phone, told Angeline the latest, and said, "That's too bad." He then thought about it longer and called Polk back. "I really want to interview for this job," he said. "How about a webcam interview? Can you ask Mr. Blank if he'd be open to that?"

Blank, one of the most successful businessmen in the country and a cofounder of the Home Depot, loved the idea. He admired the stability and success that teams like the Eagles, Colts, Steelers, and Patriots had, so he was especially interested in speaking with candidates from those teams. He had also heard a lot about Dimitroff's smarts and his "look."

"I guess at that time Thomas's hair was even longer than it is now. And I'm not sure he had a blue streak in his hair, but I think it was described to me as kind of like a blue streak," Blank says with a smile. "If you drew up a picture of what a guy from Boulder, Colorado, would look like, in a stereotypical way, it would be what was described to me about Thomas. In the case of Home Depot, we prided ourselves on building a company based on unique personalities and overachievers. So the fact that he apparently looked a little different and thought a little different about the world didn't bother me. He had a lateral view of things and I liked that."

Dimitroff knew about Blank, too. He knew Blank and Bernie Marcus's Home Depot story, how they had been fired from their jobs in 1978, come up with a concept for giant stores that would span at least sixty thousand square feet, and watched those stores become overwhelmingly popular in just a couple years. He also knew about Blank's fashion sense, which was known to be supreme even when Blank was a New England college student at Babson. So as he prepared for his noon web interview on Sunday the sixth, Dimitroff staged his wardrobe and his house.

He owned a few ties, but they were from Jerry Garcia's line. He just didn't see his Grateful Dead meshing with Blank's Gucci. He asked Angeline to buy him some appropriate ties and a dress shirt. He owned one suit, so he could go with that. As his wife shopped, he rearranged some furniture and made sure that the view behind him included a map and looked professional. Just before noon, Angeline returned with a pressed shirt and a tie that would fit in Blank's collection. Of course, when the interview began, Dimitroff was overdressed and the dapper Blank could be seen on camera in a sweat suit.

It didn't matter. The day before, the Falcons had received a hard copy of Dimitroff's PowerPoint presentation, so they were quickly engaged in conversation. Dimitroff and Blank clicked. They talked football, children, nutrition, leadership, work-family balance, and even snowboarding. They were disconnected a few times via webcam and they reconnected to talk some more. When the webcam became a pain they talked on the phone. Noon became two o'clock and two o'clock became four.

When the interview ended, the Falcons huddled with one another and Dimitroff called Scott Pioli.

"How did it go?" Pioli asked.

"I think it went well," Dimitroff answered. "We talked for four hours."

"Four hours, Thomas?" Pioli said. "You must have done great."

He found out just how great it was less than a week later, a day before the Patriots would try to continue their perfect season against Jacksonville. It was Friday the eleventh, and he and Angeline were going to dinner that night. The timing was impeccable, because shortly before they left the house Dimitroff received a phone call from Blank. "You'll be going to dinner tonight with the new GM of the Atlanta Falcons," he told his wife, and they shared a long embrace. He had a medley of quick thoughts, from how he'd have to move from his beloved Boulder, to how his salary had just more than tripled, to what his father would have thought of all this. He imagined Tom Dimitroff looking down on him and saying, "Well done, son. Well done."

In a truly perfect world, Dimitroff thought, the Falcons would have given him the job after the Super Bowl so he could enjoy his final weeks as a Patriot in a memorable season. But there was too much work to be done, from hiring a head coach to figuring out how he was going to find a quarterback to replace Vick. In just a couple days, he had gone from being a Patriot and having Tom Brady and his fifty touchdown passes to being a Falcon whose two quarterbacks, Joey Harrington and Chris Redman, had seventeen combined TD passes in 2007. The job switch happened so quickly that he didn't have time to say good-bye, face-to-face, to all the scouts he supervised. It's not like another job where you stay and give your two-week notice. He was gone. He talked with Pioli, of course, and responded to a congratulatory e-mail from Belichick.

The good news for Dimitroff was that his suddenly old team, the Patriots, would make quick work of Jacksonville in the play-offs, 31–20. It was good because it allowed the Patriots to advance to their fifth conference championship game of the decade, and it freed up one of his coaching candidates, Mike Smith, who was Jacksonville's defensive coordinator.

Unlike the previous year, when everyone anticipated another Colts-Patriots classic, the AFC Championship Game didn't generate national excitement. The more dramatic story line would have included India-napolis making yet another wintry play-off trip to New England, with a chance of ruining a perfect season. But the Colts had their own problems and were upset at home by San Diego in the divisional round, an upset that sent the Chargers to Foxboro.

The Chargers and Patriots had a bit of a history from the previous year. After a play-off loss to the Patriots, when the Chargers were the conference's top seed, LaDainian Tomlinson had said the Patriots "showed no class" in victory and added, "Maybe it comes from the head coach." In the same game, Mike Vrabel had taunted Chargers quarterback Philip Rivers, telling him that he and his teammates knew that he "would never be Drew Brees," and Rivers had called the Pa-triots' Ellis Hobbs "the sorriest corner in the league."

Any Tomlinson-vs.-the-Patriots-defense theme ended in the first quarter. The running back had a sprained medial collateral ligament, but the team didn't announce the injury to the media. So when he carried the ball just twice before spending the rest of the day on the sideline, he became a natural split-screen subject with his quarterback. Rivers had hurt his right knee against the Colts and had actually torn his ACL. He had arthroscopic surgery six days before the conference championship, just to give himself a chance to play on

Sunday. He dragged his right leg up and down the field against the Patriots, clearly affected, and he earned his opponents' respect.

No one in New England knew it, but their quarterback was hurt, too. Brady's throws were as inaccurate as they had been all season, and he threw three interceptions. His worst throw, in judgment and location, was at the San Diego two. A decent throw, or run for that matter, would have allowed the Patriots to exhale in a closer-than-expected game. But he lobbed the ball right into the middle of the defense, and it was intercepted easily by cornerback Antonio Cromartie. New England eventually won, 21–12, but consecutive win number eighteen hid some problems that would be exposed two weeks later.

In the middle of celebrating, no one was going to question two play-off defenses, the Jaguars and Chargers, adjusting to Moss and limiting him to just a single catch in both games. It would be far too negative to suggest, after a 122-yard rushing effort in the conference championship, that the Patriots couldn't expect to get that from Laurence Maroney in the Super Bowl. And it would have spoiled the party if someone had pointed out that all the mismatches seemed to be over, with the games becoming much more competitive and the points tougher to come by. It may have had something to do with Brady hurting his right foot, which was affecting his ability to move and throw with his usual accuracy. It would become a big story a couple days later when he'd be spotted by a SoHo photographer, on his way to see supermodel girlfriend Gisele Bündchen, wearing a protective boot and limping.

All of that could be dissected later. The Patriots were once again AFC champions, which was an answered prayer for many red-cheeked and frostbitten New Englanders. The forty-second Super Bowl, to be played on February 3, wasn't just at a site that was somewhere a lot warmer than Boston and Providence and Nashua, New Hampshire. It wasn't just somewhere out west where the Patriots and Giants would play for the NFL title. The game would be held at the University of Phoenix Stadium, right in the middle of the desert.

Over the years, people in New England have come to understand the differences between newspapers and magazines during Super Bowl week. It was the magazines that threw the great parties, teeming with movie stars, pop singers, pro athletes, and people whose names were on the tip of your tongue. It's the *Maxim* and *Playboy* and *Sports Illustrated* and *ESPN The Magazine* parties that Super Bowl fans want to crash, just for a chance to brush shoulders with the celebrities who might be there.

As Patriots fans knew, newspapers were different altogether. Serious newspapers were too serious to sponsor parties that anyone wanted to attend. What papers did, in the eyes of the fans, was screw up Super Bowl week. That was still the prevailing view from 1997, when the *Boston Globe* ran a breaking-news story that head coach Bill Parcells wouldn't coach the Patriots after the Super Bowl. Indeed, it was a true story and Parcells was headed to the Jets, but fans didn't want to hear it until after the game.

Eleven years later, on February 1 and 2, the newspaper industry struck again at Patriots fans, in the form of a light jab from the *New York Times* on Friday and then an uppercut from the *Boston Herald* on Saturday.

The Friday *Times* story quoted Pennsylvania senator Arlen Specter extensively. He said he was considering bringing the Spygate issue before the Senate Judiciary Committee, of which he was a ranking member, to explain why the NFL destroyed evidence that was on the tapes. Also quoted in the story was an ex-Patriots employee, Matt Walsh, who was fired in 2002. He hinted that he was in possession of something that could change the Spygate discussion, but he wanted legal protection before going forward. The story couldn't be taken completely seriously, though, after Specter's suggestion that, for the first time in the history of the country, America might need to see tapes of NFL defensive coordinators giving signals: "What if there was something on the tapes we might want to be subpoenaed, for example? You can't destroy it. That would be obstruction of justice."

The Saturday *Herald* had the more explosive piece. The paper had a source who claimed that the Patriots had taped the Saint Louis Rams' final walk-through before New England's upset win in Super Bowl XXXVI. It had been an underground rumor, similar to many others the Patriots had heard in September, but now it was in print on the day before the most significant game in team history. The story quickly made its way around the country and into a meeting with Belichick and his seven team captains.

"We had done all our preparations already," Tedy Bruschi remembers. "And he said, 'A story is out there saying that we filmed the Rams' Super Bowl walk-through, which is absolute bullshit. It's not true. But the story's out. Do you think I should address the team?' And we looked at each other as captains and said no. Because we had been through the fire already all year about Spygate and all the accusations people were putting on us. And we were supposed to double up the fire at that point? He never really addressed it during the year, either, because we just kept going and focusing on what was next. So why now?"

No matter what happened in the game, the season was going to end just as it had begun. There would be conversations about their greatness, mixed with commentary about mysterious cameras and tapes. The commissioner was on their side and believed them when they said the story was not true, but still, one day before the game was played, there was a five-hour meeting between Patriots executives and representatives of the commissioner's office. Five hours. It was an exhausting process. All they would have to do is get through one more full day, and if they did their jobs, they could be standing next to the commissioner and, finally, talking about something good.

On Sunday evening, when the Patriots' offense entered a silver-paneled domed stadium in suburban Phoenix, they could have looked across the field and noticed a man who was paid to slow them down. His name was Steve Spagnuolo, and he was New England through and through. He had an accent that could have been his dad's north Cambridge, his mom's Dorchester, or his neighbors' Grafton. He remembered the days when watching the Patriots play in a Super Bowl was a dream, especially if you had season tickets like he did in the early 1970s. The Patriots didn't win much, but he still sat in end-zone seats and yelled for his guys, Mack Herron and Steve Grogan.

Now, as defensive coordinator of the Giants, he was about to find out if his plan was going to work. He was one of the people who had disagreed with Tom Coughlin back in December: He didn't want the head coach to play all of his starters in the regular-season finale against the Patriots. He worried about injuries, and he didn't want to show too much that their first-round opponent, Tampa, could plan for. The best part about playing that game was that he had called for a number of vanilla defenses, so if the Patriots thought the same thing was coming, New York would have a slight advantage.

"To be honest with you, I thought if we could keep them under thirty, maybe in the midtwenties, then we'd have a chance of beating them," he says. "I thought that was just being realistic. The offensive line was unbelievable. The system was great. And the weapons . . ."

Spagnuolo told his defensive players to think about two things: Hit Tom Brady, and be extra attentive to yards after the catch. The Patriots were certainly going to catch the ball, but they didn't have to run free afterward. He knew his defenders were loose and confident. They were the last team to get in the play-offs, yet they went on the road and took out Tampa, Dallas, and

Green Bay. Their easy smiles were not forced. What pressure did they have to worry about as 12-point underdogs in the eyes of Las Vegas? The Patriots were the ones wearing jewelry, real and imaginary. There were the three Super Bowl rings many of them had, and there was the gradual necklace that now included eighteen "W's" that all of them had first worn in September. They weren't sneaking up on anybody.

Like most Super Bowls, you didn't have to scan the crowd long to notice the cross-section of celebrities, but what made this different was the historic nature of it. Nobody among Alicia Keys, Jesse Jackson, Peter Farrelly, Amare Stoudemire, and Pamela Anderson had ever seen a team go 19-0. Thomas Dimitroff had helped build the team, but now he was a spectator like the people around him, in great seats overlooking the forty-yard line. He sat there with Angeline, along with a couple they'd be seeing a lot of in Atlanta: new head coach Mike Smith and his wife, Julie. His new life had begun, but he couldn't help but feel that pregame belly knot for the Patriots. Scott Pioli got it, too, and there were times he'd be watching the game and unconsciously squeezing a plastic water bottle he was holding.

Even Bruschi, who was playing in his fifth Super Bowl, could feel the weight of the season descending.

"I think that we would have been considered the biggest joke in regular-season history if we would have lost in the divisional round or in the conference championship. So that was pressure. But I really felt it leading up to the game. It's supposed to be just about playing the game and executing your assignment and doing those things. But I mean, you're in the midst of a year where everyone is questioning your head coach, you know, and the validity of your world championships are questioned. It's the most pressure I've ever felt in my entire career."

Anyone watching the Super Bowl, unaware of either the Vegas line or the undefeated stakes, would have seen two equals early in the second quarter. The Patriots led 7–3 at that point, although careful observers of the team should have followed the clues that this wasn't New England's typical 2007 game. Eli Manning threw a knuckleball down the left sideline, which Ellis Hobbs picked off at the ten and returned to the Patriots' thirty-three. But strangely, an offensive line that protected and pushed better than any in the league twice couldn't generate a surge on short-yardage plays. So with an opportunity to cash in on a turnover, the Patriots couldn't pick up a first down.

A few seconds later there was another chance: Manning fumbled at his own thirty-two, and Patriots linebacker Pierre Woods landed directly on top of it. He had it. But running back Ahmad Bradshaw went to the grass, fighting and wrestling Woods for the football. He got it. The Giants didn't score when they got the ball back, but they had prevented what could have been an easy scoring chance for the Patriots.

Meanwhile Spagnuolo, who spent eight years on Philadelphia blitz master Jim Johnson's staff as a defensive backs and linebackers coach, was forcing Belichick and offensive coordinator Josh McDaniels to come up with a strong counter-move. On back-to-back plays, Brady was sacked for seven-yard losses. He hadn't been hit that hard in the previous eighteen games. The Patriots would take their 7–3 halftime lead, but there would have to be a switch.

"When they went to their nickel-and-dime packages, they had Osi Umenyiora, Michael Strahan, and Justin Tuck all on the field," McDaniels says. "So we went to a package that would have them go with their base defense and keep an extra pass rusher from coming in."

It worked for a while, but then Spagnuolo saw what was happening.

"They'd have two tight ends, two wide receivers on second and eight, second and long," he says. "Usually they'd do that to run, but we figured they wanted to pass out of it. So we put our pass rushers in against that personnel."

Halfway through the third, with the score still 7–3, Brady dropped back to pass at the New York twenty-five. He may have had something, but he didn't have time to react to it. Strahan dropped him for a six-yard loss. It was New York's fourth sack of the day. The Patriots were in field goal range in a game that looked like it would be decided late. Maybe they would have tried it if they had Adam Vinatieri, a hero of previous New England Super Bowl wins. Vinatieri was in Indianapolis, and the Patriots had replaced him with a fourth-round pick in 2006, Stephen Gostkowski, who had missed just three kicks all year. The Patriots had a fourth-and-thirteen from the New York thirty-one, and if they had elected to kick, the attempt would have been for an ever-familiar forty-eight yards.

But instead, they were going for it.

Both coordinators were excited with what they had called. McDaniels acknowledged that it's never a high-percentage play on fourth-and-thirteen, although the Patriots had played with an offensive fury the entire season. McDaniels thought Jabar Gaffney would be open in the seam. Spagnuolo had a new play for this situation called Tahoe Spin. Since the Giants usually blitzed on third- and fourth-and-long, he wanted it to appear that the weak corner was coming on a blitz. But the corner would fake the blitz and wind up playing a two-deep zone.

"Great call on Spags's part," McDaniels says.

Incomplete pass.

The third quarter was scoreless, but a few seconds into the fourth, Manning found the least-likely man in the stadium for the biggest play of the day. Tight end Kevin Boss, a six-foot-seven rookie who had caught nine passes all season, chugged for forty-five yards. That led to a short touchdown catch from David Tyree, a player whom New Englanders would never forget.

It was 10–7 Giants, with eleven minutes to play. The crowd started to sense an upset might happen when the Patriots responded to the Giants' score with just four plays, but the Giants went three and out themselves and gave the ball right back. Spagnuolo had said he'd be pleased by keeping the Patriots in the twenties, yet they hadn't even reached double digits. They had the ball at their twenty with eight minutes to play. With the way the defense had played, not allowing a play over nineteen yards all day, he could reasonably think about allowing a field goal at worst. But just as the same thought was circulating through the crowd, Brady went to work with a short passing game. Five minutes later Moss was in the end zone with a six-yard reception.

With the score 14–10 with 2:40 to play, the ball at the Giants' seventeen, did Spygate matter? Did senators and commissioners and newspaper columnists? Did ex-players and ex-coaches? What mattered was that a defense had eighty-three yards to defend, and if it could do that, the Patriots would have their fourth championship of the decade.

Their first chance to end the game came with just over ninety seconds left. The Giants had a fourth-and-one at their own thirty-seven. If they didn't pick that up, the Patriots could easily run out the clock. The Giants were going to give the ball to 265-pound Brandon Jacobs, who had an even bigger back, 270-pound Madison Hedgecock, blocking for him.

"That was my play," Bruschi says. "I went in, took on Hedgecock, and slowed him up a little bit, and Hedgecock and Jacobs, they ended up falling forward. I think about that play, just, man, maybe, should I have taken that block on different? Could I have gone over the top, which I've done many times? But I've seen that play over and over, and I did what I could to squeeze in between those offensive linemen in the B gap and get down on Hedgecock and hope that the cavalry came. And they came, it was just six inches to a foot too late."

The real just-too-late play came with seventy-five seconds left. This time it was third and five, Manning setting up from his own forty-four. He seemed to be caught between defensive ends Richard Seymour and Jarvis Green. "I look at that and say he's so in the grasp," Dimitroff says. The officials didn't agree. Manning escaped and threw a pass to the middle of the field, and Tyree was there, covered by Rodney Harrison. Tyree was supposed to be covered by Asante Samuel in the Cover 2 man scheme, but Samuel's greatest strength was his weakness, too. He was a freestyler, which had allowed him to make several big plays in his career, but this was his second Super Bowl in which he had been caught playing the wrong coverage at the worst time. In the Super Bowl win over the Eagles, he had been playing zone when he should have been playing man, and it led to a touchdown. Against the Giants, Samuel had gotten lost in the coverage, so Tyree became Harrison's problem.

Tyree reached for the ball and grabbed it with two hands stretched above his head, as if reaching for something on the top shelf. Before he could bring the ball to his body, he held it against his midnight-blue helmet. Harrison fought him for the ball the entire time, trying to dislodge it from his hands or his body. No luck. It was a huge, thirty-two-yard completion.

The Patriots were in trouble.

Sixty seconds remained.

After converting yet another third-down play, to Steve Smith, Manning had his team at the Patriots' thirteen with thirty-nine seconds left. The Patriots' defense appeared to have the percentages in their favor two minutes earlier, forcing the Giants to look out at eighty-three long yards for a touchdown. But the Giants had gained seventy of the necessary eighty-three, the end zone close enough to smell and touch. New England defenders looked to the sideline and got the defensive call from Belichick, not defensive coordinator Dean Pees. Belichick's call was not complicated. New England needed to be aggressive, so the call was for a blitz, with Hobbs playing Plaxico Burress inside for the skinny post. Hobbs had played half of the season with a labrum tear that often forced him, or a trainer, to pop his shoulder back into place to stay on the field. He also played with a persistent groin injury that led to "the trainers stretching me out on a table, with my legs spread, and giving me a shot in the balls."

He played hurt the last half of the season and through the postseason, which earned him a lot of unspoken respect in the locker room. There were times his shoulder hurt so much that he would feel stabbing pain even if he picked up a flimsy remote control and tried to hold it above his head. But on Super Bowl Sunday, no one cared about his injury. He was the target Manning chose, and when the blitz didn't arrive, he and his pain were alone on an island. "I tried to protect that slim post," he says. "Basically, it was an all-or-nothing play. When Plaxico went to the outside, I had no chance to recover." Manning had an easy touchdown pass to Burress, who was open after Hobbs bit on a route that Burress never ran.

The Patriots had a chance, maybe, at the end to get in position for a tying field goal. But for the fifth time of the evening, Brady was sacked. He tried to find what had worked in so many weeks, plays from the backyard from him to Moss, plays that had made record-holders of them both. But this was the Giants' night. They won, 17–14.

"I saw a guy walking around with hats and T-shirts that said 'Undefeated' and then he disappeared," Roosevelt Colvin says. "I had a broken foot and was supposed to be using crutches, but I was so mad that I walked back to the bus, limping the whole time."

As the Giants celebrated the greatest upset in Super Bowl history, the stadium truly rocked. Walking away from it, the crowd could be heard taunting the bunch that couldn't quite complete the historical run. "Eighteen and one," they shouted, more delirious than drunk. "Eighteen and one . . ."

"It was the closest I had come to tears since my dad passed away two years earlier," Jay Muraco says. "I hate to say that, because it's just a game. I went to the postgame party afterward, and I don't even remember who was there. I was there, but I wasn't. I didn't want to be at that party, but I also didn't want to be in my room thinking about what happened."

Bruschi was at that party, too, and the only reason he went was to give people who had come to see him permission to have a good time. He knew they would be studying him to see if it was all right for them to smile. He had short conversations with them all, told them to eat and dance, and then he left the party so he could assess what had just happened.

After the previous January in Indianapolis, when they'd blown a 21–6 halftime lead against the Colts, the Patriots didn't think things could get worse. This was worse. They had lost, and therefore the country could be satisfied with the ending of the *America Hates the Patriots* documentary. America's prize was the ability to look at the Patriots, who had raced and raged their way through eighteen games, and smirk. The Patriots would go down in history, all right, but it would be as the most famous Super Bowl runner-up the game had ever seen.

Dimitroff left the stadium, sent a sympathy text to Pioli, and rode back to his hotel on a bus full of Patriots haters. Some were fans of the Falcons, and he wasn't sure who the others were. They said things about New England that he had heard before, from fans and colleagues alike.

"We'd always hear, 'Ah, look at the Patriots scouts, you know, they think they're above everyone else; they have all the freakin' answers.' And I remember being irritated, like, 'Are you kidding me?' We never carried ourselves like that. Because of Scott and Bill, we had very definitive guidelines as far as what we were doing to help build the team, at least from our perspective as personnel guys.

"But let's call it the way it is: When you're competing with people in the NFL, you have to understand that no one in the league is truly happy for you if you win three Super Bowls."

In Atlanta, a city and franchise would be happy with one.

6.

The New Falcon Vernacular

The old joke in Atlanta was that if you wanted to get rid of your Falcons tickets, the worst thing you could do was put them on the dashboard of your parked car, windows down, in plain sight for all to see. The car might not be there when you came back to the space, but the tickets certainly would. The Falcons were born in 1966 and immediately developed a reputation: If there was greatness to be had, they'd *almost* have it. And if you loved them, truly loved them, they'd always find a way to bring a new dimension to something as old as heartbreak.

They could have had one of the all-time greats, Vince Lombardi, as their first head coach but settled instead for one of his assistants, Norb Hecker. Four coaches and twelve years later, the Falcons made their first play-off appearance. But by that time, some fans had begun to refer to owner Rankin Smith and his family as "the Clampetts" after the fictional family of *The Beverly Hillbillies*. Perception of ownership aside, the Falcons had everyone's attention in 1980 when they went on a nine-game winning streak, won twelve games, and hosted America's Team in a divisional play-off game. What luck: They were facing Tom Landry's Cowboys, but they didn't have to deal with Roger Staubach, the epitome of fourth-quarter cool. Staubach's on-field charisma and comebacks allowed Landry to pace the sideline without ever appearing to sweat or adjust his feathered fedora. Staubach's retirement meant that the new starter was Danny White, who was just as likely to throw an interception as a touchdown pass. The Falcons had the Cowboys down by 10, 27–17, just six and a half minutes away from advancing to their first conference championship game . . . and they lost, 30–27.

Oh, the Falcons had it all. They slept through the 1980s, missing the play-offs for eight consecutive seasons. In their last home game of the decade, they drew an official crowd of seven-thousand-plus to Atlanta–Fulton County Stadium. The next day, which happened to be Christmas, they were outdrawn by the NBA's Hawks, who had more than thirteen thousand fans watch them play the Cavaliers. As teams in metro

Atlanta achieved success, from national titles in football for the University of Georgia and Georgia Tech to a string of division championships and a World Series title for the Braves, the Falcons changed coaches, uniforms, and stadiums yet managed to remain the same.

They had a coach, Jerry Glanville, whose gimmick was leaving tickets for Elvis. They came up with a gimmick on offense, too, with Coach June Jones's Run and Shoot. In 1993, they could have simply checked off a contractual box that would have allowed them to match any offer that Deion Sanders received from another team. Sanders was the league's best cover corner, a rare two-sport athlete who was also a Brave, and always one play away from an interception and a new end-zone dance. But the Falcons didn't check that box, Sanders became an unrestricted free agent, and he played the next two seasons in San Francisco and Dallas, picking up Super Bowl rings with each team.

No one ever said the Falcons were without talent and smarts, on the field and in the front office. The Smith family hired Dan Reeves in 1997, which brought instant credibility. Reeves had played in the Ice Bowl, which wasn't just Packers vs. Cowboys; it was Lombardi vs. Landry. He had won a Super Bowl as a player and had taken the Broncos there three times as a head coach. He was supposedly all Landry old-school, wearing a suit and tie on game days when most of his peers were getting by with thoughtless khakis, sneakers, and team-issued pullovers. But he also knew when certain types of old got in the way of doing good business.

As soon as Reeves walked into the Falcons' offices, he noticed that the computer system was from another era. There was a bizarre operating code, and the system was not Microsoft compatible. He called for an update, revamped the scouting department, and hired Ron Hill, whom he had worked with in Denver, as one of his key personnel men. One year later, the Falcons had the most balanced and dominant team in franchise history. They won fourteen games in the regular season and earned a spot in the conference championship, where they were underdogs to the Minnesota Vikings. The Vikings had the highest-scoring offense the league had ever seen, led by two receivers ticketed for the Hall of Fame, Cris Carter and Randy Moss. But for the first time in their history, the Falcons rewarded their fans with an unexpected overtime win, 30–27, and secured a spot in Super Bowl XXXIII.

Reeves couldn't have been more familiar with the Falcons' Super Bowl opponent. He knew the quirks of the city and the region, the skills and psychology of the quarterback, and the thought process of the head coach. Instead of standing with a bunch of overmatched

Broncos on Super Bowl Sunday, Reeves was now across from them. They were led by two people he hadn't always gotten along with when he coached in Denver: head coach Mike Shanahan, who had been his offensive coordinator, and quarterback John Elway, who had famously willed the Reeves Broncos to their first Super Bowl with a ninety-eight-yard march known as the Drive. Unfortunately for Atlanta, the Falcons-Broncos matchup took on the predictable theme of *This Is Your Life*, but the subject was not Reeves; it was the Falcons, with all their tragicomic history crashing the party before the party could even start.

Really, only Falcons loyalists could appreciate the absurdity of what happened the day before the game in Miami. Falcons safety Eugene Robinson was presented with the Bart Starr Award, given to a player for his high moral character and leadership. Robinson was an outspoken Christian, nicknamed the Prophet because of his ability to dispense Bible-verse wisdom. He proudly accepted the award on a Saturday morning, smiling as he stood with his wife and two children. Later that night, he drove down Biscayne Boulevard apparently looking to pay for oral sex. He wasn't the first athlete to do it, and he wasn't even the first Christian athlete to do it, but it was just fitting that he would do it on the same night that Miami-Dade police had targeted the Biscayne area and had a sting operation in effect to curtail prostitution and drug use. So fewer than twenty-four hours before the Falcons would play the most meaningful game in their history, one of their leaders was arrested, along with twenty-four other johns, and charged with soliciting an undercover police officer for oral sex. The Falcons had gone from the *Hillbillies* to *Night Court*.

Robinson played the next day, but of course, he was on the wrong end of the biggest play of the Super Bowl: Elway noticed that Robinson was badly out of position, and in a 10–3 game, the quarterback found receiver Rod Smith for an eighty-yard scoring play that officially lit the torch for the blowout. The Falcons would trail by as many as 25 points before losing 34–19.

There were more complicated days ahead for the Falcons in terms of producing consistent and reliable teams. Reeves displayed some foresight before the 1999 draft, but he didn't feel comfortable carrying out a plan that didn't have a lot of in-house support from his personnel staff. The New England Patriots were willing to trade their first-round pick, originally number 20 overall, for Falcons running back Jamal Anderson. Reeves was ecstatic. He liked the twenty-six-year-old back, but Anderson had carried the ball more than four hundred times in 1998 and he wanted to get paid. As a former running back himself, Reeves knew the team had already gotten the best from Anderson. If someone was willing to give up a first-rounder for an All-Pro power back who had carried the ball that much, as well as take on Anderson's contract demands, Reeves thought they should leap at the deal. They didn't, and two games into the season, Anderson had blown out his knee.

The franchise began to change two years later, in 2001. While they had played football for thirty-five years and never had back-to-back winning seasons, the Falcons suddenly had hope. A bold play had been made for the number one pick in the draft, which would be used to select Virginia Tech quarterback Michael Vick. Reeves was captivated by Vick, and long before the Falcons had traded with San Diego for the top pick, the coach walked around the office and referred to Vick as "the Offensive Weapon." He envisioned building an offense around a quarterback with a sprinter's speed and a right fielder's strong arm. Vick was a kid, just twenty years old on draft day, but all the football people from either school, old and new alike, could see how gifted he was. There wasn't a player like him in the league. If he could ever gather his multiple strands of talent and weave them together, he would lead and entertain and win. At least that was the dream.

As Vick was emerging in his first season with the Falcons, there was a deal being brokered between Taylor Smith, son of the Falcons' founder, and a local businessman who had already starred in the average American employee's daydream. Imagine: You and a couple friends start a business, but not just any business. You start a franchise that revolutionizes the marketplace, makes billionaires of you all, and crests as your former employer, who fired you, goes broke and belly-up. That was part of Arthur Blank's story, the part that began in 1978 when, at the age of thirty-six, he was fired from his management job at a place called Handy Dan Hardware. Blank, Bernie Marcus, and Ken Langone were among those who decided that they would come up with a chain of stores that were bigger than the competitions'. This idealistic place, the Home Depot, would have more inventory, more engagement between employees and customers, better prices, and a philosophy of working—living, really—that couldn't be altered.

"Bernie and I decided that before we began to think about succession planning and before we thought of who should become the next assistant manager and store managers and district managers, regional vice presidents, presidents, etc., our first question should always be, 'Are they ambassadors for our culture?'"

Blank says. "It's 'Do they believe in our culture? Do they live our culture?' So that became more important than anything else they were doing. They could have been really good at whatever their job was, but if they weren't great cultural leaders and weren't strong when it came to character, integrity, trust, and didn't understand what we were about, then they weren't going to be promoted. It didn't matter how good they were at their job."

Blank bought the Falcons toward the end of the 2001 season, paying $545 million. In the beginning, Blank would be no different from many of the league owners whom he was now joining: On day one, nearly all of them have earnest smiles and a fresh-faced naiveté, confident that universal business principles and common sense can be applied to running an NFL team, too; by their second or third year, there's the realization that, for example, conceiving and building Home Depot is one thing, while inheriting an NFL team, scars and all, is quite another. If you're lucky, your kind of coach, your kind of front office, and your kind of team will already be in place. Realistically, it'll take some firing, hiring, and maybe some mistakes before the organization is truly yours, in deed and principle. After that expensive and often humbling initiation, there's usually an experienced "You don't know what you don't know" gaze reserved for the league's next wide-eyed new owner.

For most Falcons employees, Blank's arrival was a good thing. The new owner made it clear that he wanted the best of whatever money, persuasion, or goodwill could buy the Falcons. Best board of directors. Best facilities. Best marketing team. He was not some king in a tower, shouting instructions to peasants. He had a sharp sense of humor and a disarming smile, and his background allowed him to relate to a wide variety of people. He grew up in Queens, which could quickly be heard in his voice, and his family of four had shared a one-bedroom apartment. He and his brother had the bedroom and his parents slept near the foyer on a pullout couch. He was a smart kid but far from an entitled one. His father died when Arthur was fifteen, leaving his mother widowed at thirty-seven. He attended Babson College, just outside of Boston, and graduated in three years. He was a lifelong high achiever and visionary, taking over a franchise that was his opposite.

On the day he was approved by the league and officially took control of the Falcons, he was advised by Patriots owner Robert Kraft that there were many similarities between his previous business and the NFL, but one thing that was not similar was media coverage. It was going to be a new world for him, Kraft warned, so he'd have to prepare for it. Blank listened and invited the Falcons' head of football communications, Reggie Roberts, to his home to talk.

"It was the first time in my career an owner had reached out to me like that," says Roberts, who had worked in the league a dozen years before Blank arrived with the Falcons. "We spent more than an hour talking, and he asked a lot of questions about me, as a person, in addition to getting my professional ideas on how we should approach the media. He gave his ideas, but he also listened to mine."

The presence of Blank improved the work experience for most, but not Reeves. Blank had said he wanted the best of all available things, and that included the best coach and GM, too. Reeves had proved ten times over that he could coach, but the owner didn't want the head coach to also be in charge of picking the players. It may have been different if Reeves had been exceptional when it came to the draft, simultaneously picking for the present and future, but he wasn't. So it wasn't a secret to Reeves or anyone else that Blank was looking for someone to replace part of the job that the head coach had been accustomed to doing.

He first looked to Tampa, whose GM was Rich McKay. The deal broke down when the Buccaneers asked for compensation. But Blank nearly landed an executive superstar a month before the 2002 draft. He reached out to Ron Wolf, who had helped build championship teams in Oakland and Green Bay, and offered him the most lucrative GM contract in the league at the time: $16 million over four years. Wolf, who was sixty-three, turned it down because he wondered if he had the energy and preparation to do the job well.

From Blank's perspective, searching for a top GM made sense. But the search, the temporary solutions, the near misses, the consultants, and the coaching changes that would follow created a philosophical maze in his scouting department. There would be no true absorbing of the system for the scouts, because just as they would go to sink into it, the rules of the system would change. They'd be going from a 4-3 defense to a 3-4 and back to a 4-3. They'd be told to focus on power backs one day and then change-of-pace backs the next. They needed smaller offensive linemen for one coach's zone blocking scheme, and suddenly they were looking for three-hundred-plus-pound brutes for another.

The confusion started shortly after the 2002 draft. On draft day, Reeves and Ron Hill shared the thought that they were sitting on a sleeper pick. The Falcons were picking eighteenth, and leading up to the draft, they hadn't heard a single draftnik or "secret source" whisper that anyone in front of them was thinking of selecting Syracuse pass rusher Dwight Freeney. That was their guy. They'd design special schemes for him in defensive coordinator Wade Phillips's 3-4, with Freeney's speed and instincts too much for most offensive linemen to account for. In some ways, he'd be the Vick of their defense. But the Colts, picking eleventh, saw the same talent that Atlanta did and drafted the six-foot defensive end who was supposed to slip in the draft due to his less-than-ideal height. When it was time for the Falcons to pick, their consolation prize was a 250-pound running back named T. J. Duckett.

It turned out that the 2002 draft was Reeves's last one as a decision-maker. After the draft, the personnel department had to deal with some awkward office politics. Reeves was still the coach, of course, but the man he brought in to help him in personnel, Hill, was now responsible for picking the players. So, theoretically, Hill could draft players and Reeves, as caretaker of the fifty-three-man roster, could cut them. Both men handled the move with grace, although it was obvious the arrangement wouldn't and couldn't last. It was no way to build a team, and more important, Blank continued to search for a GM who was going to replace at least one of them, if not both.

On the field, second-year quarterback Vick was becoming everything that Reeves imagined. As traditional as Reeves was in some ways, he had told his staff early on that they were to adjust to Vick and not the other way around. So at its core, the Falcons' offense was basic, but the improvisation of Vick made it appear complex. He was a legitimate threat to score each time he tucked the ball away and headed upfield. He hadn't mastered the nuances of the passing game, but everyone could see the enormity of his talent, so there was excitement and curiosity when he painted outside the lines or acted like he didn't see lines at all. He was getting away with things on the field that weren't supposed to be possible in the NFL, or with the laws of gravity, from making defenders grasp at air because they thought they had him to flicking a pass sixty yards without so much as a grunt.

The team's season highlight came in the play offs when the Falcons traveled to Green Bay. Vick was a Pro Bowler, and his nearly eight hundred yards rushing got him more respect as a runner than a passer. On a 20-degree Wisconsin night, he did just enough of both as Atlanta jumped to a 24–0 halftime lead. The final was 27–7, a victory convincing enough to make you believe in illusions. It appeared that Vick had grown up and the Falcons had turned a corner, and neither was true.

The problem wasn't just a loss the next week in Philadelphia in the divisional round. It was about team-building, from expecting accountability of leaders, such as Vick, to coming up with something more than a Top 40 music roster, good for today but ultimately not good enough to be timeless. What the Falcons needed was a system, a program. Yet the last major act of the Reeves-Hill administration was a shortsighted trade: The Falcons gave up their first-round pick, number 23 overall, for Buffalo Bills receiver Peerless Price. They projected him as a number one receiver and gave him a fat contract to match. It was the type of deal that most smart franchises agonized over before making, if they made it at all. The superficial logic was that no player of that caliber would be available for the Falcons at spot 23, a line of thinking that didn't factor in a team's ability to either trade the pick up, down, or away for future picks. Nor did it acknowledge cost control. Pick 23, which turned out to be running back Willis McGahee, got a contract that could have been worth $15 million in total, with incentives, but included just $4 million in actual guarantees. With a $10 million signing bonus alone, the Falcons had guaranteed Price more than twice McGahee's compensation.

It's one of the reasons the Steelers, whom Blank respected for their stability, hadn't been without a first-round pick since 1967. For better or worse, whether Hall of Famer or bust or in between, they had made their first-round picks practically every year the Falcons had been in existence. On draft day 2003, as the Falcons sat out the first round, the Steelers traded up to spot 16 for USC safety Troy Polamalu; the Falcons, with less draft capital after the trade for Price, were locked into spot 55 and took Penn State safety Bryan Scott.

There was more than the obvious numerical gap between picks 16 and 55. It was symbolic of the chasm that existed between one of the NFL's most stable football factories, in Pittsburgh, and a football operation in Atlanta whose long-term thoughts were akin to quotes on a daily calendar: It says one thing on the first, so you go in that direction, and if it says something completely different on the second, you happily contradict your path and go there. For the Falcons to become the football version of Home Depot, Blank was going to have to find a personnel man who could change the thinking from day-to-day and season-to-season to something greater, more thoughtful, and more permanent. Bad luck wasn't keeping the Falcons from back-to-back winning seasons. Bad thinking was.

In 2003, Blank was still five years away from meeting Thomas Dimitroff, who was going into his second draft with the Patriots. Dimitroff was thirty-six, the same age Blank was when he began to give definition to the thought of Home Depot. From afar, based on nothing but appearances and pop-culture stereotyping, both men could easily have been mistaken for something they weren't. Blank, sixty-one, believed in risk-taking just as much as the cycling and snowboarding scout did, if not more. Dimitroff, perceived as the anything-goes hippie, believed that the key to a strong organization was "clearly defined, indisputable roles" as well as unmistakable leadership. They put different flourishes and accents on their big ideas, a borough echoing from one man and Boulder from the other, but the ideas in many cases were identical.

If you believe in karma, people meet when or if they are supposed to, so Blank and Dimitroff weren't ready for each other in August 2003. Blank still didn't have a GM, but what bothered him and all of Atlanta more was that he didn't have a quarterback. Vick broke his right fibula in a preseason game, and the most optimistic news was that he'd miss just six weeks. That seemed ambitious when Vick showed up at a press conference seemingly mummified in a black cast. He was going to be out for a while, and Reeves was going to learn what it was like to build a franchise around a quarterback who's not able to play.

When the NFL season started, the Falcons didn't start with it. They won their first game, lost their next seven, won one more, and then lost the next three. At 2-10, the future didn't look good for Reeves. After missing the first twelve games, Vick returned in December against Carolina. He played as if the broken leg had been a publicity stunt. The Panthers would wind up in the Super Bowl, against the Patriots, but they had no defense for Vick. He looked as quick as normal, if not quicker. He threw for 179 yards and ran for 141 more.

Anyone from Panthers coach John Fox to defensive end Julius Peppers could tell you what an athlete he was, but it wasn't just athleticism that led thousands of people and dozens of corporate sponsors to the Georgia Dome. He was a stylist and a showman, as much as local musicians Usher and Cee Lo Green were. He was as much a home-run hitter as Chipper Jones was. And he sparked passionate debates about categorizing, great quarterback or great athlete, as much as any stance-taking politician could. What he couldn't do, as Reeves learned after win number three, was save jobs. The coach knew that Blank was going to fire him at the end of the year, so he asked to leave with three regular-season games remaining.

It didn't take long for Blank to finally get his GM, Tampa's McKay, who was also team president. It was a good hire. McKay was smart, respected around the league, and had presided over a Super Bowl winner with the 2002 Buccaneers. But, no disrespect to McKay, some scouts had exasperated sighs when given the news.

Another system?

Another head coach?

What's it going to be *this* time?

McKay was schooled in the Tampa 2, a 4-3 defense that doesn't work unless the middle linebacker can run like a defensive back and the defensive ends can fly to the quarterback. Defensive backs primarily play zone to prevent big plays. Essentially, scouting for the Tampa 2 is a lot different from scouting for the 3-4 that Reeves and Phillips taught. McKay hired Jim Mora, the younger, to be his head coach, and Mora promised to do something that Reeves never wanted to: put Vick in a specific system and see if he could thrive in it. When McKay brought in longtime personnel man Tim Ruskell to be assistant general manager, a scouting system was in place, too.

No matter what the stats revealed, Michael Vick wouldn't be able to be better in Atlanta than he was in 2004. He was still that rare artist, a pianist who could play a Steinway beautifully without studying it. He was also living a bit of a double life, and in 2004 no one had begun to chip away at it yet. The Falcons won eleven games in the first year of McKay-Mora and advanced to the conference championship before losing to Philadelphia.

The franchise revolved around Vick as an athlete and marketer. When he was in the Falcons' offices in Flowery Branch, Vick was comfortable. He talked about his interest in wine and being on his boat in Chesapeake Bay. If employees had their kids around, he would strike up conversations and sign autographs. But as much as he painted as he saw fit on the field, he did the same in his personal life. He worked on his game on his own terms, which was not much. He kept company with petty criminals from Newport News, Virginia, his hometown. Reeves knew he had some issues when the Falcons drafted him, but no one knew the extent. Yet the Falcons knew that he had to be monitored and worked with, long before his life started to fall apart, because there were far too many problematic signs.

"We were cool. Obviously there were no hints of the slovenliness that he would eventually admit to," says Darryl Orlando Ledbetter, an *Atlanta Journal-Constitution* sportswriter who covered Vick on the Falcons beat. "I never got the sense from him that he was ever committed to being great. He always thought his athletic ability would bail him out of everything. And you know, whether it was Virginia Tech or the Falcons, he always had somebody running behind him, trying to clean up the mess that he or his friends had left."

It was no coincidence that as glimpses of Vick's private life began to be revealed to the public, one layer at a time, the Falcons began to sink with him. Only in hindsight does anyone mention that the organization had an in-house replacement available with a third-round pick from McKay's first Falcons draft, quarterback Matt Schaub. Fans would have never forgiven the franchise if it had picked Schaub over Vick. Instead, the Falcons braced for the public-relations hits and prepared press releases, having no idea what they were actually protecting and defending.

During the 2004 season, when everyone was paying attention to the field, two of Vick's friends had been entangled in the case of a stolen Rolex at the Atlanta airport. The case didn't receive a lot of coverage. In April 2005, a woman who described herself as Vick's ex-girlfriend sued him for knowingly giving her a sexually transmitted disease. He never told her that he was infected with genital herpes and, according to the lawsuit, used the alias "Ron Mexico" to receive treatment. The case was settled out of court a year later. "That whole situation was a by-product of thinking that you're above the law," Ledbetter says.

"And now the young woman has health problems for life."

In November 2006, after the Falcons lost at home to New Orleans, Vick responded to hecklers by twice holding up his middle finger. He was fined $20,000 and apologized repeatedly the next day in a press conference. He was unraveling and so were the Falcons. They went 2-6 in the second half of 2005 and finished 8-8. They were 7-9 in 2006, one of the reasons Mora lost his job. Ten days after former Louisville head coach Bobby Petrino was settling into the position vacated by Mora, in January 2007, there was yet another Vick airport incident, this time in Miami. He tried to get a twenty-ounce water bottle past security, but it was confiscated and initially tossed into a recycling bin. It was quickly retrieved when Vick seemed to show a special interest in it. The bottle had a hidden compartment that smelled of marijuana. He was cleared a few days later when the tested bottle showed no marijuana traces.

Finally, the biggest secret of all was exposed four days before the 2007 draft. Police raided a property owned by Vick in Virginia and found evidence of a dogfighting operation. There was a federal raid in July, and a week before the Falcons opened training camp, Vick and three others (including Quanis Phillips, one

of the friends from the Rolex incident at the airport)
were indicted by a federal grand jury. They faced
charges ranging from dogfighting to interstate gambling. The more news that trickled out, the worse Vick
looked. Dogs had been trained to fight to kill if necessary, and when they could not perform, they were
killed by their owners. Vick and others were linked
to sickening acts, accused of either shooting, drown-
ing, or hanging the dogs when there was no longer any
use for them. When the story first broke, Vick told his
employers that he wasn't involved and that his name
would be cleared. Those in denial believed him, but
as one Falcons employee put it, "They're not going to
be on the world news indicting you one day and then
the next wake up and say, 'Oh, by the way, we got this
wrong.'"

When training camp started, the emphasis was on
the word "camp": The animal-rights camp, with out-
raged activists, was on one side; the Vick camp, with
supporters wearing his jerseys, was on another; and
above all an airplane flew with a sign that read NEW
TEAM NAME: DOG KILLERS.

Vick was down, so that meant the franchise was,
too. Everyone was going to have to start over. For Vick,
that meant nearly two years of prison time. For Petrino,
it meant going back to college, because a franchise

without Vick was not what he had signed up for. For Atlanta it meant learning how to trust, once again, a franchise that took more than it gave. And for Blank, going into his sixth season of ownership, it meant going back in time.

He didn't know what Home Depot would become in 1978, but at least he knew what was being put into it. There were no surprises in the foundation. He knew how much time and thought he had put into making it work, how Bernie Marcus had spent his fiftieth birthday stocking the shelves himself at night, sweating profusely because he wanted to save money and not run the air conditioning when there were no customers in the building. That was real. What Blank tried to build on with the Falcons was a fraud. How could you build something great with a superstar who has shameful blood on his hands while you have your own sweat on yours? How can you be a partner with someone whose time and energy is spent establishing another "company," not the one that gave him stardom and wealth and a platform in the first place? Blank was going to have to go back to the time when the Home Depot was an idea and not a building. It was a few men who depended on one another, guys who thought nothing of getting their hands dirty and bringing a great idea to life, one nail at a time.

———

The first e-mail came from Bernie Marcus, which was a bit of a surprise because as Blank says, "He never writes e-mails. He has a computer, and I think he's just learning to turn it on." The next e-mail came from Pat Farrah, another Home Depot cofounder. "When it came to merchandising, Pat would think of fifty ideas, and forty-eight would drive me directly into bankruptcy. But the other two were so brilliant that nobody would ever think of them. And if you did those two and did them well, you were going to put yourself years ahead of everybody else."

The e-mails were reminders of how good business was supposed to look and feel. They reminded Blank, who was at the low point of his ownership, to think about what had worked in the past before rushing forward with a plan to remake the Falcons. He listened to his friends and former partners and began the process of interviewing several coaching and GM candidates in person. One of the candidates, Bill Parcells, did him a huge favor, although it probably didn't feel that way at the time.

Parcells was in place as the next Atlanta football czar. If it had been a wedding, Parcells and the Falcons would have already exchanged rings and been close to the "If anyone has any objections to this union . . ." stage. The deal fell apart, and Parcells went to Miami.

It would have been a splash to have Parcells in Atlanta, but would it have been the right move? He could build a team quickly and bring legitimacy, but he could also be there for three years. Or one. It would have been yet another temporary solution, and besides, it was too easy. Anybody can point out the best football minds who have already had decades of success. It's harder, but more rewarding, to find a team builder for the next generation. It might be someone whose name doesn't sell tickets, but the quality teams he puts together does.

By late 2007 and in January 2008, Blank had heard from and met with dozens of candidates. Nothing clicked for him like the webcam interview with Thomas Dimitroff did. When the interview ended, Blank wasn't the only one convinced that the Falcons had found a franchise fixer. Dean Stamoulis, who represented independent recruiting consultant Russell Reynolds and took notes during all the Falcons interviews, said Dimitroff's performance was the best of them all. Through his work at Russell Reynolds, Stamoulis had sat in on dozens of interviews around the country and world, trying to help corporations find leaders or retain them. As soon as Dimitroff appeared on the webcam screen, Stamoulis began writing.

Offbeat look, he wrote. *What's with the hair?*

Dimitroff's brown hair was long and at the top it appeared to be teased and moussed. He often made fun of his look, calling himself Jimmy Neutron, the Nickelodeon cartoon character with the same hairstyle. Mindful of Dimitroff's love for Boulder and the city's agreeable and laid-back reputation, Stamoulis also wrote, *We may want to get this guy drug-tested.*

After a few minutes, Stamoulis, who has a background in industrial and organizational psychology, saw beneath the superficial surface and found what he considered to be Dimitroff's brilliance. It wasn't just that the GM-to-be effortlessly quoted Thoreau as he was making a point about football. He was able to show his smarts and flexibility by talking about the game of football for a few minutes and then showing an understanding of football business ten minutes later. Stamoulis made a flurry of notes: *Able to see the big picture . . . Clearly smart . . . amazing focus on detail . . . amazing rigor . . . Profoundly driven . . . Get the feeling that he has a mental model for what the job is and has spent a lot of time thinking it through.*

"You had to be intelligent, and you had to be able to present your ideas in an intelligent manner. Arthur had been used to dealing with Rich, so you're dealing with a smart person who is used to hearing smart football people," says Les Snead, the Falcons pro personnel director who was part of the GM search committee. "You couldn't just be 'the Old Football Guy.' You know what I mean? Thomas came off as intelligent, organized, clear, and there was an innovative side to him. I don't think Arthur Blank's ever worried about, 'Hey, this guy can do a toe-side turn on a snowboard.' If anything, Arthur kind of likes people like that."

Dimitroff got the job and headed to Atlanta. His temporary home was the Ritz-Carlton in Buckhead, close to Blank's family office. When Dimitroff went to the office one day to interview a coaching candidate, Mike Smith, he had an experience similar to the Web interview. Talking about football philosophy was easy and fun with the Jacksonville defensive coordinator, and it made the two men lose track of time. Blank opened the door several times to check on them and they'd alternate saying, "Just give us a few more minutes." A few more minutes would become forty-five minutes here, an hour there. The two had never formally met, but they saw too many things the same way. Smith was a natural leader, the son of schoolteachers and the oldest of eight children. He was a football guy to his core, but with his silver hair and effortless grin he looked like a more muscular version of the comedian

Steve Martin. He and Dimitroff could have spent the whole day talking schemes and players if they wanted, since both of them had devoted so much of their lives to the game, but they were more interested in talking about building. If football was such a critical part of their lives, why not figure out how to build an organization that would allow them to enjoy football, in one place, for years?

Dimitroff had been imagining his ideal football environment for most of his professional life. It amused him when he would be in a football crowd and get strange looks for something he wore or something he said. Scott Pioli knew him better than most, so he could get away with calling him "Eurotrash" for his trendy clothing style. But he knew there was a real belief among many in the league that credible football people were supposed to look or sound a certain way, which is like everyone else. It was an odd dynamic that existed among coaches and personnel people: Everyone wanted to win a Super Bowl, which separates you from the pack; yet if you were perceived as too separate from the pack in your pursuit of winning, it drew scoffs.

"I know there was a time with certain people, there was a whole self-righteous perception thing from people toward me," Dimitroff says. "And that was not it at all. I never, ever, proselytized about my vegan diet, or my approach, or my environmental bent. Never. Only to people who were interested in talking about it. I was very mindful of that. And you know, a lot of people knew my dad in the business. And on the ribbing side, they would often say, 'In so many ways, you're like your father . . . but in other ways, you're so not like your dad.'

"I think all of us in football, in general, are a bit myopic. I know when I was just getting started in the NFL, there was an element of rigidity in how you should dress, shave, wear your hair, speak, and behave politically. I always wanted to create a culture where everyone is passionate and intensely involved in their work, but there's also enough levity to make the journey enjoyable.

"We're all driven, focused, serious, tough-ass football people. All of us in this business are that way. But I think we all crave something outside of that realm, too. We all need relief. I remember back in the day, some coaches would be aghast that you'd take ninety minutes out of the day to have a workout and have lunch. I mean, it's something I don't even have to address: There's a time to work and there's a time to pull back. Everyone in the building is very aware of that."

During that first interview, Dimitroff and Smith had talked about building a culture in football that was vibrant, authentic, and honest. They both hated the thought, for example, of leaving the job of releasing a player to someone else. They agreed that when it was time to release someone, the best way to do it was for them to be in the room together and be honest about the decision to move on. It was the best way to treat people.

It's one thing to have a theoretical philosophy and something different to have to put your thoughts into practice. Within a couple weeks on the job, Dimitroff made two moves that earned him instant respect among the scouts and let them know what kind of leader, and man, he was.

The first move proved that he was practical and adaptable. The scouts had spent the fall preparing for the draft, using the language of their own scouting system. Dimitroff was planning to overhaul the system and install the one used by the Patriots, which was difficult to learn quickly. Since Dimitroff had been the college director in New England, he was confident that he knew the draft, even if he knew it in terminology that his new staff didn't understand. So he agreed that any kind of system change should wait until after the draft, and in the meantime he would begin to communicate in the language that they had been using.

"But I wanted to make it clear that a change was coming," he says. "I wanted them to start thinking in the new Falcon vernacular."

It's a good thing he didn't make them start thinking about it immediately, because it was going to take a Dimitroff scouting seminar, and most likely a full year, for everyone to be fluent in it. It was a revolutionary grading scale that was based on the value of a specific position. It forced a scout to go deeper, eliminate gray areas, and say exactly what they projected a player would be in the NFL. The idea was for the grade, with 1 being the lowest, 9 being the highest, and 6 representing a starter, to reflect the value to the team. For example, based on today's NFL, it made sense that a number two running back would have a 5.9 grade, which the scale says is a backup, and for a third receiver or third corner to have a 6.3, which the scale considers a starter. The grade factors in a passing-heavy league, where third corners and receivers are heavily valued.

The scale was also one of comparatives. The idea was to know the Falcons' roster, one to fifty-three, and be able to provide a snapshot for who a prospect is compared to his Falcon counterpart. It wasn't good enough to say that a player was a "first-round pick" (you'd be thrown out of the room for that) or someone who could start "by his second year in the league."

The system was created and tweaked to make it leaner and more specific. What was the player's value to the Falcons? And ultimately, who on our roster is this kid from Texas or Alabama or USC going to replace?

It was a system full of numbers, colors, and upper- and lowercase letters that the scouts would have to learn, too. It had numerous columns for athletic ability, positional strength, and change of direction. It also had grades for character, which took on greater importance given where the franchise had just been.

The new Falcon vernacular wasn't just the grading scale that they were about to learn. It was an emphasis on consistency, transparency, and loyalty. What annoyed the new GM more than anything was waffling, especially from leadership that was supposed to be setting a tone. As liberal as he was in many aspects of his life, he couldn't compromise when it came to inconsistency. He'd call people out on it. He'd call himself out on it. He wanted anyone working for him to know what he was thinking, whether they liked to hear it or not; that's why he felt compelled to have a conversation with a man he respected, college scouting director Phil Emery.

Emery had been intrigued by the scouting process since his sophomore year at Wayne State University in Michigan, his home state. He was a member of the football team then, and he remembered seeing a scout, sixteen-millimeter projector in tow, on his way to the football office. He thought it probably was one of the best jobs in the country, being able to travel, meet new people, and see some of the top athletes in America. He had overseen the previous three drafts in Atlanta as director, drafts that had produced players such as Roddy White, Jonathan Babineaux, Stephen Nicholas, and Justin Blalock. The Michael Vick situation had brought ridicule to the entire organization, but there were many smart football men like Emery who wanted to prove that there was actual talent beneath the rubble.

Dimitroff told Emery that he liked his work, but he was making Dave Caldwell the new college director. Caldwell had worked several years with the Colts, and when he and Dimitroff saw each other on the road, they talked football and had similar ideas. When Dimitroff was hired, there were two guys he knew he had to get: Caldwell and Lionel Vital, who had worked with two generations of Dimitroffs. Emery was offered a job as national scout, but there was no way around it: It was a demotion.

He was crushed.

"I felt a genuine loss and underwent somewhat of a personal grieving period that most likely anyone goes through when you lose your 'spot' in life," Emery says.

Dimitroff told him that news of the change was just between them, and he wanted Emery to keep his standing as college director through the upcoming draft. Emery appreciated how the difficult situation was handled, and Dimitroff made a note of how much class and professionalism Emery displayed the entire time.

"I worked very hard at developing a positive relationship with Thomas and Dave," Emery says. "I wanted everyone to feel comfortable around me after the transition so I could continue to contribute positively to the scouting process. I decided for that to happen I needed to be the most positive person in the building about the new direction we were taking through Thomas's leadership."

No one would have guessed that Dimitroff and Emery had ever had an issue. As the Falcons got closer to the April draft, Emery was right there next to the GM as he tried to figure out which player would be taken with the third overall pick. Emery traveled with a group of executives and coaches to private workouts for Matt Ryan, Joe Flacco, Chad Henne, and Glenn Dorsey. Emery respected Dimitroff. And Dimitroff respected him so much that, when a better opportunity arose for Emery a year later, he was his top advocate.

Office dynamics aside, there was plenty of work to do on the Falcons' roster. Any GM, whether in the

NFL or fantasy football, could see that the team's top need was a quarterback. Vick had taken the franchise out at the knees, so even when he was finished serving his nearly two-year prison sentence he wasn't going to return. But the Vick issue was complicated. He had been so charming, to ownership, his teammates, and his fans, that he'd actually had an impact on the Falcons even after he was gone.

Five players, Roddy White, Joe Horn, Alge Crumpler, DeAngelo Hall, and Chris Houston, had all been fined by the NFL for on-field tributes to Vick in 2007. On the morning of December 10, Vick received his prison sentence. That night, the Falcons played a home game against New Orleans. White wore a black T-shirt with white lettering that read FREE MIKE VICK. The shirt was under his jersey, but it was revealed when Horn pulled up the jersey so the crowd and cameras could see it. Hall was on the field before the game with a Vick poster. The other players wore black eye strips with written tributes to Vick.

Dimitroff believed he could get a quarterback in the draft, but clearly replacing the quarterback wasn't the only issue. Among other things, the Falcons needed to be psychologically free of Vick, too. They needed help everywhere. They didn't have a reliable left tackle who could protect a quarterback; they were either too old at the position, with thirty-six-year-old Wayne Gandy, or too young and questionable, with twenty-three-year-old Quinn Ojinnaka. They had been ranked in the league's bottom four on offense and defense. Their leading rusher, Warrick Dunn, rushed for just 720 yards and averaged just over 3 yards per carry.

They also had a couple players who got the GM's attention more for their attitude than their play. One of those players was Hall, a cornerback who had been a top-ten pick in 2004. His 2007 season had been filled with controversy. It started with a bizarre September episode in which he melted down on the field with interference and unsportsmanlike-conduct penalties, and then had to be restrained on the sideline after yelling at his coaches. It ended with the Vick tribute. He had been selected to the Pro Bowl the previous two seasons, and those selections fed an ego that was already outsized. He was exactly the kind of player who could undermine the good intentions of a new leadership team, so he quickly became part of Dimitroff's history: He was the first player the new GM traded.

A couple years earlier, Dimitroff had been in Indianapolis at the Scouting Combine when he entered an elevator with a Hall of Famer. He immediately recognized Al Davis, the legendary owner of the Oakland Raiders. Dimitroff introduced himself: "Hello, Mr. Davis. I'm Thomas Dimitroff . . ." Davis smiled before the Patriots' director of college scouting could continue. "Ah, Dimitroff," Davis said. "I knew your father." They had a brief and pleasant chat.

In March 2008, after just two months on the job, Dimitroff talked with Davis about acquiring Hall. Throughout his career, Davis had been riveted by fast receivers and corners. He envisioned pairing Hall with the Raiders' Nnamdi Asomugha, considered to be the best corner in the NFL. Dimitroff was looking for multiple draft picks so he could start to fill in some of the numerous holes on his roster. They agreed that the Raiders would send the Falcons a second-round pick in 2008 and a fifth-rounder in 2009. The Raiders would happily take Hall and sign him to a $70 million contract with $24 million in guarantees.

"I'm just relieved, happy to be out of a bad situation in Atlanta, a situation that wasn't the right fit for me," Hall told his hometown paper, the *Virginian-Pilot*. "I'm happy to go to Oakland where I'm wanted, to team up with Nnamdi Asomugha and create a great secondary. I think you can argue me and Nnamdi will probably be the two best corners ever to team up, side by side . . . I'm a Pro Bowl player, he's a Pro Bowl player. It's just going to be great to have another guy alongside me that I feel confident can hold his own weight. I don't have to worry about teams avoiding me, because they can't avoid both of us."

For considerably less cash than the Raiders spent on Hall, the Falcons had made their mark in free agency three weeks earlier by signing the best available running back, Michael Turner. He had spent his entire career as a backup in San Diego, but Turner projected well as a starter. There was no question Turner's 250-pound body could take the punishment of being an every-down back, so Dimitroff thought that offering him a contract with $15 million in guarantees was worth the risk.

When it was time for Dimitroff to make his first draft pick for the Falcons, there wasn't much uncertainty. A few nights before the draft he talked to Scott Pioli, whose Patriots were scheduled to pick seventh by virtue of their trade with the 49ers the year before. There didn't have to be much secrecy with Pioli regarding the pick because there was zero chance the Patriots would be drafting Boston College quarterback Matt Ryan.

"Are you sure about him, Thomas?" Pioli asked, knowing the gamble of taking a quarterback that high. A miss at that position in the top five was the quickest route to unemployment.

"Definitely," Dimitroff replied.

He had seen all the throws on tape and in person. He had interviewed him. At times, he even allowed himself to think that Ryan had certain leadership qualities that reminded him of Tom Brady. There was no hesitation on draft day when it was time for the Falcons to pick. They took Ryan. As the draft got into the early teens, there was a furious run on tackles. Over a span of eight picks, five tackles were selected. The Falcons needed someone to protect Ryan, so they made a trade with Washington, using the second-rounder they got from Oakland to help them get back into the first round. They selected USC's Sam Baker.

They still had a second-rounder, even after the trade for Baker, and they used that one on Oklahoma middle linebacker Curtis Lofton, whom they expected to be an immediate starter.

After the draft, it was time to spend more money. Ryan was signed to a six-year contract for $72 million. Dimitroff had been told by a former GM, Ernie Accorsi, to concentrate on one area of team-building at a time. Don't try to fix everything all at once because it could become overwhelming. In fewer than six months on the job, Dimitroff had hired a new coach, installed a new grading system, signed the top free-agent running back on the market, traded a former top-ten pick, and made a strong financial commitment to a top-ten pick of his own.

He believed that all of the additions would be good fits in Atlanta. These Falcons were long-term builders now.

7.

New England Departure, Kansas City Arrival

About thirty minutes before the first game of the 2008 regular season, Scott Pioli walked unnoticed toward the club level of Gillette Stadium. He was on his way to the coaches' box, where he always sat in the front row and watched the games. It was amazing: He had been going through this routine for nearly a decade, having helped assemble four Super Bowl teams and three champions, yet he blended into a crowd of Patriots fans without so much as a "Hey, aren't you . . . ?"

He didn't mind the anonymity, and on a few occasions he was teased about it mercilessly. Once, he had driven to work and parked his car in front of a stadium sign that read RESERVED FOR SCOTT PIOLI. He remained in the car to finish a cell phone conversation he was having and he was interrupted by a security guard's hasty rap on the window.

"Excuse me, sir. You're going to have to move. This space is for Scott Pioli."

Pioli smiled.

"I *am* Scott Pioli."

There was the time in New Orleans when he couldn't get into the Patriots' Super Bowl party because security didn't recognize him. Another time, he and Dallas were at dinner outside of Boston with another couple, Berj and Regina Najarian. Berj, one of his closest friends, was Bill Belichick's executive assistant. The couples had planned to go to a restaurant run by celebrity chef Ming Tsai, and when they arrived, the chef put on a show for them. He was thrilled to see Berj and asked several football questions, but he didn't know much about the other guy.

"What do you do for work?" the chef asked Pioli.

"I work for the Patriots, too," he replied.

"Really? What do you do?"

For the rest of that night, it was the punch line that the couples kept coming back to, over wine and laughter, putting the emphasis on different words to keep the joke going. "So, Scott, what *do* you *do*?" They messed with him for a while about that one. He could take it, and it was even funnier because everyone at the table knew just how thorough his work with the Patriots was. The NFL knew who Pioli was, too, and that's why he had become known more for turning down job interviews than going on them. And those were just the teams that had followed procedure and asked the Patriots for permission to speak with him; a couple teams had gone the back-channel route, procedure be damned, and let Pioli know that his own universe could exist in their city, with total football control and all the money and perks he'd ever need. He always said no, easily, because money and power would never be the combination that would lure him away from New England.

Maybe people didn't know his face, but they knew his name and respected his brain. He was the man on the other side of the ampersand, Belichick & Pioli, whom everyone mentioned from the Combine until the day after the draft. It was the duo that helped turn the cliché about the draft, the inexact science of it all, into a myth. The Patriots had been extremely exact in round one with their picks, with most of them either known as among the best in the league at their positions or at least solid contributors to championship-level teams. The first-round aberration came with Laurence Maroney, and they could go back to their notes on him and study the intense internal disagreements that preceded the pick. Good drafts were a huge reason Pioli sat in that home coaches' box and, from 2001 through 2007, watched his team win fifty-five of its sixty-six home games, a winning percentage of 83.

Similar expectations were in place for the 2008 season. The Spygate heat from the previous September had cooled, and by the spring it had made its way to *South Park*, with Belichick's "I misinterpreted the rules" being the fodder for an episode on the irreverent cartoon. Belichick and Patriots owner Robert Kraft had apologized for the incident again at the owners' meetings, with Kraft's contrition coming off so sincerely that he was given a standing ovation. In an extraordinary move, the *Boston Herald* ran apologies on its front and back pages for publishing a false story on the eve of the Super Bowl. It turned out the paper's claim that the Patriots had taped a Saint Louis Rams walk-through before the Super Bowl couldn't be supported, so the *Herald* ran large bold-type headlines that read SORRY, PATS and OUR MISTAKE. Even senator Arlen Specter, who had appointed himself as a watchdog of Spygate conspiracies, began to get distracted by other things and was on his way to making news for an abrupt switch to the Democratic Party.

On the first Sunday in September 2008, the only sour sign from the past year actually hung in the north end zone of Gillette. It was a banner commemorating the "16-0 regular season." The rest of the story, the postseason postscript, is what made the new addition so unsightly for most fans. As Pioli sat in the coaches' box, with plenty of time before kickoff, he ignored the banner and instead looked to the field and the red uniforms of the opponent, the Kansas City Chiefs. When he saw the jagged white arrowhead with the red interlocking "KC" in the classic logo, he didn't think of how young the Chiefs were and how the Patriots were heavy favorites in the opener. Every time he saw Kansas City, he thought of the connections, personal and visceral, he had made with the franchise.

One of Pioli's personal connections had been with the best of all, the late Lamar Hunt, who died in December 2006. Not only had Hunt founded the Chiefs, he'd founded the entire American Football League in 1960. At the time, he was still in his late twenties. He was the reason a team like the Patriots, an AFL original, had life, and it was his ingenuity that led to the merger between the AFL and NFL. He was a wealthy man without airs, "relentlessly modest," as the *Dallas Morning News* put it, as legendary for his humility as he was for his contributions to pro football, soccer, and tennis. He was a Hall of Famer in all three sports, elected in three different decades. He wasn't a bad investor, either: He and seven others invested in the Chicago Bulls in 1966, a deal that would eventually allow him to enjoy having six championship rings and Michael Jordan on his side. Even his nickname, Games, was understated given his impact on pro sports.

Pioli met Hunt for the first time in 2004. They were at the owners' meetings in Palm Beach, and one day after business had been done, Pioli wandered off to a hospitality suite. He entered the room at the luxurious Breakers Hotel, an oceanfront resort, and found it to be nearly empty. There was one man in there and Pioli did a double take when he saw him. He recognized Hunt and suddenly became a nervous fan. He had deep respect for the history of the league, so he knew the story of Hunt as well as many other men who first met in hotels that weren't nearly as posh as the Breakers. They were the ones who built the league that made Pioli's NFL life possible. It was one of the subjects Pioli was passionate about, and sometimes he'd start talking about it and become so emotional that he'd well up with tears. After fidgeting and talking himself in and out of saying something, he finally decided to say hello to Hunt, and the two had a friendly and short conversation.

After New England won its third Super Bowl in February 2005, Pioli received a handwritten note from the man whose family was responsible for naming the game the Patriots had just won. It was the Hunt children's 1960s toy, the bounce-to-the-sky Super Ball, that sparked an idea and led to their father giving the championship game its now-famous moniker. He was also the one who decided that Roman numerals should be attached to the game because they had a "dignified" look. So he sent that congratulatory note after Super Bowl XXXIX, and Pioli wrote a note of his own to Hunt after the Chiefs beat the Patriots in November 2005. Pioli was surprised when he received yet another letter from Hunt, once again handwritten, a few weeks later. He thanked Pioli for the thoughtful note, mentioned that the Chiefs had been lucky that day against the Patriots, applauded Pioli on his "very important part in the team-building process there in New England," and wished "continued success to [Pioli] and the organization." He was genuinely happy for someone else's success, so true to his character he modestly concluded, "I kind of look at it like everyone in the NFL is in this 'project' together. I feel very fortunate to have been able to be a small part of it for a lot of years. Regards, Lamar Hunt."

"It was very typical for my dad to drop people notes. In fact, he was famous for it, and we all still marvel at his ability to produce either short notes or long memos on a daily basis," says Clark Hunt, one of Lamar's three sons. "He would absolutely turn them out. And everybody who's ever worked for him has a file of Lamar Hunt letters. And they're very interesting, on a wide range of subjects, and it really shows his creativity, because he was always an idea guy. But he was also one of the best people I knew in terms of being thoughtful and just dropping people notes. 'Hey, congratulations, I read that you won this award.' Or, 'Congrats on the Super Bowl.'

"It's not like today, where people are hitting stuff on their BlackBerry or where the English is garbled at best. His writing was very well thought out and there were no missed commas or missed periods or anything like that. I don't know what he would think about all the e-mail and texting and Twitter and so forth."

In his notes to Pioli, Hunt never made a reference to his cancer, first diagnosed in his prostate in 1998. It wouldn't be completely accurate to say he "battled" health problems from that moment on, because it would paint the picture of someone whose body and spirit were noticeably beaten. The truth is that Hunt lived, played, and worked around any issue that arose, and he embraced that philosophy until his death. He took a two-week trip to the Caribbean shortly after publicly announcing he had prostate cancer. He was always watching or listening to his Chiefs, whether he was at

Arrowhead or in some hospital room. And he spun out big ideas, as usual, but maybe even Lamar Hunt didn't dream that the Patriots executive he encouraged would one day become a Chief.

Unfortunately for Chiefs fans, they knew long before the 2008 season began that the championship drought in Kansas City was going to continue. It had been fifteen years since they'd won a play-off game and thirty-eight since they'd won a Super Bowl. They'd pieced together four wins in 2007, and when the season was over they fully committed to the kids. Jared Allen, their best defensive player, was traded for three draft picks, and eleven of the twelve players the Chiefs selected on draft day made the 2008 roster. Not one of those picks was a quarterback, although they could have had Joe Flacco if they wanted him, so they entered Gillette with Brodie Croyle as their starter.

It was game time. Pioli settled into his seat next to Ernie Adams, a longtime Belichick adviser. As usual, the coaches' box came to life. It was an audio box, as it buzzed with coaches' observations and curses, but it was a future box, too, because anyone who experienced the game there was always several seconds ahead of the crowd. If you put on a headset, you were getting the director's cut of the game, mostly narrated by Belichick, Josh McDaniels, and defensive coordinator Dean Pees, with cameos from Adams and various coaches. You knew the proper name and purpose of each play, long before the huddle broke. You knew exactly who blew the assignment, who made the key block, and what Belichick instantly thought of it all, minus the filter of *It is what it is.*

Seven and a half minutes into the season, the buzz in the box stopped. The headsets went quiet. It was one of the first times that those in the box saw things exactly the same way as the sixty-eight thousand fans on the other side of the glass. Tom Brady had dropped back to pass and was hit low by safety Bernard Pollard. Brady's left leg bent too far just as he was throwing and his anterior cruciate ligament snapped. There was an alarming scream, startling even Pollard, and Brady instinctively held his injured knee and leg. The gesture was the obvious giveaway: This was serious and season-ending. For a few seconds, no coach said anything, and the silence hung there the way it does in the room after a tasteless joke. What do you say after *that*? Around the NFL, coaches are trained not to become overly emotional about injuries. So the noise in the box and headsets returned slowly, eventually building back up to the point where it was before Brady got hurt. They knew they were going to beat the Chiefs, even if their eventual 17–10 win would be much tougher than anyone expected. But that wasn't the story. The real story was that everyone in the organization was going to have to accept that the Patriots' starting quarterback for the rest of the season was going to be Matt Cassel.

Finding a replacement for Tom Brady isn't in anyone's job description, but technically that was the simplistic answer to the *What do you do?* question Pioli had gotten at that Boston restaurant. The reason he spent hours upon hours away from home was because he was either on or presiding over a constant talent search to be discussed and debated with his staff. For Pioli and his staff, that debate was never at the top of the roster, at quarterback. It was somewhere in the thirty-to-fifty-three range, for Brady's backup. On the weekend of the 2005 draft, the Patriots weren't thinking of someone who could take snaps behind Brady. Their first four picks that year were guard Logan Mankins, cornerback Ellis Hobbs, tackle Nick Kaczur, and safety James Sanders. They had two seventh-round picks, which was a wasteland for many teams. The Packers and Giants, who had found productive players like Donald Driver, Mark Tauscher, Ahmad Bradshaw, Derrick Ward, and Kevin Walter in the seventh, as well as the Patriots, were among the rare teams that saw and selected reliable players at the low end of the draft. Pioli and Belichick had become draft students in their time working together, so they knew the typical profiles of what teams faced in the last round.

"If you look at the player and say, 'Okay, we think that they're going to develop based on their work ethic, their intelligence, their commitment,' then that's a good seventh-round pick. But there are lots of guys in the seventh round that don't have that, in all honesty," Belichick says. "They're just not good enough. You just draft them to cut. Then there are some character guys. Those guys that have slid down the board and their character is an issue. There are some players where you say, 'Look, I do not want this guy on my team under any circumstances.' There are other guys that you say, 'Okay, this guy's got problems but we think we can handle it.' We think we can . . . I wouldn't say *really* get him straightened out; I'd say we think we can handle and manage the problem."

The Patriots' first seventh-rounder in '05, Cassel, was part of the initial group that Belichick described. But the projection was more complicated because he had barely played in college. He backed up Heisman Trophy winners Carson Palmer and Matt Leinart at USC, and by the time he got to New England it was as if he was backing up Hollywood itself. Brady had championships and Super Bowl MVPs. He had contracts and endorsements worth millions. He was pursued by women so attractive that they were insulted if you simply called them beautiful. Cassel? He had a spot on the team.

In his first two seasons in the league, Cassel was once again surrounded by Heisman Trophy winners. But these guys, Doug Flutie and Vinny Testaverde, had won the trophy before Cassel had started first grade. He really didn't have to worry about being replaced by men in their early forties. But 2008 was different. The Patriots spent a third-round pick on a quarterback named Kevin O'Connell, and that was viewed as an indictment of Cassel's skills. Things got shakier when Cassel didn't look good in the preseason, yet he made the team and beat out the rookie for the backup job.

Halfway through the first quarter of 2008, he did more than take over for the injured Brady. He was now one of those people responsible for making the nightmare in the desert disappear. That Super Bowl loss to the Giants had deeply affected some players and coaches to the point where they sometimes had 2007 flashbacks. They were haunted by calls and plays they could have made but didn't. Tedy Bruschi had been ready to announce his retirement if they won, but the loss stung him so much that he was determined to return so the football memory in the Phoenix suburbs wouldn't be his final one. The man who would be calling plays for Cassel, McDaniels, had spent a restless off-season thinking of the game, too.

"You know, some of us were fortunate enough to be there in '01 and '03 and '04, and those years, statistically, weren't the same as '07. But the ending was better," he says. "And the taste in your mouth was a whole different thing. And I think that's what sticks with you. I know it made me want to get back to that game in a worse way, just to try to have that feeling that we had in '01, '03, and '04 again."

Just as there was a sense that the dynamics were changing in 2004, which was the final season Belichick had Romeo Crennel and Charlie Weis as his coordinators, there was also a feeling that 2008 represented something different. It wasn't just the loss of Brady. It was the knowledge that owners from other teams might come knocking after the season, taking away someone else from the Patriots' fountain of winning. The brand, whether the Patriots wanted to use that word or not, had been established. Belichick wasn't going to leave, so teams were looking for the next best thing, someone the head coach had shined on, as if they would get what he had by osmosis. McDaniels was one of the prime candidates to leave. He had gotten the league's attention the previous two years with his offensive diversity. One year he took an offense that lost its top two receivers and turned it into a top-ten unit, and the next season he called the plays for the most explosive offensive force in NFL history. He was confident and smart and had worked with Belichick for the previous seven seasons. It was a tough résumé to ignore.

The 2008 season was also the ground floor of a different locker-room mix, the nexus of a championship Patriots generation with a generation that was a combination of youth and imports. Bruschi, Mike Vrabel, and Rodney Harrison were in their early to midthirties. This wasn't going to be their team for long. They could try to be enforcers like they were five years earlier, but there were too many new guys to reach. There were times Bruschi and Vrabel would be sitting at their lockers and Vrabel would turn to Bruschi and say, "So this is the next generation, huh? *This* is the next generation?"

The next generation provided speed and athleticism that the veterans no longer had, but the veterans knew what it took to build the infrastructure of a championship locker room. The next generation was looser and louder than the generation that came before them, which was okay, except that the wise veterans wondered why a group that had accomplished nothing was seemingly so relaxed. It was evolution, and it happened in football as well as dozens of other industries in

America. It wouldn't bring down the Patriots in 2008, but a few bad seeds were in place for problems in the near future.

One game into Cassel's career as a starter, it was obvious that the Patriots were going to be a lot better than expected at quarterback. In the week leading up to their second game of the season, in New York against the Jets, there had been wild rumors and hysteria. If it wasn't a call to bring in free agent Daunte Culpepper to be the quarterback, it was a report that Chris Simms and Tim Rattay were coming to town. No one wanted to hear about the system and how no street free agent could possibly be better for the Patriots than Cassel, who was carefully selected as one of the right fifty-three. It was hard for many to grasp that the Patriots didn't see Cassel as a scrub. He was going into his fourth season in New England for an obvious reason: Belichick and Pioli believed in him.

His first test was against Eric Mangini's Jets, who had devoted three straight drafts to beating the Patriots. Center Nick Mangold was drafted with nose tackle Vince Wilfork in mind, linebacker Vernon Gholston was brought in to be a hybrid player similar to what Willie McGinest was with the Patriots, and the Jets had cashed in some draft chips, Patriot-like, to move up the board and select cornerback Darrelle Revis.

They believed Revis could defend any receiver, large or small, and when they graded him before the draft, he received their version of straight A's. They used green dots to indicate when a player was exceptional, and he had those dots in intelligence, character, athletic ability, strength, speed, and even his ability to return kicks and punts.

Cassel was smart enough not to throw too many balls in Revis's direction, which meant there were times he'd hold the football and take sacks. He was going to have to work on that, but it was clear to McDaniels that the offense wouldn't have to be radically modified when Cassel ran it. They started him off slowly against the Jets, and he passed for 165 yards in an impressive 19–10 win. By the time the Patriots saw the Jets again, in mid-November, Cassel would be running the offense with no restrictions. In some games, he'd put up Brady-like numbers, which put him on the path to a Brady-like contract.

In November, a little more than a week before Thanksgiving, Pioli decided that he could take a scouting trip and visit a friend at the same time. So he headed to Atlanta to see how Thomas Dimitroff was doing. The Falcons had already surpassed their four-win total from the previous season, and each of their new additions was contributing as planned, if not better. Quarterback

Matt Ryan, the team's first-round pick, was playing with poise and was the favorite to win Rookie of the Year. Running back Michael Turner, the team's top free-agent target, immediately lived up to expectations by breaking the team's single-game rushing record in the first game of the season. Curtis Lofton, a second-round pick, looked like a natural as a starting middle linebacker. In a 24–0 shutout of the Raiders, Lofton and the rest of the defense couldn't have played better as they allowed just three first downs the entire game. As for the Raiders and their new cornerback, former Falcon DeAngelo Hall, Al Davis regretted trading two picks for him and handing him a $70 million contract. Halfway through the year, Hall had played so poorly, giving up more yards than any corner in football, that he was released.

Dimitroff's father always had career advice for him, even in casual settings, and one of the things he told his younger son was to be himself if an opportunity to run a department ever came his way. Pioli noticed that Dimitroff was living his father's words. This had become a mission for Dimitroff. He knew there had been raised eyebrows around the league when Arthur Blank hired a college director who'd never managed day-to-day in an office, as a general manager would have to do. He knew he was also viewed by some old-guard traditionalists as some New Age freak, a forty-two-year-old outdoors lover with his head in the clouds. But he was confident that he didn't have to compromise all his interests just to look the part of a hard-core football man, whatever that was. The Falcons' office became a reflection of him, from scouting philosophy to patronizing Whole Foods.

Les Snead, the player personnel director, had the office closest to the general manager's, and he got used to the consistent aroma of cooked chickpeas, tomatoes, and rice coming from Dimitroff's direction. "It always smells good," Snead says, "but I'm not sure about the taste." Dimitroff's executive assistant Laura Moore, a former Virginia Tech soccer player, quickly learned to build certain things into his schedule: reading time, limited appointments before ten A.M., and a workout. She also learned to listen carefully for context clues because some of the words he used were as long as sectionals. "Each person in the office has a word he's used on them that they don't understand," she says. "Sometimes he'll see the look on my face and say, 'Do you know what that means?'" His office was equipped with an expensive stationary bike, which received monthly maintenance from Atlanta Cycle. Sometimes he'd be in there riding and watching film, and sometimes it was just a ride to the sounds of the Zac Brown Band.

Moore knew that if she couldn't find Dimitroff in the building, there was a good chance he was just several feet away, outside. Shortly after taking the job, he met with the superintendent of the grounds crew, Jim Hewitt, and asked what it would take to build a two-mile bike path at the facility. Hewitt cleared some of the refuse from the area, and in lieu of workouts, Dimitroff and scout Robinson Payne did the rest. They'd spend forty-five minutes to an hour each time they went out there, bushwhacking and raking, until they finally had a path on which the serious cyclist could ride or just walk and clear his mind. "Sometimes I'll be out there on my cell," Dimitroff says, "which will get you a dirty look on a bike path in Boulder."

Pioli was also impressed that Dimitroff had taken the essence of the Patriots' scouting system and tweaked it to make it more relevant to a 4-3 defense, which head coach Mike Smith and his defensive coordinator, Brian VanGorder, preferred. The Patriots were a team with bulk, with defensive ends Richard Seymour and Ty Warren both over three hundred pounds. Dimitroff was drawn to athleticism and fluidity, and he could now have an Atlanta roster with lighter, faster defensive ends and linebackers who wouldn't have been system fits in New England.

When the two friends weren't touring the facility, they were working and talking. They scouted a University of Miami–Georgia Tech game in midtown, watching Tech coach Paul Johnson's triple-option offense produce 472 yards on the ground. They sat in the same suite as an unusual man, Clay Matthews Sr., who was on the verge of representing three generations of NFL history: He played in the league, as did his sons Clay Jr. and Bruce, and his grandson, Clay III, was going to be a first-round pick in the spring. They talked about the future, specifically Pioli's job future, and they weren't sure at the time if they were discussing a move that Pioli wanted to make in the next year or if it was something more far off. Pioli was proud of Dimitroff and inspired by him. Not only had he left the Patriot nest and had instant success, he'd done it his way. He wasn't trying to be Belichick, Pioli, or even his father. He had ideas about the way he'd like to see football operations run, and he was putting those ideas in place. For Pioli, the trip to Atlanta only solidified what he was already starting to believe, that the time for him to leave New England was approaching, too. It wasn't a money chase, because if he'd wanted that he could have had it years earlier. It wasn't a quest for more power, to be the man, because in his mind that went against everything football was supposed to be. There wasn't a rift to speak of between him and Belichick.

"The thing that happens with some people is that they taste success and think they're smarter than they are. I never got to the point where I thought I was smarter than Bill," he says. "Without Bill, I'm at a completely different station in my football career. Probably still wallowing in the Ohio Valley Conference somewhere. And dreaming about making it to the NFL."

If the right opportunity were there, maybe it would be time to go simply because of renewal. After all, Pioli had worked with Belichick every year but one since he was twenty-seven, and now he was forty-three. Maybe it was healthy to go somewhere else and find the next New England, so to speak. The Patriots were well run and established. How great would it be, how *pure* would it be, to go somewhere and be part of a group that revived some team's football heartbeat? How much fun would it be to bring together a passionate group of players who hungered to achieve something greater than their individual selves?

That's how Pioli thought of football, and it explained a lot of things about his life, past and present. It's the reason he was a bit withdrawn, feeling hollow and embarrassed, when he was honored as an all–New England player in college, at Central Connecticut.

The honor was flattering, but it was far from the ultimate because it was an honor that didn't bring in his teammates.

He really was the personification of the group activity the Patriots did before every Super Bowl, choosing to be introduced as a team. It was why, when he pulled into his garage at home in New England, he still parked near a sign that read A WIZARD LIVES HERE. That was a sign from high school, when boosters went around his hometown of Washingtonville, New York, and rallied the football players, the Wizards, before their games. He still loved a Wizards team that went undefeated, just as much as he loved the Patriots, because they got together and did something that their individual talent said wasn't possible. He was a professional evaluator, used to analyzing the best athletes in the world, but when he described his high school teammates he made them all sound like people you should've watched or read about.

"I never got into pro football to see if I could run a team and 'do it on my own.' What does that prove? What does it even mean?" he says. "I love team-building. I love the idea of like-minded people coming together and creating greatness that is never just about one person. At some point you find that the brotherhood of relationships far exceeds any individual glory that you could ever be given."

It's not something he worked on. It's just who he was. People often told him he had the one-liner wit of his father-in-law, which he did, but his ability to create laughs sometimes hid an introverted side. The Patriots essentially had a one-voice policy, which meant no one in football operations except Belichick could speak to the media without permission. Pioli could have done twice as many media interviews if he wanted and been entertaining along the way, especially if he were interested in doing something like a weekly music segment on a radio station. He knew music like he knew football, and he could have put a happy face on what many perceived to be a dour and businesslike Patriots franchise. But he didn't want to, no disrespect to the deejays and journalists. As long as the policy was in place, he was content to do his job, completely and anonymously, while Belichick dealt with the media.

Over the years, his success had brought him the type of income that blue-collar workers like his dad never had. He appreciated and enjoyed the life the NFL provided, but anyone who was around him could see that it was important for him to stay connected to people who knew him when. He was still close to several friends and teammates from high school, and he celebrated many Super Bowls with his college roommate, Ralph Marchant. He didn't romanticize the life he had growing up, because there were some moments he wouldn't want to relive, but there was something eternally grounding in what he had experienced. He always seemed to be conscious of the world he was in, with chartered flights, million-dollar player contracts, and billion-dollar TV deals, vs. the world he came from, where no one he knew talked about signing bonuses or even contracts.

"I grew up with two parents who hated their jobs, really hated them," he says. "My father had a wife, four kids, a house payment, a car payment, and a high school education. He didn't have choices. He didn't have options. The way he lived was the way it was going to be."

Ron and Diane Pioli did the best they could with what they had, with Ron working at the local phone company and, at times, driving a cab and working as a plumber. It's probably the reason Pioli had no tolerance for slackers or complainers in the NFL. They wouldn't last long around him, whether they were just-getting-by scouts or underachieving players. He had seen too much achievement from people who didn't have nearly the resources or support network that someone working in the NFL does.

He watched as his sister, Lisa, two years older than he is, relied on her smarts, her creativity, her drive, and her family to finally carve out the life that she truly wanted. That was in jeopardy in high school when Lisa got pregnant at eighteen, three months before graduation. She got into a bad marriage and divorced, so she was a single mother trying to find her way. She started going to school at Orange County Community College and then went to work at Sharper Electronics. The company had a tuition-reimbursement program, and it would cover the entire cost of a class if the employee came away with A's. Lisa got A's. She went to night school, year after year, with her parents watching her daughter.

"You know, three years ago she just finished her master's," Pioli says. "She's got her bachelor's and her master's. Magna cum laude. Put herself through school. She's remarried now, too, to the greatest guy in the world, and she just got her first full-time teaching job. She's incredible."

No matter where he worked, and no matter how much money he made, there was something infused in Pioli that appreciated that thing, that hard struggle on the way to achievement. It's why he could appreciate Cassel, the seventh-rounder who produced back-to-back four-hundred-yard passing games in November and was looking like he belonged as an NFL starter.

It's the reason he could understand how cool it was to have rare, original hardcover copies of Ernest

Hemingway's novels, which he and Dallas owned, yet when he quoted a writer it was usually a Jersey guy named Springsteen. It was fitting that he was drawn to Bruce, a musician loved by the mainstream who sometimes grappled with his mainstream success. *Darkness on the Edge of Town* was the result of Springsteen sanding away at all the things he perceived to be overly commercial and finding something raw and genuine instead. It turned out to be an authentic album and a great one, of course, but it never had singles that were as popular as the ones on *Born to Run*.

Pioli had loved Springsteen since he was a teenager, and when Ron Pioli had asked years ago what the hell all that noise was his son was always listening to, he tried to connect with his father by highlighting some lyrics in "Badlands." There was a line that Scott found powerful, a line that he thought a workingman like his father could relate to: *Poor man wanna be rich / Rich man wanna be king / And a king ain't satisfied / Until he rules everything.* But fathers and their teenage sons don't always view things the same way, especially when it comes to music. Ron didn't see at the time that the music was Scott's literature, and it was literature that would help him understand his own small town and deepen his appreciation for the everyday people who made it run.

One month before the 2008 season began, Springsteen had a concert at Gillette. For the first time ever, Pioli, the Bruce devotee, got a chance to meet him afterward. He expected the meeting to be brief, five minutes max. But they began talking about those lyrics from "Badlands" and family dynamics and New Jersey and New York. There were tears in Pioli's eyes and there were tears in Springsteen's, too. Springsteen's manager kept popping into the room telling him that he had to go, and the Boss kept waving him off. They had connected.

Months later, it all made sense. If Pioli ever left New England, it would probably be for a place where he and others could go back to their football roots, strip away hype and distractions, and have their own *Darkness on the Edge of Town*.

After beating the Seahawks in Seattle the first week of December, the Patriots were 8-5 and headed toward a bunched finish in the AFC play-off standings. It was one of those years where someone with double-digit wins wasn't going to make the postseason. Unless the Patriots got some help, they were going to be that team. The problem was both simple and predictable: The Patriots had no problems against teams that weren't going to the play-offs and struggled against teams that were.

Cassel seemed to get better and better by the snap. He still took far too many sacks, but he wasn't a repeat offender in making mistakes. You'd see a flaw one game and it would be corrected the next. What the quarterback couldn't do was rewrite the losses, with all five of them coming in the conference, nor could he change New England's 2-4 record against likely play-off teams. He did exactly what the team needed the final three games of the season, throwing a combined seven touchdown passes to just one interception. The Patriots won all three, including a finale in Buffalo where the wind gusts were so ferocious that they caused the goalposts to sway. Cassel threw just eight times in the 13–0 win.

The only play-off hope for the Patriots, with eleven wins, rested on the shoulders of Mangini and Brett Favre. The Jets, playing at home, needed to beat the Dolphins. If that happened, the division would belong to New England for the sixth consecutive season. Favre was all over the place in the game, wildly under- and overthrowing his targets all day. He threw three interceptions, and when the season was over archaeologists would have all they needed when they looked at the quarterback's final totals: twenty-two touchdowns, twenty-two interceptions. He helped, and then he didn't. He didn't help himself, the Patriots, or Mangini in the final game of the season.

The Jets lost, completing the one and only season of Favre's career in New York. It also completed the season for the 11-5 Patriots, who lost the divisional tie-breaker to the Dolphins. For Mangini, whose team had lost four of its last five games, the loss cost him his job. He had lasted just three seasons in New York, a surprisingly short run for a man who had made the playoffs in his first year; was given a made-for-the-tabloids nickname, Mangenius; and had begun thinking long-term for the Jets. He was excited about his roster, and he felt like he had a bit of a secret weapon in information technology. He had helped design a computer system that he believed to be one of a kind. It quickly crunched and spit out data that Mangini believed many personnel departments in the league were missing. He had developed it on his own and had spent hours with computer programmers building and refining it. As much as he respected the Patriots' approach to the draft, he didn't think they or anyone else had technology that was so specific.

He would have to leave the intel in New York and move on to another job. As surprising as his firing was, the instant pursuit of him was just as stunning. The season had ended on December 28, and within forty-eight hours Mangini was being heavily recruited by the Cleveland Browns. Mangini was familiar with some other top recruits on the market, too. Their names were Josh McDaniels and Scott Pioli.

In an odd twist, Browns owner Randy Lerner wanted to hire Mangini and Pioli. It didn't seem to cross Lerner's mind that he could pick just one; it was like saying you were a fan of the Jets and Patriots or Yankees and Red Sox. It wasn't possible. There was three years' worth of issues that needed to be worked out between the two, and working it out together on a new job seemed to be a level of dysfunction that even the sensationalist TV shrinks wouldn't want to touch.

Still, Pioli liked Lerner. He had been raised in the Shaker Heights section of Cleveland, the son of billionaire Al Lerner, who was a minority owner of the original Cleveland Browns. Al Lerner had a role in helping the Browns move to Baltimore in 1995, and he was the reason the "new" Browns returned in 1998 when he paid $530 million for an expansion team. Al Lerner died four years later, and Randy assumed control of the team. Pioli and Randy Lerner knew some of the same people in Cleveland, starting with Indians executive Mark Shapiro, who was one of Pioli's best friends (and Mangini's brother-in-law). Lerner had received permission to speak with Pioli, and Pioli felt it was his obligation to talk with a man for whom he had a lot of respect. They met on New Year's Eve in Providence, on Lerner's private plane. When Pioli got to the plane, in the early afternoon, two people departed and he walked on. Seven hours later he was still there, laughing and talking despite the driving snowstorm that was ruining many Rhode Islanders' New Year's plans.

They talked about football; the Browns; Browns history; Lerner's family; Pioli's family; the city of Cleveland, which Pioli loved; and team-building. The conversation was flowing so well that it wouldn't have been shocking if Lerner had asked Pioli to fly back to Cleveland with him and become the new boss of the Browns by New Year's Day. But there were a couple of issues, one that they couldn't get around and one that Pioli didn't want to get around.

The first issue, obviously, was Mangini. Lerner asked Pioli flat-out if he could work with Mangini. It was complicated. The two of them had grown up together in the business, working in Cleveland, Baltimore, New York, and New England at the same time. They had been part of that brotherhood that Pioli described, but it was going to be very difficult to reestablish trust after the way things ended in New England.

There was also the matter of another scheduled interview Pioli had five days later, with the Kansas City Chiefs. Lerner let Pioli know that the Browns job was his if he wanted it, but Pioli didn't want to make that commitment without talking to the Chiefs first. He didn't think it was right to schedule an interview and then cancel it. Besides, he didn't *want* to cancel it.

Lerner and Pioli shook hands, and Pioli left to deal with the snowstorm. Lerner went back to Cleveland to deal with a storm of a different kind in his organization, which was about to hire its third head coach in the last six years. It would also be Lerner's second swing at the Belichick Tree, since the man he was going to hire, Mangini, was replacing Romeo Crennel, who had three losing seasons in his four years with the Browns.

As both Pioli and McDaniels went on interviews, it seemed that they went out of their way to avoid each other. Everyone in the Patriots organization knew how Mangini was viewed there, and no one wanted to even give the appearance that he was being disloyal to Belichick. So Pioli never asked McDaniels what he was thinking, and McDaniels never approached Pioli about what his plans were. They were a ready-made GM-coach combo that would have worked well together, but there wasn't so much as a whisper in the office about what they were going to do in the future.

On the first Monday of 2009, January 5, Pioli sat in the Hunt Sports Group offices in Dallas. The Chiefs were originally the Dallas Texans, and when the franchise moved to Kansas City in 1963, Lamar Hunt kept his home in Texas. When Arrowhead was built in the early 1970s, a multilevel apartment was included for the Hunts to use. The shuttling between Texas and Missouri worked for the Hunts, so they continued to be headquartered in Dallas while the team played in Kansas City.

Pioli had met the Chiefs' chairman of the board, Clark Hunt, just once, and it was years earlier at a league labor seminar in Dallas. They had barely spoken then, quickly going through a handshake, the way you do when you have an assembly line of people to meet. But going into his interview, Pioli had done his research on Hunt and had been impressed. Hunt was just six weeks older than Pioli, yet this relatively young man was considered one of the league's brightest minds. He had been a scholar and an athlete at Southern Methodist University, where he graduated number one in his class and was an academic All-American on the soccer team. As an SMU undergraduate and MBA student, his favorite classes had been ones focusing on capital markets trading, so naturally the company where he had his first full-time job was a fit: Goldman Sachs, the New York City investment banking and securities giant.

"You talk about something that'll grow you up fast," he says with a laugh. "I had had summer jobs, but nothing like working for Goldman Sachs. They're happy to throw you right into the fire. They're a lot like a professional sports team: They have a big draft class every year, firm-wide. The area I was in, there were maybe fifty of us. They work your tail off for two years and then hold on to a few people in the class. There are others that they want to go back to business school, with the thought that they'll bring them back. And then there are some that probably need to do something else."

Hunt was a draft pick who made it, getting an opportunity to work first in New York and then Los Angeles. He could have stayed with the firm as long as he wanted, but it made more sense for him to work with his dad, someone he considered "a creative genius." He attended league meetings with his father, helped him with the founding and operating of Major League Soccer, and provided advice whenever it was needed. They spent so much time together that there weren't many secrets, but there was at least one. Clark had no idea that his father was trading letters with Pioli. When his father passed toward the end of the 2006 season, Clark, then forty-one, became the youngest owner in the NFL.

He had been in the top decision-making seat for a year when the fans demanded that he make a change. At the end of the 2007 season, in which the Chiefs were 4-12, many fans wanted Hunt to move on from Carl Peterson, the longtime president, CEO, and general manager. Hunt didn't think it was the right time. He retained Peterson and head coach Herm Edwards. But fourteen games into the 2008 season, Peterson resigned and Hunt said that the new GM would have input on Edwards's job. He had heard many stories about Pioli, and one of the things he heard most often was that just getting Pioli to interview for the job would be a long shot.

"That was probably the biggest concern," Hunt says. "That he might not be interested."

Pioli was ready to leave New England, so he was interested, and thanks to a legendary letter-writer named Lamar Hunt, he automatically had positive thoughts about the Kansas City Chiefs.

Even before the interview in Dallas began, the handful of people who would interview Pioli was able to understand how frugal he could be. He could have stayed in any area hotel he wanted on Sunday night, the night before his all-day interview. The tab was on the Chiefs, yet Pioli selected a fairly shabby place near the Dallas/ Fort Worth airport, a hotel where if they left the light on for you, the light would flicker.

On Monday morning, his interviewers quickly saw his focus and convictions, too. Pioli looked around a conference room and saw Clark Hunt, Daniel Hunt, team president Denny Thum, and Ryan Petkoff, who handled PR for the Hunts. He handed them all folders that included several pages of observations, salary-cap information, and thoughts he had about leading a winning franchise. Unsolicited, he apologized to them for not having the "book" that some candidates came to the table with during interviews.

"I don't have one and I never will," he said to them. "I've never understood how and when people can create a book when you're working for someone and you have a job to do. You're supposed to be working for that team. Robert Kraft doesn't pay me to write books."

There was silence. They stared at Pioli and then stared at one another. It hadn't occurred to Pioli that they didn't care if he had a book or not. Clark Hunt was just happy that he had gotten Pioli through the door for an interview, something, amazingly, that no one had done since 1992. That was for Pioli's first NFL job, with Bill Belichick. Since that time, he had advanced to different positions without putting on his best suit, talking about his personal highlights, and telling a potential employer that references were available upon request.

They moved on.

The interview wasn't as casual as the one with Lerner, but it was just as smooth. Clark Hunt wanted to know about Pioli's family as much as he wanted to hear about the Patriots and team-building. The conversation lasted eight hours, with a couple of food breaks, and there were both pointed and poignant moments. One of the sharpest and most direct questions of the day happened when Pioli was asked about Spygate and what his role was in it. He said that as one of the leaders in the organization, he had to take part of the responsibility for something that happened on his watch.

Clark Hunt asked him if he would consider retaining Edwards, whom Hunt credited with the push for a Chiefs youth movement after the 2006 season. Hunt respected Edwards's honest assessment of where they were. It's not always easy to endorse the kids because, inevitably, the head coach who endorsed them usually isn't around to watch them grow up. Pioli said that of course he would consider Edwards and speak with him before making any decisions, although there were no promises that Edwards would be retained.

At one point, Pioli had to do a complicated verbal tiptoe. He realized how much the Chiefs meant to the Hunts, and he had obviously been awed by Lamar Hunt, but he needed to address a few things with the organization without coming off as disrespectful. He wanted to investigate why there had been a twenty-two-year gap between division titles, 1971 to 1993, and he wanted to understand why there was a perception of a Chiefs juggernaut, as recently as the late 1990s, when in reality there had been just three play-off wins in the previous twenty years. He wondered if the problem wasn't just on the field.

"There's this living, breathing dysfunction with football organizations," he said, "and it pits lifetime employees vs. temporary employees. It's insane. You need the help of all these people to do the job well. It's not just players. It's equipment people, the grounds crew, community relations, marketing . . ."

He didn't know these interviewers the way he knew Lerner, but this was a more complete conversation. There were plenty of laughs mixed in with some hard-core football talk. As Pioli spoke, the Chiefs realized how fortunate they were. Technically, they were talking to the Patriots' vice president of player personnel, so, by NFL rules, offering a person in that position a GM's job was a promotion. The league wanted to eliminate teams stealing one another's front-office people for lateral moves, so a hierarchy was established. Even though Pioli really was the GM in New England, he wasn't as far as the masthead was concerned. What it meant for Pioli was that he was free to take the Chiefs job if he wanted it. It was clear that they wanted him.

"He was obviously prepared, which is sort of one of his hallmarks," Hunt says. "But it's just sort of his thoughtful, analytical personality that really came through, and I felt like I was having a different conversation with him than I had had with the other people. Not that the others were all the same, because they weren't, there was just something that was deeper, more thoughtful, about this conversation that I was having with Scott."

For Pioli, his long day in Dallas led to some intricate emotional moments during his trip back to New England. He was on the verge of a new beginning, and the possibilities of that journey were exciting. But beginning something in Kansas City would mean, officially, that he had finished something with the Patriots. He thought about what that meant and it made his heart heavy, even though he knew it was time to go somewhere else. He was going to excitedly accept the Chiefs' offer to become their new GM, and there would be a random moment when he'd say to himself, "Man, I'm working for the Kansas City Chiefs. Lamar Hunt's team." Working for Lamar Hunt's team would mean telling the man who brought him to the NFL, Bill Belichick, that he'd no longer be a part of his team.

What the public saw from the New England Patriots most of the time was a cardboard stiffness. Engaging them in a relaxed, on-the-record conversation was like trying to converse with the generic computer voice that repeated your four or five menu options. Belichick had convinced most of them that the media were a distraction, and despite their real personalities, they became men of steel when the cameras came on.

There were no cameras in Foxboro in the middle of January, so steel gave way to flesh, muscle fiber, and blood. The Patriots weren't trying to "manage expectations" or "focus on the next game." They were just a bunch of guys sad that they were losing two more three-time champions, Scott Pioli and Josh McDaniels. McDaniels was going to Denver, where at thirty-two years old he'd be the youngest coach in the league. It had been easy for him the night before, when Belichick had left him a message congratulating him on getting the job. The coach said he was happy for McDaniels and his wife, Laura, and their three kids. But then there was the next day, when McDaniels had to see Belichick.

He walked into Belichick's office with every intention of speaking, but he couldn't say anything. He was so appreciative of everything the coach had done for him, he couldn't quite put it in a sentence or two to express his gratitude. Every time he tried to get out a word, his voice would start cracking and he'd have to quickly stop or everything was going to fall apart. Belichick put up his hands, told him not to worry about speaking, and gave him some advice.

"Things are about to change for you. They always do," the coach said. "You're not going to be playing a lot of golf, I can tell you that. But don't let the important things change. Whatever you do, make sure Laura is okay with it. This is going to be a big change for her, too. Make sure you keep up a good relationship with your kids."

Belichick also reminded him to bring young people into the system whom he could train, just as Belichick had done with McDaniels. Later, it was Laura McDaniels's turn to cry. The couple was being driven to the airport when a call came in from Tom Brady. McDaniels put him on speaker and, within seconds, Laura's makeup was running.

"You're going to do a great job out there," Brady said. "I'm going to miss you, man. I love you."

There was a feeling in Foxboro that it was only a matter of time before McDaniels left. With Pioli, the instinctive reaction for people was not to give him a hug and say, "Congratulations." It was more, "You're kidding, right?" Even when permission was sought and granted, even when he went on lengthy interviews with the Browns and Chiefs, there was a belief that Pioli wasn't going anywhere.

How could he leave? He was part of a unique NFL partnership with Belichick. They had talked drafts, salary caps, free agents, and trades hundreds of times. But that was just the silhouette of their relationship. They had spent some fun times on Nantucket, with their families seeing so much of each other that it was practically a merger. It was as if Scott and Dallas had four kids, with Mia being the youngest and Belichick's three, Amanda, Stephen, and Brian, acting as big sister and brothers. They loved each other, even when times were difficult. When Belichick and his wife, Debby, divorced, the Piolis refused to take sides. They couldn't. They loved them both and they stayed close to each of them.

Pioli was leaving? So what was going to happen to that ampersand? Belichick & . . . what, exactly? Pioli was one of those employees whom bosses always appreciate but don't really understand until they're gone. They're the ones who are so competent at their jobs that you don't notice that they're actually mastering a couple other duties that aren't necessarily in the job description. Pioli could scout, negotiate, stack a board, manage a cap, and be a voice of reason.

When Pioli told Brady that he was leaving, the quarterback laughed. He thought he was joking. They were standing in the team's weight room, Brady sweating himself back into shape after the knee injury that took his 2008 season. After being convinced that it wasn't a prank, Brady stared for a long time and didn't have much to say. On the record, the Patriots always said that job switches were not surprising and part of the uncertain NFL. But they had gotten used to putting on the armor of who they were supposed to be. Truly, moves like these made them wince. Whether it was good players who "got it" or executives and coaches who helped build it, it hurt to see champions walk out the door.

Robert and Jonathan Kraft both cried when they heard the news, and Pioli cried with them. The consolation was that they both had great things to say about the Hunt family. They knew Pioli was going to work for a good man, and they knew how many times this day *could* have happened if he had been inclined to make every available dollar on the market.

Down the hall and around the corner from the Krafts' offices, a woman named Nancy Meier was red-eyed, too. She had worked with the Patriots since the 1970s, and she knew people the way Pioli knew players. She had become close to the Piolis and looked out for them. Sometimes she picked up things, whether it was someone's integrity or insincerity, before her boss did. If he didn't ask her opinion on something that she'd noticed, she felt that it was her obligation to tell him.

He was going to miss Berj Najarian, who indeed knew what Pioli had done as an employee and a friend going back to the time when the two met in New York, in 1997. Najarian's office adjoined Belichick's, so a trip to see the head coach usually meant a trip to see Najarian, too. They had spent time together professionally and socially over the past decade, and it was hard to imagine that getting together now would suddenly require some elaborate planning that had never existed before.

As for Belichick, their meeting was not what it should have been. There were no great speeches, no wise words, no reminiscing about what they had done. The Patriots would release perhaps the most heartfelt statement of the Belichick era, in which the head coach would glow about the contributions of Pioli. "It has been extremely gratifying for me to follow Scott's career ascension from the bottom of the totem pole in Cleveland to his place as a pillar of championship teams in New England," the statement read. "Now, with the opportunity to steer his own ship and a vision of building a winner, there is no more capable, hardworking, loyal, team-oriented person than Scott Pioli."

But those words weren't said face-to-face. Frankly, the absence of a blessing hurt Pioli, although Belichick may have been going through the same shock Brady had. Pioli had never been close to leaving before, so there was reason to believe that he would come back from the Cleveland and Kansas City interviews and say, "Okay, Bill. Now that those fifteen hours of interviews are over, what are we thinking about in free agency?" The other franchise losses had been different and somewhat expected. Charlie Weis and Romeo Crennel were looking for head-coaching jobs a full year before they left Foxboro. McDaniels and Eric Mangini were both in their early thirties, quickly climbing from position coaches to coordinators, so it was inevitable that they'd take the next step.

Pioli wasn't like any of them. Belichick hadn't brought Weis and Crennel to the NFL. The coach had hired McDaniels and Mangini, but neither had the professional and personal history with him that Pioli had. And no one else would have it again because the Belichick of the twenty-first century never would do what the Belichick of the 1980s did. There's no way he would be as trusting as he was then and reward a friend of a friend with a chance to watch film with him. He'd gotten lucky with Pioli, a young employee who'd never crossed or betrayed him. But times had changed; you couldn't take those chances anymore.

The new era had begun in Foxboro. There were fewer and fewer people who knew what Belichick wanted and what he thought without even talking to him. There were fewer people capable of cracking open a beer with him and just playfully busting him, the way that old and secure friends do. The building still had smart evaluators and good players, for sure, just fewer of them. Belichick often emphasized that his teams should keep their heads down and not seek attention, but his brilliance and their brilliance drew attention. The NFL gathered and picked away at what it could of his fruits, from players to coaches and now, with the losses of Thomas Dimitroff and Pioli in back-to-back years, executives.

For the first time since 1997, it was time for everyone to be accountable for himself, independent of the others. Belichick was faced with replenishing the team, the coaching staff, and the scouting department. Pioli would be out on his own, no longer anonymous, putting himself in position to receive more credit and blame than he ever had in the past. Dimitroff was in Atlanta, trying to prove that he could build a champion with the heart of his father's old-school toughness, and he could do it while eating tofu and wearing True Religion jeans.

Pioli and Belichick had built three championship teams together and nearly touched perfection another time. But it was the "together" part of football that always struck Pioli. It was why one of his best memories was standing on the field in the Superdome, after the Super Bowl win over the Rams, and being thanked by players like Mike Compton, Jermaine Wiggins, and Joe Andruzzi.

"We all had given each other something that no one else could give us," he says.

It was why he could appreciate the meticulous craftsmanship and deep thought that was poured into some of the fine art that Dallas brought into their home, yet one of the pieces of art that stirred his soul was actually a football photo. He had purchased and framed it after his first visit to Arrowhead, in 1998. He had seen it as he walked through the press box, and he stared at it for the longest time, falling in love with the game again as he looked.

The picture was taken on Christmas Day 1971. The Chiefs were playing the Dolphins in a marathon playoff game at Kansas City's Municipal Stadium. Len Dawson, the "16" on his jersey still perfectly clean, was giving instructions in the huddle. Wendell Hayes's pants were a combination of white, brown, and grass-stain green. Jim Tyrer's helmet was scratched and had streaks of brown, yet he leaned in intensely, ready for more. Ed Podolak was exhausted, bent over with both hands on his knees.

"I think it's one of the great pictures in NFL history," Pioli says. "It's the essence of football."

Now he was off to Kansas City, to see if the essence of football could be re-created.

8.

A Tale of Three Cities

Scott Pioli had been in Kansas City for less than a month, and he already knew that his instincts in his job interview had been correct. On that long day in Dallas, when all subjects seemed to be fair game, Pioli had asked his interviewers if some of the problems with the Chiefs extended beyond the football field and into other areas of the organization. He had been too polite to answer the question himself that day, but now that he was one of them he could say it with authority.

Yes.

The Chiefs were officially a mess, and what happened on the field was just a representation of what was happening in parts of the office. He noticed things, big and small, that irritated him. He was no obsessive accounting guy, but he was practical and didn't believe in wasting money. His conservative estimate was that he could save the Chiefs at least $10,000, easily, just by informing employees not to print everything in color. As for the majority of the team's scouts, they either hadn't asked some of their peers in New England what it was like to work for Pioli or the job wasn't that important to them. Pioli had spent most of his career working for Bill Belichick and Bill Parcells, and he was just as organized as they were, if not more. The scouts had to know that their reports would be scrutinized, that they would be required to give opinions and should be prepared to defend them, and that there would be very few moments to sit and do nothing.

As Pioli began talking at his first gathering with the Chiefs' scouts, he heard a bright chime from a laptop computer. It was hard for any of the scouts to hide in that situation. They were seated at a conference table, and everyone could see what everyone else was doing. Seconds after the laptop alert, one of the scouts began tapping away at his keyboard.

"What are you doing?" Pioli asked.

"I got an e-mail," the scout replied, furrowing his brow. The only thing missing from the response was, "Duh!" He seemed annoyed that the boss even asked, and the other scouts reacted as if this type of behavior was normal in this setting. Pioli was too surprised to erupt. This group was going to need a strong talking-to, sooner rather than later.

Shortly after, Pioli was watching film with the scouts in a darkened room. From his seat in front, he could hear giggling behind him. He turned around once, certain that a quick glare would send the message to knock off the nonsense. It didn't. There was more laughter. He turned again and stared a couple seconds longer. Still, it was clear that a couple guys were distracted and amused by something else. Finally, he stopped the film and turned on the lights.

"What's on the computer? Turn it around so I can see it," he said.

A couple of sheepish scouts showed him the computer screen, which revealed a silly picture that had been making the rounds online. Pioli knew then that he had a couple of options: He could either ban laptops from scouting meetings, or he could find a bunch of new college scouts.

There was too much work to be done in Kansas City for anyone to be feeling comfortable. Pioli had noticed that two scouts on his staff, Terry Delp and former Chiefs receiver Willie Davis, appeared to be curious and conscientious as they took notes and asked questions. Eventually, the scouting staff would be reshaped as radically as the team on the field, and Delp and Davis would be the only holdovers on the college side while Ray Farmer would stay as director of pro personnel. As for that team that had won two games the previous year, Pioli had mentioned something to Clark Hunt during the initial interview that got the owner's attention.

"He told me he could tell just from watching tape how out of shape the team was," Hunt says. "No one had made the observation before. It's always easy to look at the big guys and say they're out of shape, but he pointed to all aspects of the team and identified conditioning as one of the problems. One thing about Scott is that he'll always tell you the truth, whether you want to hear it or not, so I appreciated that."

It was one of the reasons he had to find a new head coach. Pioli kept his word to Hunt and considered retaining Herm Edwards, whom he liked personally. Everyone in the league had a good story to tell about the affable Edwards, who could probably win anyone's Make a Fast Friend contest. But there needed to be a new voice and new direction with the players. Pioli took a week and a half to meet with Edwards and watch film, and then he made the decision to replace him. In early February 2009, two weeks after the dismissal of Edwards, Pioli hired Arizona Cardinals offensive coordinator Todd Haley, a coach who was equally talented and brash.

Haley grew up in Pittsburgh and was a preteen when Bradshaw-to-Swann was a staple of 1970s Super Bowls. He was in Pittsburgh because his father, Dick, was the ace personnel man of the Steeler dynasty. Todd lived for scouting trips with his dad. Dick Haley would take a mini tape recorder, wrap a game program around it, and sit in the stands as he uttered fragmented observations about players into the recorder. Todd would do whatever he could to help, whether it was writing things down or, a couple times during long scouting trips in Florida, driving the car so his father could take catnaps (Dick never told his wife, Carolyn, about that; Haley wasn't legally able to drive when his father put him behind the wheel).

Todd Haley's football education resulted in a double major: He learned scouting from his father and was a young coach on Parcells's all-star coaching staff with the Jets in the late 1990s. The coaches there included Belichick, Charlie Weis, and Romeo Crennel. Haley had an exceptional eye for detail, and he had a difficult time holding his tongue if he didn't believe things were being done properly. As a thirty-one-year-old assistant who should have known better, he questioned one of Parcells's motivational tactics. The Jets were 2-3, had an upcoming Monday-night game against the Patriots, and were practicing with a focus that underwhelmed their head coach. So Parcells instructed all coaches to follow him and left the players on the field to coach themselves. After a while, Haley, not understanding the classic Parcells mind game, piped up: "So we're quitting? We're giving up?" To which the quick-witted Parcells, referencing Haley's love for and background in golf, sarcastically replied, "Yeah, we're fucking quitting . . . just like you quit when you couldn't golf."

The Jets beat the Patriots, won ten of their final eleven games, and went all the way to the conference championship game before losing to the Broncos. Lesson learned for the young Haley. Parcells liked him, though, and so did Pioli, who was the Jets' player personnel director when Haley was there. Pioli believed that the young Chiefs could benefit from the knowledge and discipline that he expected Haley to bring.

On Haley's birthday, February 28, his boss had already put the bow on a thoughtful present. No one understood the Patriots' salary cap, Belichick, and the art of making a deal with the coach better than Pioli. February 27 was the first day of free agency and the new league year, so Pioli knew that if he wanted to pry Matt Cassel from the Patriots, he'd have to move fast and present a specific compensation package that Belichick would find attractive. Everyone knew Cassel had to be traded. Tom Brady's rehab had gone well, and the

Patriots were expecting him to return to health and his starting job in 2009. Thus Cassel was the only backup player in the league designated as his team's franchise player. The Patriots had done that in early February to protect themselves from Cassel slipping away as an unrestricted free agent, but it meant the team had to commit $14 million to its backup quarterback.

Pioli's knowledge and hustle worked to his advantage. He'd heard rumors that his old colleague and new divisional rival, Josh McDaniels, was trying to construct a three-team deal that would net the Patriots a first-round pick and land Cassel in Denver. McDaniels was just thirty-two, but he already had tremendous power in Denver. There was a general manager, Brian Xanders, in place, but McDaniels had final say over the roster. Pioli was ready with a deal before McDaniels was and offered the Chiefs' second-round pick, the third choice in the round, for Cassel and thirty-three-year-old linebacker Mike Vrabel. It was the first and smartest offer the Patriots received. Pioli understood that the Patriots were going to have to act quickly with Cassel so they could be players in free agency; he was aware that Belichick viewed the second round as the sweet spot in the upcoming draft; he knew how skeptical Belichick was of three-team trades; and he was one of the few people who realized that Vrabel, adored in

New England, was most likely going to be cut due to his age and cap number.

The deal went through and, officially, the Chiefs gained a starting quarterback while the Patriots traded one. But anyone who had been around the Patriots the previous eight seasons knew better. Vrabel was a quarterback, too, a leader in every way imaginable. He was advanced enough to know game plans as well as the coaches, yet he had enough jokester in him to interrupt tense team meetings with mock questions that would have Belichick laughing out loud. He was the only person on the team who could get away with that. He was a movie junkie with an encyclopedic memory, so he'd entertain his teammates by reciting one-liners that applied to whatever conversation they were having. He was the symbol of who the Patriots were, the godfather of the seemingly unremarkable free-agent class that helped engineer the upset of the Rams in Super Bowl XXXVI. Pro football is defined by seasonal job changes, but fans and teammates alike allowed themselves to believe that Vrabel would be an exception.

"I've seen a lot of good football players leave here, but the Vrabel trade is the one that really got up underneath my skin," says Vince Wilfork, a teammate for five seasons. "That trade ticks me off. Right now. Still. When I heard about it I said, 'What the fuck is going on?' If you want to talk about the Patriot Way, you start with Vrabel. He's smart. He's great off the field. He knows what he's doing on the field.

"Let me tell you, if the play clock was running down and we didn't have a play on defense, he gave us one. He didn't look to the coaches for reassurances. He did it himself. He always knew what defense we could and couldn't be in."

All those traits are why Pioli wanted him in Kansas City, even though Vrabel would be thirty-four by the first game of the regular season. Vrabel didn't run as well as he used to, and his brain sometimes processed plays that his body could no longer make. But the Patriots were going to miss him and players like him. Even the Patriots' system, perceived as diva-proof, would be challenged by its share of whiny and self-absorbed athletes who would carry some influence in the locker room. It was inevitable, and it's exactly what Vrabel saw unfolding at times during the 2008 season. While the Patriots would spend 2009 in transition, searching to define their new identity, the Chiefs were going to be trying to learn the fundamentals of winning. Vrabel was going to help in the locker room with a style that wasn't too heavy-handed or preachy. He was going to be able to show a young team how to think and act while also retaining an ability to be seen as one of the guys.

Unfortunately for Pioli, he wasn't going to be able to have Vrabel and Chiefs legend Tony Gonzalez in the same locker room. It wasn't personal, but Gonzalez wanted out of town. He had been selected to nine Pro Bowls and was regarded as one of the best tight ends of all time, but he'd never won a play-off game in his career. He was the same age as Vrabel, and he wanted to switch places with him. Vrabel had come from a team that had won eleven games in 2008; the Chiefs hadn't won eleven games the previous two seasons combined.

Gonzalez had nearly done it all in his NFL career. He got open as well as anyone in the league. He supported his teammates, even when they said silly things, like the time former Chiefs quarterback Elvis Grbac criticized him during a postgame press conference and said he and others needed to start making some plays. Maybe Gonzalez let it slide because he saw the comedy in a quarterback who was personally responsible for three turnovers in that game calling someone else out. He was charitable. He was so concerned about connecting with the Latino community in Kansas City that he spent a month of vacation time in Mexico, taking Spanish classes and living with a family that didn't speak English. When Carl Peterson was the leading man in football operations, Gonzalez's dissatisfaction with the deal Peterson offered him went public, which is usually a PR nightmare for an athlete. But in the first-name game, people liked Tony much more than they liked Carl, so it was okay. Once, while having dinner in California, he even saved a choking Chargers fan's life by giving him the Heimlich, even if he had only seen it done before on TV.

The Chiefs obviously weren't eager to trade him, and Pioli even met with him to sell him on the turnaround that was coming in Kansas City. Gonzalez determined that it was time to go, so eight weeks after acquiring Cassel and Vrabel, Pioli had to find a team that was willing to handsomely pay the tight end and the Chiefs. It wasn't difficult. All he had to do was contact a friend of his, who was coming off a season in which he was named the league's executive of the year. In voting among forty coaches, general managers, and personnel types, Thomas Dimitroff was recognized as the best in the league. Dimitroff didn't see it as validation. He was looking for more than an eleven-win regular season and a first-round loss in the play-offs. But the award meant that the league had recognized the difficulty of what he had inherited and appreciated how he had turned a bad situation into a respectable one. Dimitroff was looking to add more unpredictability to the Falcons' offense. He offered Pioli a second-round pick in 2010 and was prepared to hand Gonzalez the last big contract of his career. It was a deal. Gonzalez was off to a winner, and the new Chiefs were going to have to find their way without him.

Meanwhile, Pioli was going to have to find a scouting staff that could be trained to converse in the same system he had known the previous nine seasons. He needed a staff that would be able to identify stars like Gonzalez, of course, but also players like Vrabel. While in New England, the linebacker was selected to just one Pro Bowl, but he was as important to the team's success and psyche as anyone in the organization. Those types of players, talented and uncelebrated, fantasy football draft leftovers, could help win championships. Pioli was going to need a new director of college scouting to help him, someone with a knack for digging beneath the surface and seeing talent even when it's not always obvious to everyone else. The perfect man for the job was out there, and he was someone his best friend in the business, Dimitroff, could vouch for.

Dimitroff had worked with Phil Emery for a year and had been awed by him. Emery handled his demotion from college director to national scout gracefully, so much so that Dimitroff told him, "I think you deserve another chance. If anything comes up, I'll help you get it." When Dimitroff said it, Pioli was still working in New England. But when Pioli moved to Kansas City and began making changes in the organization, it made sense for Dimitroff: Pioli and Emery were a match.

Pioli and Emery had met just once, briefly, about ten years earlier in Syracuse. But it was as if Emery possessed every quality that the Chiefs needed. He spent seven years as the head strength and conditioning coach at the Naval Academy, so structure and attention to detail were a part of his repertoire. Since he had worked the previous season in Atlanta, he already had some familiarity with the system that Pioli was going to ask him to teach the scouts. But beyond the technique of scouting, Emery was able to negotiate the nearly invisible line between evaluating and being overly judgmental.

"It's funny; scouts are very judgmental people by nature," Dimitroff says. "We evaluate players, we evaluate their character, we evaluate their decisions. After a while, we end up thinking that we have everything figured out, from the grocery store clerk to our wives."

Both Dimitroff and Pioli had enough experience with a wide variety of people to not fall into some easy scouting traps. One of Pioli's red flags is when a scout questions a player's intelligence. From experience, Pioli has seen intelligent young men labeled as something else simply because of the way they speak or perhaps due to a learning disability. It was a description that bothered him and if you were a scout who was going to throw it out there, you'd better have a stack of evidence to support the charge. Dimitroff laughs at a time, not so long ago, when some NFL scouts and evaluators would mark a player down on character because of multiple tattoos. He remembers presumptuous conversations about gang activity, based primarily on tattoos and where a player grew up.

There were many reasons Emery wasn't going to be lured into surface judgments. He had too many stories, humorous and humbling, that proved that what you see isn't always what you get. He never thought, for example, that he would find the love of his life in a small town where Billy the Kid once roamed. Emery was a graduate assistant at Western New Mexico University, located in the mining town of Silver City, in the early 1980s. There were barely ten thousand people in town and not a whole lot of single women. That's why it was such a surprise to Emery when he was introduced to an attractive young woman who was working as a speech-language therapist in a local school district. She was from New York City, the daughter of a Wall Street broker and a school nurse. She may have been a New Yorker, but she had a Silver City connection: She was dating the son of the biggest cattle rancher in town. Until she met Emery. They were married in Silver City just three months after they began dating.

Phil and Beth Emery loved each other and football, and they had to because the game took them across the country. They lived in the Southwest, Southeast, Mid-South, Midwest, and Mid-Atlantic. Phil was coaching at the time, but he always thought of scouting. When he was at Navy, he developed a friendship with Andy Dengler, a scout for the Jaguars. He'd ask Dengler dozens of questions about the business, and it became clear that Emery's true passion and future were in scouting. A mutual friend of Emery and Dengler's, Tim Mincey, mentioned that there were some openings in Chicago, and in 1998, Emery got his NFL break as a Southeast area scout for the Bears.

He brought depth, patience, and open-mindedness to the job, and it wasn't just because he loved football. He learned a lot about subtlety and nuance from Beth, who was a skilled expressionist oil painter. Beth already had a degree from Northern Arizona University in the speech-language field, and she was such an accomplished artist that she got a second degree, in studio art, from Florida State. Like most parents, Phil and Beth saw life differently after the birth of their daughter, April. Throughout her early development, April was as active and bright as most kids her age. When she was six, she started having infrequent seizures, usually when she was going into or coming out of sleep.

It wasn't long before the seizures occurred more frequently and at odd times. Clearly, there was a neurological disorder, although doctors couldn't immediately say what it was. When they determined that Phil and Beth's six-year-old girl had epilepsy, they attempted to control it with medication. They tried a half-dozen medications over the next several years, and none could combat the severity of the seizures. Phil and Beth's prayers, initially, were to get back to what they considered normal. They had been to the best hospitals, from Thomas Jefferson in Philadelphia to Shands in Gainesville. They had authorized different surgeries and procedures, from the corpus callostomy to the vagus nerve stimulation. They had seen a lot of medications, and they were going to see more, as many as fifteen. Eventually they got to the point where they embraced the life that they had as their normal family life.

"Once we reached the point of true realization that some of the special-needs issues my daughter has were permanent, and after we worked through the sense of loss that realization brings for her and to us, we were forced to look at life and all people in a different light," Emery says.

They learned many new things, and some things they already knew they had reconfirmed, such as their love for one another. You learn the depth of your relationship when something unexpected happens to the family. There was enough growth and acceptance that they were able to offer advice and wisdom to other couples who were first experiencing what the Emerys had years earlier. Even that became an opportunity to learn, because while some families listen, as Emery puts it, some aren't able "because they don't think they're going there. There's some denial because they don't believe they're like you; they don't believe their kid is that kid."

Phil and Beth both got past the stage where they were overwhelmed with feelings of loss and what used to be. The emphasis was on living and enjoying what they had. They understood that there would be around-the-clock monitoring of April and that their knowledge, and helpers' knowledge, of her medications and patterns could be the difference between spending the night at home and spending it in the emergency room. That was their new life. But there would still be Phil's scouting and Beth's painting. There would still be family dinners and family vacations. There would still be father-daughter drives where they'd listen to music on the radio, stop for lunch, go bargain shopping, and talk football.

It didn't matter if the job was in Atlanta or Kansas City and if the man in charge was named Dimitroff or

Pioli. Phil Emery was not only going to manage your scouts and help you efficiently evaluate the best players for your team, he was someone you could trust. "He dots the i's and crosses the t's," Dimitroff says, "and then goes back to dot and cross again." He appeared to be all business with his deliberate speech and purposeful walk that could be heard long before he was seen. But what made him so good at what he did was that he realized that an appearance was just the beginning of the story. It's one of the many lessons he and Beth have learned over the twenty-one years April has been battling epilepsy.

"More than a learning process, it's been a maturing process," he says. "We matured in patience. We matured in seeing the grace and perfection in people, no matter what their perceived imperfections may be. I think we both learned to reach out and help others in a way that we may not have before.

"Although my daughter has been through numerous surgeries and has several physical limitations, when she awakes in the morning and I look down at her, I see what any parent does when they see their child: an example of God's grace and what His picture of beauty is."

In a sense, the old guys with Patriots rings should have seen where things were headed toward the end of the 2008 season. They were the players in the locker room who were born in the 1970s, which meant they were operating with an entirely different set of winning and pop-culture references than most of their teammates. Of the seventeen players on the roster who had won at least one title in New England, thirteen of them were born in the seventies, and eight of them had played at the now-demolished Foxboro Stadium.

They were like those wise heads at the park who still do newspaper crosswords, play chess, and talk about some of the greats they've seen while youths with iPads and iPhones tweet and text around them. The elite eight, which included the likes of Vrabel, Kevin Faulk, Richard Seymour, and Tedy Bruschi, could remember when Gillette Stadium was just a hole in the ground. They remembered when there was no such thing as an outdoor mall called Patriot Place, with high-priced restaurants, two theaters, and a four-star hotel with spa services. Back in the day, the team's hall of fame was not housed in a modern, well-designed building with memorabilia and exhibits. No, the hall was actually just a wall with framed jerseys hanging there.

All of the old guys were close to that symbolic wall, closer to being plaques than future Patriots. In September 2008, one of the best they'd ever seen, Troy Brown, went to the wall. He had spent his entire fifteen-year career as a Patriot and defied the age of specialization by specializing in everything. In January 2009, Rodney Harrison was attending events in Tampa prior to Super Bowl XLIII and unintentionally hinted about his future when he referred to the Patriots as "they." In February, Vrabel was traded. Rosevelt Colvin had literally come in off the couch late in the 2008 season, but by 2009 he knew his future was as a UPS franchisee, running a store in Indianapolis, his hometown. Bruschi had been about two minutes and eighty-three yards from retiring in February 2008, but when the New York Giants pulled off the biggest upset in Super Bowl history, Bruschi knew he had to return. You can't always choose your endings, but sometimes you can, and he decided that game, with all of its near misses, was not the taste he wanted to be left with going into retirement.

There was a bit of a twist developing in Foxboro when Bruschi came back to play in 2008, and it's one of the most difficult things to explain in sports. Who knows why the power shifts in a locker room from one season to the next? Was it based on popularity, common interests, performance, contract status, or who talked the loudest? Or was it a little of all of them? The power in the room was changing in 2008 and it had officially changed by training camp in 2009, and that fact alone was fine. There were times as young players when

Bruschi, Faulk, and Seymour followed policy rather than set it, so a new power group was to be expected. The problem was that it wasn't always clear what the agenda of some of the leaders was.

Some of them were seventies players, too, but they had never won with the Patriots. One of them was Adalius Thomas, a 270-pound linebacker with the speed and smarts to play anywhere on defense. Thomas, who turned thirty-two during '09 training camp, had arrived in New England in 2007 as a highly regarded and highly paid free agent from the Ravens. Free agency in itself is a gamble, but the Patriots had reeled off a string of hits there, in all shapes and sizes, since 2000. Even in cases where the signees were unproductive or not on board with Patriot business, none had the ability to make a dent in team culture. It was too strong. But late in 2008 and during camp of '09, Thomas proved that he and the culture were different from what had been seen in the past.

"I remember that he just started to question a lot of things in meetings. 'Why are we doing that? . . . Why don't we just do this? . . . What is that, man?' He stopped buying in on what the coaches thought," Bruschi says. "He really did think he had all the answers, you know? And that's what he turned into: the answer man. That's when I was on my way out, and I was glad to get out at that point. It just so happens that he was one of the most demonstrative guys that I had ever been around. Loud voice. Very strong opinions, on football and otherwise.

"A lot of guys would gravitate to him, actually. I don't know how he got to the point of helping us almost go 19-0 to, all of a sudden, he was being a distraction. And being very critical of what was going on in the organization in a bad way. He was outspoken to a lot of guys, trying to rally them. I think he really resented the way he ended up being used in the defense."

That's how Thomas was long before his issues with Belichick became public. In late August 2009, Bruschi was starting to see and feel that he wasn't going to be around Thomas or any other Patriot for much longer. He was a thirty-six-year-old linebacker, something his body reminded him of daily. He had hurt his left knee at the end of the '08 season and thought that getting it "scoped" in the off-season would help him. But when he ran early in camp, the knee throbbed and swelled and it forced him to take three weeks off to rest it.

And then there was something he couldn't escape. Film. He liked to watch it as intensely as the coaches did, and he took great pride in his careful viewing as it led him to insights that some players missed. One day in camp, the coaches were trying to show the team how a particular defense was supposed to be run. The coaches would show 2009 film of the defense and compare it to film from 2001, when the defense was executed the way they wanted. Bruschi was uncomfortable as he sat there and thought, "Damn, I'm slow." The film said it all. If he saw it and said it, he knew the coaches were seeing and saying the same thing.

As for the locker room, it was so different that it was hard to articulate. Bruschi loved some of the new guys, like Jerod Mayo, a young man with an old soul. Mayo had been a top-ten pick who didn't act like one. On draft day, when the best of the best are invited to New York, often wearing made-for-the-occasion tailored suits, Mayo had been home in Virginia with his family raking leaves. He was a worker there and a worker in Foxboro. In the off-season, he'd come to the stadium and watch film, even when there were no coaches to be found. He loved the game, and it could be seen by the way he played middle linebacker, never turning down an opportunity to plug a hole or run sideline to sideline. There weren't a lot of Mayos, though.

Some of the new-era Patriots didn't know what they didn't know, and they weren't always eager to learn. If Thomas was the free-agent definition of that mentality, Laurence Maroney was the representative for the draft picks. Maroney coasted on his natural talent, which was considerable, and it didn't seem to affect him that he was a better player his first year in the pros than he was in his fourth. He wasn't *improving*. That was probably the biggest division between the generations. Guys like Brown, Faulk, Bruschi, and Vrabel had improved during their careers. Mistakes bothered them. They'd fight to find and correct the errors before the coaches did. Between them they had appeared in three Pro Bowls, but they had a dozen Super Bowl rings, and that's what they practiced and played for. It's something they thought about when they were at the office and at home. It was just a different ethic, a different outlook, a different time.

Four and a half years after he first told Belichick and team owner Robert Kraft that he was retiring, following his stroke, Bruschi officially did it two weeks before the first game of the 2009 season. There was something inspiring and unsettling about his standing at a lectern saying good-bye. The day before the news broke, he was an old linebacker trying to contribute to the team. But on the morning of his retirement he looked young and energetic. He didn't have a hair out of place, a contrast to his postgame on-field interviews when he still breathed out the rage of the game, even after wins, and his hair was tussled from his helmet. He wore a stylish tan jacket and a light-blue shirt and he didn't look down once at notes as he eloquently explained that he had accomplished all that he had wanted in his thirteen-season career. The only thing missing was a producer whispering in his ear to wrap up his point and move on to the next one; a career in television wasn't far away.

It was an unusual day, as thousands of New Englanders watched the retirement on live TV. Those viewers sat on the edge of their seats as they saw Belichick come as close to crying as anyone had seen publicly in his entire Patriots career. He spoke softly. His voice shook and cracked. He gave Bruschi the ultimate compliment: "If you ask me to sum up how I feel about Tedy Bruschi in five seconds . . . He's the perfect player . . . he's the perfect player. He has helped create a tradition here that we're all proud of. The torch has been passed, and we'll try to carry it on."

Bruschi had improved over his career, through coaching and practice, but he did certain things that couldn't be taught. No one told him that he needed to be the locker-room enforcer. He just did it, and it was a continuation of what he had done in high school and college. In high school, he had blasted a kid who was half-stepping through a drill that the coach wanted them all to do. That was just him. In the near-perfect season, Bruschi had called Belichick off the team bus and told him that he didn't like his postgame message to the team. He wanted to be coached harder, and Belichick obliged the next day by tearing into the team and using Bruschi as a frequent target.

You can't teach a player to be that. And since Bruschi was one of the first players people thought of when they mentioned the Patriots and their championship, maybe it was true that you could no longer teach a player to be a Patriot. You either were or you weren't. Clearly Bruschi was at peace with his decision, but the organization was losing yet another employee who knew how to do championship-level things that couldn't always be explained.

A week after Bruschi retired, it was time for another farewell. Seymour, who was a month away from his thirtieth birthday, was traded to the Raiders for a first-round pick in 2011. Seymour was Belichick's first number one draft pick with the Patriots, a rare three-hundred-plus-pound lineman who could actually be described as svelte. He had been a great player for the Patriots and going into 2009 he was still expected to be very good. But he was hoping to negotiate a new contract with the team, and talks hadn't gone all that well. He fully expected 2009 to be his last season in New England, but the preseason trade surprised and hurt him. While Bruschi's final press conference was cordial and featured an emotional Belichick, Seymour's departure was more businesslike.

He received the news during a short Sunday-morning phone call from Belichick, and the Patriots released a statement thanking him for all he'd done over his eight seasons in New England.

Belichick had achieved some historic things in his career, and now there was a new mountain facing him. He still had Tom Brady, who played the most important position on the field and had won 77 percent of his regular-season starts. But Bruschi and Seymour, teammates since 2001, had a record of 111-34 in their Patriots careers. They'd played eight home play-off games without losing, won two conference titles on the road, and been to four Super Bowls. There sure seemed to be a lot of wins, and brains, leaving Foxboro. The head coach would likely be able to replace the production of the players he lost, and no one doubted that he could get his team in position to win even more rings. But he'd have to deal with other rings, the circus kind, first.

On a Wednesday morning, December 9, there were a few certainties in New England that no Patriot could ignore. One was their record, 7-5, which had them on a play-off pace but as a team playing without a first-round bye. They couldn't catch the top-seeded Colts, who were 12-0, and the number two seed, the Chargers, were 9-3 and on a seven-game winning streak. There was also the matter of their record on the road,

1-5, with the single win coming in London against Tampa. The Patriots were not a good road team but they were a memorable one.

They'd lost in overtime to the Broncos and Josh McDaniels, allowing the first-year coach to begin his career 5-0; they'd lost by three touchdowns in New Orleans, a night of high artistry for Drew Brees, who missed on just five throws and threw five touchdown passes; and they'd lost in Indianapolis after leading by 17 early in the fourth quarter. The Colts loss had its own shorthand: fourth and two. With the Patriots leading by six with two minutes to play and the ball at their own twenty-eight, Belichick called for the offense to go for it on fourth and two. They came up short, gave Peyton Manning a short field, and lost by a point.

In football terms, the road was a tricky place for the Patriots. In everyday New England life, the same was true: You never knew what wintry hand you'd be dealt in the Northeast, even if it wasn't technically winter, so you had to prepare for everything. That's what Belichick reminded his players of when he saw them on December 7. They had the next day off, but if they were in town they probably heard about the storm that was supposed to arrive the next morning. On the Wednesday when they were expected back at the office, the Patriots saw a New England that was slammed with an exotic bad-weather mix. Depending on where you lived, you experienced a foot of snow, a half foot of snow, a sleet special, or high winds with rain. Making things worse, some early-morning drivers in the snow-bound areas went to the roads and saw no plows in sight. "What a cluster," they thought. "Typical."

The Foxboro streets were a mess and the stand-still traffic planted the seeds for road rage, yet every Patriot made it to work on time except for four guys: Gary Guyton, Derrick Burgess, Randy Moss, and Adalius Thomas. They would soon be known in the media as the Tardy Boys. When they checked in late at the office, they were sent home. Guyton, Burgess, and Moss didn't have much to say about the punishment, but Thomas did. He had long been at odds with the coaching staff, going back to the previous season. It got worse in October when he was a healthy scratch for a game against the Titans. When asked about being in-active and his role going forward he replied, "Ask Bill. He has all the answers."

In early 2007, Belichick had returned from the Pro Bowl excited about Thomas's intelligence and versa-tility. Later that season, Thomas handed out T-shirts with HUMBLE PIE emblazoned on them, a tribute to Beli-chick's style of keeping players grounded and focused on the next game. But the joking had ended a year later, and by December 2009 no one was getting what was expected. Thomas was not the playmaker the Patriots thought he was, and they didn't use him all over the field like he thought they would. Being sent home for lateness due to a snowstorm seemed to insult his pride and intelligence. His next-door neighbor Ty Warren had taken the same route to work from nearby North Attleborough and gotten there in plenty of time. But Thomas didn't want to focus on the stories of the forty-nine teammates who made it. He complained about the weather and the gridlocked traffic and quipped, "What do you do? It's not *The Jetsons*. I can't jump up and just fly."

His strongest comment came when he seemed to address Belichick directly: "Motivation is for kindergartners. I'm not a kindergartner. Sending somebody home, that's like, 'You're expelled until you come back and make good grades.' Get that shit out of here. That's ridiculous."

There were four games left in the season and in Thomas's Patriots career. The Patriots were headed to the play-offs, unlike the Falcons and Chiefs, but like those teams, they were going to look back at the 2009 season and be inspired to remodel.

While the Chiefs were just a bad and slow defense in the middle of December, giving up at least 34 points in five of their twelve games, and the Patriots were good but not great with an 8-5 record, the Atlanta Falcons were stuck in a place that mortified their general manager. They were average.

Thomas Dimitroff was more competitive than anyone realized, and it's part of the reason you really had to know him before he allowed you to watch a game with him. The Falcons' owner, Arthur Blank, was similar in that way, so they often watched games together and even commiserated over them, win or lose, on Sunday nights. Sometimes they'd talk on the phone and Blank would say, "Why don't you come over?" Dimitroff would make the two-mile drive to Blank's house and they'd relive the afternoon again.

The Falcons were 6-7 after losing at home to the Saints on December 13. The week before, in a game that was part homecoming, part purging, and part plain-old gawking, the Eagles had come to town with Michael Vick as their backup quarterback. Vick had been released from a federal prison in Kansas in May and had a brief, respectful conversation with Dimitroff in June.

"Hello, Michael. This is Thomas Dimitroff, general manager of the Falcons."

"I know who you are," Vick had replied.

"I wanted to call and tell you that we're relinquishing your contractual rights."

Vick, still suspended by the NFL at the time for his dogfighting and gambling activity, thanked him for the personal call and they both hung up. Even with a player who was clearly out of the Falcons' plans, Dimitroff wanted to stick to his policy of being direct and honest with every player who was part of a team transaction. The move to release Vick was not a surprise, and after being reinstated by the commissioner, the quarterback landed in Philadelphia.

His return to Atlanta, nearly three full seasons after he had last played there, proved what a provocative figure he was in the city. Dean Stamoulis, the Russell Reynolds consultant whom the Falcons hired to help them move forward after Vick, was amazed at how Blank and team president Rich McKay continued to refer to the quarterback. "Even in the darkest days of the franchise, Arthur and Rich clearly felt that Michael was still a good kid who did something wrong," Stamoulis says. They had company, in the stands and in the organization. When Vick walked on the field before the game, he saw Reggie Roberts, the Falcons' director of football communication.

"I know you're pissed at me," Vick said, putting an arm around the man who'd written several press releases on Vick's behalf, trying his best to clean up issues the former franchise star had created.

"No, Michael, I'm not," Roberts said. "I believe in forgiveness. I love you."

The Atlanta crowd was undecided when the game started, some cheering and some booing, but when Vick ran for a touchdown and threw for another in a 34–7 victory, all he heard was applause. As much of a showman as he was during his years with the Falcons, Vick had never been able to lead them to back-to-back winning seasons. In fact, no one in team history had. That would have to be the modest goal for the rest of the regular season, and it's something that bothered the GM much more than he was willing to admit publicly.

In his two seasons as an Atlanta executive, Dimitroff had already done many things that were the opposite of his Patriots teachings. He scouted and built for a 4-3 defense, and he had actually tried building a bridge between football operations and marketing and promotions. There were times in New England where the football operations people were often skeptical of anything the marketers suggested. The way Dimitroff felt about a winning record with no play-offs was purely New England. It was a reason to yell and challenge and demand more from everyone.

The Patriots didn't make the play-offs in Dimitroff's first year working there, 2002, and he noticed how angry and tense people were well after they had been eliminated from play-off contention. A day after the final team meeting of the year that season, Belichick had a legal pad with his top team priorities circled. He'd also given special projects to the assistant coaches, challenging them to see things that would prevent them from the hell of being play-off observers.

Dimitroff's obsession was equal to that in January 2010. The Patriots had been embarrassed in a wild-card game by the Ravens, the first home play-off loss for Belichick and Tom Brady in New England. The Chiefs had won their final game of the year to go 4-12. Dimitroff's Falcons, meanwhile, had gone 9-7 with a late three-game winning streak. Although he appreciated the phone call from Pioli in which his friend told him he should be proud of how the team finished, Dimitroff longed for the days when the play-offs were just the beginning of the journey, not the destination.

All three teams were going to have to do fairly dramatic things for the 2010 season to be different from what they'd watched in 2009. For the Chiefs, it was going to be the continued strengthening of their staff, which would extend to a stronger roster. For the Patriots, it would be reclaiming a locker room that heard a lot of talking from Adalius Thomas during the

season and was going to hear more talk from Randy
Moss in the future regarding his contract. For the
Falcons, it was going to be a combination of tweaking and spending a lot of cash. There would also be a
constant reminder from the GM, something he'd written to himself in a list of notes on his iPad: *Be true to
yourself; be bold.*

9.

Let's Make a Deal

B ill Belichick didn't wait tables after college. He didn't pursue a career in music, write the first few chapters of his novel, or backpack through Europe trying to find himself. As soon as he graduated from Connecticut's Wesleyan University in 1975, when he was twenty-three, he went straight to a job in the NFL. Since that start with the Baltimore Colts, where his $1,300 annual salary was just 15 percent of the national average, he's spent every day of his working life in the league.

Longevity and experience certainly don't mean everything, but they do allow you to exhale and think clearly when major decisions need to be made. They're also reminders that no matter how disappointing a particular year may be, like 2009 was for Belichick, there's probably something in your thirty-five-season treasure trove labeled HOW TO FIX IT. After all, Belichick is the only active head coach with victories against Chuck Noll, Bill Cowher, and Mike Tomlin, or every coach the Pittsburgh Steelers have had since the NFL/AFL merger in 1970. He's seen the arrival of six expansion teams and he's seen six teams move, including one, the Browns, that he was coaching. He's been around so long that the man who hired him out of college, Ted Marchibroda, was the same man who replaced him as head coach twenty-one years later when the Browns left Cleveland and became the Baltimore Ravens.

Based on what the coach had already seen in his career, his 2009 Patriots weren't a team in need of an overhaul. What they needed for future improvement was a good rewiring job. Their final game had been in January 2010, when, after fifteen minutes, they found themselves trailing 24–0 in a home play-off game.

The Patriots literally have a "Needs Book" on every team in the league, which includes everything from which fourth corner is likely to be replaced in the off-season to which prospects visited leading up to the draft. One day after the eventual 33–14 loss to the Ravens, Belichick began writing in the most important Needs Book the Patriots had on their Foxboro shelves:

(John H. Reid/Getty Images)

Bill Belichick had big ideas about turning the Browns into winners. He had an all-star cast on his coaching and personnel staffs, but when it was time to bring his scientific player-evaluation system to the field, he wasn't surrounded by enough of the right players.

(Heinz Kluetmeier/Getty Images)

Not many people in America expected red, white, and blue confetti to be falling on the New England Patriots after facing the mighty Saint Louis Rams in Super Bowl XXXVI. The game's MVP was quarterback Tom Brady, pictured here celebrating next to Belichick's father, Steve (blue sweater).

(Courtesy of AP Photos)

Belichick hired Scott Pioli as a low-paid scouting assistant in 1992. Ten years later, Belichick and Pioli became synonymous with team-building at a championship level.

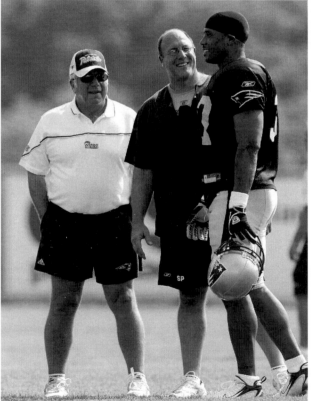

(Courtesy of AP Photos)

After a letdown in 2002, the Patriots needed reinforcements. Pioli and Patriots owner Robert Kraft found a safety with the temperament of a linebacker in free agent Rodney Harrison. A couple of longtime Patriots veterans had to train Harrison how to be their kind of enforcer.

Wide receiver Randy Moss was a controversial acquisition for the Patriots in 2007. Touchdown catches like this one against the Cincinnati Bengals became so routine that it carried Moss, Brady, and the Patriots to a historic regular season.

For six seasons, Michael Vick wasn't just the Falcons' quarterback; he was one of Atlanta's most dazzling entertainers, too. But in 2007, his secret life brought the franchise to its knees.

(Atlanta Falcons/Jimmy Cribb)

One of the best decisions Arthur Blank and a few partners made came in 1978, when they cofounded retail giant the Home Depot. Thirty years later, the stylish owner of the Falcons had to figure out the best way to restore trust and stability to the team.

(Atlanta Falcons/Jimmy Cribb)

When Belichick and Thomas Dimitroff first worked together, it was a head coach–groundskeeper relationship. Years later they would speak as fellow team-builders.

Dimitroff witnessed the seamless relationship between Belichick and Pioli in New England. He wanted to have something similar with his head coach in Atlanta. He interviewed bigger names, like Rex Ryan, but went with the smart and steady Mike Smith.

Many Belichick disciples were able to leave Foxboro and still enjoy a good relationship with their mentor. But this photo of Belichick and former Jets and Browns head coach Eric Mangini, who used to be one of Belichick's star pupils, says it all.

(Atlanta Falcons/Jimmy Cribb)

Lionel Vital has worked with two generations of Dimitroffs. When Thomas got the job in Atlanta, one of his first calls was to Vital, a man who always gives unfiltered analyses of players.

(Courtesy of AP Photos)

AFL founder Lamar Hunt, playing football here with five-year-old son Clark in 1970, is credited with numerous sports innovations. One is naming the Super Bowl, which the Chiefs won in January 1970—and haven't returned to since.

(Courtesy of AP Photos)

Clark Hunt had no idea that Pioli had connections to the Chiefs long before Kansas City asked permission to interview him. Hunt thought getting Pioli to interview was a coup; having him accept the offer to be general manager was even better.

(Courtesy of AP Photos)

Quarterback Matt Cassel's fortunes literally changed when Brady was injured against the Chiefs in the first game of the 2008 season. The next time Cassel saw a Kansas City uniform, he was wearing it and Pioli was once again one of his bosses.

(Atlanta Falcons/Jimmy Cribb)

Officially, the drafting of Alabama receiver Julio Jones was an organizational decision shared by the likes of Blank and Smith. But Dimitroff had begun dreaming of the possibility six months before it happened. On the afternoon of the draft, Dimitroff told one of the people he respects most in the league of his plan to acquire Jones. The response was "I wouldn't do it."

(Courtesy of AP Photos)

Pioli, a student of NFL history, hired the son of a legendary scout as his first head coach. Todd Haley's scouting genes allowed him to see a lot, and his fiery tongue was a guarantee that he'd always share what he saw.

(Courtesy of Kansas City Chiefs)

Belichick often gave a young Pioli unsolicited family advice. And to this day, when he's on the job, Pioli has managed to stay close to his eight-year-old daughter, Mia.

their own. Belichick was able to write with conviction and specifically say what needed to change, from new bodies to new soul.

While there wasn't a single redeeming thing from the play-off loss, the team-building challenge that followed was something that excited and even regenerated the coach. There isn't a definitive line between Belichick the Coach and Belichick the Builder, because he's equally passionate about both tasks. He's a student and admirer of the process, and his love for it all, from the big picture to the minutiae, is probably why he's never complained of burnout or hinted at taking a break. Noll, for example, was coasting toward the end of a Hall of Fame career in his fifties and was happily retired by fifty-nine. But by the time Belichick celebrated his fifty-eighth birthday, on April 16, he was filled with his usual zeal about the upcoming draft and seemed to have a firm grasp on what would make the Patriots better in 2010.

One of his first moves had been solidified more than a month earlier, in the first week of March, when he re-signed a draft pick he never expected to have. The Patriots had selected University of Miami defensive tackle Vince Wilfork with the twenty-first overall pick in 2004, although that was far from the original plan. On the morning of that draft, Belichick and Scott Pioli had both agreed that Steven Jackson, a running back from Oregon State, would be their pick. But as the draft moved into the early teens and the Bears, expected to take Wilfork at 14, went with Tommie Harris instead, the Patriots were forced to reconsider.

They loved Jackson, but they couldn't allow someone with Wilfork's ability to slip by them. They took him at 21 and tried to flip their other first-rounder, number 32, and get themselves back in the midtwenties so they could take Jackson, too. But at least three or four teams had the same thought and the Rams, slotted to pick twenty-sixth, were able to make a deal with Cincinnati and move up two spots to grab Jackson at 24. The Patriots stayed at 32 and selected Georgia tight end Ben Watson.

As the Patriots expected, Wilfork had turned into a star. When they studied film of him at Miami, there wasn't a single play of his performing the two-gap technique that they were going to ask him to perfect in the pros. Yet he learned to do it quickly, and along the way he came to have a better understanding of Belichick as well.

"When I first got there I'd say, 'Hey, Coach.' And sometimes he'd speak and sometimes he wouldn't," Wilfork says. "I remember asking one of the guys, 'What's up with Coach? He doesn't always talk.' And the answer I got was, 'You'd better be glad. If he starts talking to you, that probably means there's gonna be a problem.'"

Over the years, as Wilfork developed into one of the best nose tackles in the league, worthy of the March 2010 contract that earned him an $18 million signing bonus, he found that the player's analysis had been far too cynical.

"Let's face it," Wilfork says with a laugh, "there are two Bills: There's the coach who can be an asshole, and he knows it, and there's the man I get to see, who's nothing like what you see in the media. I know I can talk to him about football, but I usually don't. We talk about personal things, family things. He's a very smart guy and he gives good advice, but he's a great listener. I really feel that I can talk to him about anything."

Belichick knew that Wilfork was one of the essential Patriots, along with players such as Tom Brady, Jerod Mayo, and Kevin Faulk. They were part of a trustworthy veteran core who didn't need to be hounded into doing extra film study or getting to the weight room early. They did that on their own and encouraged teammates to do the same. To simplify everything Belichick had written in his 2010 Needs Book, the key was to find good players with those same traits. Some of the good players the Patriots wanted were in-house

and were re-signed, like Wilfork, Faulk, and cornerback Leigh Bodden. Some of them were veteran free
agents without flash, similar to ones the Patriots had
signed at the beginning of their run, like Alge Crumpler and Gerard Warren. And others could be found
during an event that Belichick had studied for years,
so much so that no one in the league was as consistently active during it as he was, nor, in some cases,
as willing as he was to wait for his players. It was the
draft, probably the single biggest reason he'd had a
ten-season stretch in which his teams won at least ten
games eight times.

As far back as the 1990s in Cleveland, he and Mike
Lombardi had begun talking about ways to build a
streamlined system in which college and pro scouts
had the same grading scale and were therefore speaking the same language. The building plan was interrupted when Belichick was fired, but the idea began
to be resurrected in 1997 when he went to the Jets and
had an office next to Pioli's. When they left New York
for New England in 2000, Belichick and Pioli refined
and burnished the system until it truly became what
Belichick had imagined. Anyone who has ever programmed a system knows that no matter what firewalls
and fail-safes are in place, it can still break down. Belichick had been around long enough to see that, too. He

had received a fair amount of resistance from at least one of his coaches at the time, Brian Daboll, and a few strong voices on his scouting staff when it came to the 2006 draft. Laurence Maroney was taken in the first round and Chad Jackson was taken in the second. The Patriots moved up for Jackson, and in the spot they vacated, Green Bay took receiver Greg Jennings, who had more catches in his first four NFL games than Jackson did in his career. Chad Jackson: the definition of a system breakdown.

"He was a better athlete than he was a football player," Belichick says. "He was an exceptional athlete, had some football skills, but the athletic skills didn't all translate over to the football field. Some of the things that we asked him to do weren't really his strengths. They were more weaknesses for him, actually. We weren't able to get to his strengths in our offensive system, so it was a bad fit and it was, to a certain degree, I'd say a misevaluation.

"I don't think Chad really understood how to use some of the exceptional athletic ability that he had, and in a lot of cases he made it not as difficult for the defenders to cover him as he could have. But over a period of time he still was never really able to do that. He was never able to convert his athleticism to attacking the defense or defender."

Belichick hadn't listened to the anti-Jackson chorus in Foxboro before the 2006 draft, and four years later, the new challenge for Belichick was to avoid costly mistakes like Jackson and to do it in an organization with fewer people willing to confront him. Even Pioli, who had known Belichick for more than twenty years, admitted that it's easy for self-doubt to creep in when you have an opinion that is the opposite of Belichick's. The respect for his knowledge and his résumé automatically gives you pause when you have a counterpoint to his point. But with that said, Pioli still had his disagreements with Belichick, as did Thomas Dimitroff, Charlie Weis, Eric Mangini, and Romeo Crennel. It was business, rarely personal. The question going forward was whether that checks-and-balances resistance, on the coaching staff and in the personnel department, still existed in Foxboro.

By 2010, Belichick had spent so long thinking in the system, teaching it, tweaking it, communicating in it, practically living in it, that the entire draft process had become an enjoyable obsession for him. He was addicted to the strategy and possibilities of it, the same way some people are hooked on *Tetris* or *Grand Theft Auto*. He had already been compulsive about draft homework, diving into it with a tireless rigor and curiosity so he could have a feel for first- and seventh-rounders alike, and then the NFL did him a favor.

For the purpose of increased television ratings, the league decided that the draft would be a three-day, mostly nighttime event starting with Thursday in Eastern Standard prime time. Round one would be on Thursday at seven thirty; rounds two and three would start at six on Friday; and rounds four through seven would be completed by Saturday evening. It was perfect for Belichick: more time to strategize, plot, and scheme; more time to figure out, for the current year and the next, how to accumulate draft picks that other teams would see as attractive trade bait.

"My philosophy is that you've got to know the whole draft," Belichick says. "Now, if you're picking at thirty-two, do you need to know the top-ten players? Do you need to know Matt Ryan vs. Joe Flacco? Well, you're not going to draft a quarterback and they're not going to be there anyway, so no. But you might want to move up in the first to take someone else, so I think you've got to know to a point, 'If one of these three guys happens to be there at, say, twenty-two or twenty-three, then we've got to be ready to get on the phone and see if we can make a deal.' And if you can't, I think you always have to have the philosophy that you have to pick. You might want to get out of the pick and you can't, so you always have to have a card to turn in.

"Really, it's just knowing the draft from A to Z. And not just the top of the draft or the end of the first round. Because if you want to move within the draft, you've got to understand where you're moving to or what you're moving from."

Belichick talked about trades so much because, he says, "I think teams know we're open for business." He didn't make trades for the sake of it, although it sometimes appeared that way to fans who were used to counting down with the clock and waiting for the commissioner to announce the newest Patriot. If Belichick could pick up an extra choice and still come away with players he had targeted for a specific section of the draft, he'd almost always do it.

As he left his Gillette Stadium office and climbed one flight of stairs to the draft room for round one on April 22, he knew he was in a strong position. His team held four of the first fifty-three picks: the twenty-second pick in the first round and three second-rounders. When possible, he liked to come out of a draft with extra picks for the following year. Part of his work had already been done in that category with the 2009 trade of Richard Seymour, which brought back a 2011 first-rounder from the Raiders. So, preferably, an extra second- or third-rounder for 2011 would be ideal if someone made the right offer. He also went into that room confident that he knew how the league perceived the player he wanted to pick in the first round.

"It's such a process, and part of it is knowing what the league thinks," he says. "We have players on our board and we look up there and say, 'We're probably higher on this player than any other team in the league.' You see mock drafts out there and the player is not mentioned in the first round. In any of them. Scouts talk, and you kind of get a feel that no one else sees the player quite like we do. On the flip side, there are guys that we might take, say, in the third round and we know someone's going to take him in the first. So, again, it comes back to homework."

Belichick settled into his chair, in a room where the trading spirit remained but a familiar face was no longer there. It was the second draft in a row without Pioli, which meant it was just the third time in the previous nineteen seasons that Belichick and Pioli weren't on the same team. The pairing had been so dynamic and slightly taken for granted that when Pioli moved to Kansas City, portions of his duties were split between four employees: Nick Caserio moved from director of college scouting to director of player personnel; Jon Robinson became the new college scouting director; Jason Licht became director of pro personnel; and Floyd Reese, a longtime general manager with the

Titans, became a senior adviser primarily in charge of negotiating contracts.

The draft began and the first handful of picks went as expected. Belichick had his mind on defensive backs, and the first one to come off the board was safety Eric Berry, who went to Pioli's Chiefs at number 5. The Browns took the first corner, Florida's Joe Haden, at 7. There were just a couple wrinkles in the top fifteen, and none of them affected the Patriots. The Jaguars took a defensive tackle from Cal, Tyson Alualu, at 10, higher than most people projected. And in a draft so thin on true pass rushers that teams were willing to stretch to invent them, the Eagles traded up to 13 to select Brandon Graham, a defensive end from Michigan.

Through nineteen picks, the draft had unfolded the way the Patriots wanted. Tim Tebow, whom Belichick and Caserio had taken to dinner in Boston's North End just three weeks earlier, was still there. Belichick believed the Florida quarterback was rising in other draft rooms, and he knew there was some mystery about the Patriots' interest, so that meant there might be a market for Tebow when the Patriots picked at 22. Oklahoma State receiver Dez Bryant was also on the board, and the Patriots knew that Dallas coveted him and that created a trade market as well. Most important, the man

Belichick wanted all along, Rutgers cornerback Devin McCourty, was still available.

"I think a lot of people had McCourty in the second round," Belichick says. "Right or wrong, I think that was kind of the league's take on him. There weren't a lot of people willing to step up and take him in the first round. That was my sense of it. So if you don't feel there's that big of a market for the player, you can back off a bit if you have the chance and accumulate picks."

As pick 22 approached, the phone rang and the ID let Belichick know there would be a familiar voice on the other end. The ringing line flashed "Denver." Josh McDaniels wanted Georgia Tech receiver Demaryius Thomas and was willing to swap pick 24 for 22 with a fourth-rounder, pick 113, to go with it.

Deal.

As pick 24 approached, the phone rang again. It was the Cowboys. They were offering a third, pick 90, for the right to move up from 27. They also wanted the Patriots to give them a fourth, pick 119, which was fine since New England had just acquired a more valuable fourth minutes earlier. It hadn't been much of a gamble to move down from 22 to 27, and if the Patriots really wanted to test their theory, they could have moved behind the Jets at 29, too. The Needs Book predicted the Jets would take a corner, and Belichick thought

New York had Boise's Kyle Wilson rated higher than McCourty, but why risk it? The Patriots selected McCourty at 27 and walked away from round one with the player they wanted and two extra picks they hadn't owned at the beginning of the night.

The next day, for rounds two and three, the Patriots made so many deals that a family tree was needed to keep up with the origin of the picks. While tight end Jermaine Gresham had been drafted by the Bengals in the first round, the Patriots believed Arizona's Rob Gronkowski was better. The problem was that back surgery had caused him to miss the entire season, and if he hadn't he might have gone in the top fifteen. The Patriots thought that Baltimore might be interested in the tight end, too, so they moved from pick 44 to pick 42. It was one spot ahead of the Ravens and the deal, with the Raiders, cost them a sixth.

"When you move back, it's always easy to move up again if you need to," Belichick says. "You should have enough to do it after the trades you've made."

The best deal of the night came with the sandwich pick of the Patriots' original second-rounders, number 47. They'd already turned the first one, number 44, into 42. And their last one, number 53, was still on the board. So when Belichick saw at least a half dozen players whom he thought were comparable for pick 47, he indeed was open for business when Arizona called and dangled two picks, 58 and 89. He liked the value of the deal, and it gave him tremendous flexibility now in the third, where the Patriots suddenly had back-to-back picks that they didn't have a couple days earlier. It would put the team in position for a sweetheart of an offer in the next couple hours.

There was no trading, surprisingly, of pick 53 and Florida defensive end Jermaine Cunningham was selected. But the status quo didn't last long. The recently acquired pick, 58, was on the move again, and it was headed to the Texans in exchange for picks 62 and 150. The Patriots wanted another Florida player, Brandon Spikes, to play inside linebacker for them and he was taken at 62. As for pick 150, it usually didn't work this way, but they had a plan for it. To them, the pick said Zoltan Mesko.

"Normally when you trade back in the second and pick up a fifth, you're not thinking about a specific player in the fifth," Belichick says. "You don't know who's going to be there. It's just value. But we really felt Mesko would be there in the fifth and we said, 'Okay, we might get him in the sixth, but he's really the only punter we would draft. So even if it's a round early, we're going to take him in the fifth and go with him as our punter.'"

Toward the end of the second day of the draft, with the Patriots and the rest of the league thinking about closing time and resetting for the morning, the black office phones in the draft room rang again. This time it was Carolina. The Panthers had gone 8-8 in 2009 with veteran Jake Delhomme as their starting quarterback. Once upon a time, Delhomme had put a scare into the Patriots in one of the most entertaining Super Bowls ever played, XXXVIII. But the Panthers saw his miserable eight-touchdown, eighteen-interception season and decided it was time to go young. They had twenty-five-year-old Matt Moore as his backup, and they had drafted Notre Dame quarterback Jimmy Clausen at pick 48. They had their eyes on pick 89, one of the few remaining picks that could be traded in the third round (the rest were compensatory picks and could not be moved). The Panthers wanted a quarterback. Kind of. They liked Appalachian State's Armanti Edwards, who was a record-setting quarterback in college, but he was being projected as a receiver in the pros.

Anyway, the Panthers were willing to trade their 2011 second-rounder for 89. It was too good to walk away from, and not just because the Patriots already owned pick 90. Even if all the Panthers' dreams were realized in 2010 and they won the Super Bowl, the Patriots would still move up twenty-five spots, from 89 to 64, just for being willing to wait. But the Panthers weren't going to win and they knew it. Head coach John Fox was in a lame-duck situation, and there was an air of desperation to do something.

That's where longevity and experience paid off for Belichick as well. He didn't have to worry about the classic GM-vs.–head coach debate, with one man planning for the long term while the other fights for right now, knowing that he's judged on the present and this year's wins and losses. For Belichick, with hands in both fields, he was able to have a more balanced view of things. He'd loved New England since he was a teenager, and there was no desire to bolt from the Patriots. He agreed to the deal, satisfied with the players he'd selected and confident that he'd like what was coming to him in the future, whether that future was the next day or the next year.

On the final day of the draft, the Patriots got to cash in on the fourth they'd gotten from Denver. At 113 they took Florida tight end Aaron Hernandez, whose talent alone was first- or second-round quality. But many teams thought he was a character risk and let him slide to day three. The Patriots figured they could get Hernandez straightened out and with multiple picks, they felt they could take a gamble.

Another draft had been completed, with teams from Foxboro to Atlanta to Kansas City excited about what they had done. The day after the draft, the Patriots finally released Adalius Thomas, ending a bitter relationship that had begun with such promise. After all the moves by all the teams, no one would know for sure what it all meant until the players took the field, which, coincidentally, was scheduled to happen during training camp with the Patriots and Falcons. It didn't happen often, but sometimes teams practiced together to break up the monotony of camp. The Saints were also scheduled to hold practices with the Patriots in Foxboro.

In August, the Patriots headed south to the Falcons' immaculate facility in Flowery Branch, Georgia. With stately brick buildings and carefully landscaped fields, the complex looked like a small college campus. It was the Falcons' daily home, and they had built dormitories on site to make it camp-compatible as well.

Both teams appreciated the change in routine, from players to ownership. Arthur Blank had often asked Thomas Dimitroff about Belichick, and Dimitroff told him that the Belichick of press conferences didn't do him justice. The owner was skeptical until he chatted with Belichick one day and was surprised to be greeted with a hug and a string of one-liners. Dimitroff and head coach Mike Smith shared plenty of laughs with Belichick as well, although both general manager and head coach found themselves inching toward Tom

Brady so they could see how he practiced and share some insight with Matt Ryan.

"It was an eye-opening two days for me," Smith says. "I saw an intense player who was in control of every offensive piece on the field. Everything that was happening on offense, from route adjustments to plays that were called from the coaching staff, he had a hand in it. I could see the trust level between the offensive staff and Brady, and the players and Brady. I thought it was very revealing."

Dimitroff had made some comparisons to Brady, traits-wise, when he was studying and writing an evaluation of Ryan. It surprised him during one of the practices when Brady headed his way and struck up a brief conversation. He told him he was impressed with what he and Smith had done with the Falcons and he said that he was a Matt Ryan fan as well.

"There are some quarterbacks who have a unique way of ripping the team with an element of positivity to it," Dimitroff says. "There are guys who try to do that and it flops, and the team just has a disdain for the quarterback. But Tom and Matt, with their seriousness, passion, and competitiveness, they're special. They're just people you want to be around."

Although it was still football practice, the joint Falcons-Patriots work session had felt like a vacation.

When it was over and both teams resumed normal business, it seemed that the season opener suddenly hovered. The Falcons would open in Pittsburgh, and the Patriots would be home against Cincinnati.

As Dimitroff prepared for the season, trying to be in a dozen places at once, he missed a call placed to his cell phone. It was Belichick. The coach left a voice mail that surprised and humbled Dimitroff. They had come a long way from a head coach–groundskeeper dynamic, and even a head coach–director of college scouting relationship. It was one team builder to another, showing admiration. Belichick wished the team luck going into the season and, he added, based on how the team was built and conceived, he thought the Falcons' season would turn out just fine.

On the first Saturday in October, seemingly a lifetime away from spring and the 2011 NFL draft, Dimitroff stood in his office and admired a board. The names and early rankings of the top college players in the country were listed there, and Dimitroff stared at the neatly labeled magnetic strips as if transfixed.

A friend from Boulder, ex-racer and current bike shop owner Doug Emerson, was visiting for the weekend and Dimitroff explained to him how the board came to be ordered, or stacked. He then talked about

the athleticism of two of the nation's most gifted receivers, Julio Jones and A. J. Green, and that's when it
became apparent to Emerson just how riveted Dimitroff was by the players and the process.

"Dude," Emerson said, beginning to chuckle.
"You're such a nerd!"

And Emerson, who'd had two-hour talks with Dimitroff on the bike paths of Colorado, the subjects ranging from literature to politics, had seen just a glimpse
of it. Two months earlier, during a break from practice
and the punishing Georgia sun, Dimitroff had called
the scouting staff into the draft room for an informal
session. He wanted to be sure everyone was clear on
what he meant when he said he was looking to add explosive, "urgent athletes" to the Falcons. The staff pro-
ceeded to have nerdy arguments about what was and
was not athleticism.

The general manager, a wordsmith, was known for
coming up with handles that would make his thoughts
portable and memorable. When he first got to the
Falcons, he said that he and head coach Mike Smith
were on a "malcontent inquisition." When a member of
the organization loosely and frequently referred to the
Super Bowl in a newspaper interview, Dimitroff's in-
house response was that the organization had to remain
"semantically responsible" when publicly talking about

winning championships. The new catchphrase, "urgent athleticism," qualified as a true obsession.

As he paced his office and studied that board, Dimitroff openly wondered what it would take to put the Falcons in position to select one of those receivers. He had focused on offense in his first draft, taking Ryan and left tackle Sam Baker. In his second draft, he went defense by selecting tackle Peria Jerry in the first, although Jerry got hurt and missed most of the season. He added to the defense in round three, taking Missouri linebacker Sean Weatherspoon because of his speed and ability to cover. For his fourth draft, he was thinking about getting into position for one of those alpha receivers. "If there was a way to trade some of the lower-round picks and move up, I'd do it," he said. "If you're telling me the cost to significantly move up is lower-to-middle-round picks, then why not? I guess I look at it differently than a lot of people."

In Dimitroff's third year as GM, the entire organization was looking to define itself with greater expectations. The team had paid millions of dollars for a soulful marketing campaign, "Rise Up," with a rousing video of a mass choir singing behind actor and Falcons fan Samuel L. Jackson. For Dimitroff, rising up had to be more than consecutive winning seasons. He already counted on that, and he wanted Atlanta fans to feel the same way, even if that hadn't been anyone's reality in the first forty-two years of the franchise. The next step was to win big games and continue to add the right kind of impact players to the roster.

Dimitroff challenged himself and his staff to build a team that was a consistent contender, filled with enough "captain-characteristic" players as mainstays. When he took the job, he brought along a color-coded scouting matrix that would bring even more specificity to the scouting process. It could be read quickly, and a series of numbers, four 7.5s, for example, told a precise story of what kind of player he could expect to see on film. The numerical snapshot also included a dot, with green the mark for a captain and black for someone who would go in a high-risk, skull-and-crossbones column on the team's board. High-risk didn't just mean an arrest or an expulsion from school. High-maintenance could equate to high-risk, too. Dimitroff was conscious of the locker-room mix and knew that one too many "me" guys could undermine years of planning. He was a political liberal and he could tolerate a lot of different things, but he wasn't going to employ players who required so much special management that they'd distract coaches and other players from focusing on their jobs.

The Falcons passed on so many black-dotters in the 2010 draft that team owner Arthur Blank called for further investigation. Blank wanted to be sure the Falcons weren't being too extreme with their grading standards. Dimitroff did some research and reported that a handful of teams, the Chargers, Chiefs, and Colts among them, had not selected a single player from the Falcons' skull-and-crossbones list, either. He told Blank that he had no issues being in such a small group since he had immense respect for each of those teams' GMs.

Besides, a lot of what teams saw as high-risk or not, or even urgently athletic or not, was subjective. When Dimitroff was with the Patriots, he could watch the same film as Scott Pioli and Bill Belichick and sometimes the three of them would walk away seeing different things. He had learned a lot of football and management from them both, but *becoming* them was never the point; he was an extension of a Belichick Tree, not a Belichick Monolith. So he hadn't been surprised in April when his high risk became Belichick's late second-round value and the Patriots selected Florida linebacker Brandon Spikes. It was the same story in the fourth round, when one man's "character concern" was another's "this is by far the best player on the board," and that's how the Patriots wound up with another Florida player, talented tight end Aaron Hernandez.

It was important for him to have a vision for where he was trying to take the football-operations arm of the franchise and to make sure he wasn't straying too far from his core while doing it. Before the season began, he typed a few notes in his iPad about general-managing in his third year. *Be true to yourself,* he wrote. *Remember your roots: tough, honest, organic. Keep it real.*

After their first game of the season, an overtime loss in Pittsburgh, the Falcons had impressed by winning their next two. They crushed the Cardinals 41–7, and went on the road to division rival New Orleans the next week and beat the Saints in overtime, 27–24. Dimitroff was thrilled that the team was making his job harder with each successful week they had: The more they won, the lower their first-round pick would be in the spring, which would make it more complex to leap from the back of the room to the front.

Dimitroff didn't mind. He loved to win, and he wasn't afraid of doing something unconventional to make it happen.

At twelve fifteen Sunday afternoon, about forty-five minutes before game time, Lionel Vital stood on the Georgia Dome field watching players from the 49ers and Falcons go through warm-up drills. Vital, or "L" as Dimitroff sometimes calls him, didn't miss much, even when someone came over to say hello. His brown eyes instinctively scanned the field, left to right, always noticing something that he could use later.

It was easy to see why Vital, the Falcons' assistant director of player personnel, initially thought of a career in law enforcement after his NFL playing days were over in the late 1980s. Bald, about five feet nine inches, muscular, and someone who smiles as long as you do it first, Vital had the look of a man who could knock heads and not overtalk while doing it. He was forty-eight and had four daughters and three grandkids, but he was not someone you'd bet against in the weight room. He had to have a title, but it did a poor job of describing who he was to the Falcons' general manager. Vital grew up in Louisiana and officially had six brothers and sisters, but he considered Dimitroff a seventh sibling. They'd known each other for more than twenty years. Vital worked for Belichick in Cleveland and with Dimitroff's father on the Browns' scouting staff in the early 1990s. He twice scouted for the Ravens, as well as the Jets and Patriots. He knows Dimitroff so well that he swore that if you gave him just a brief description of where Dimitroff was, he can tell you what he's thinking.

"The thing about Thomas is, he could be standing on the other side of the field, and I know what he thinks about certain things," he says. "I know how he ticks. And he knows me, too. He could be in a room with fifty guys, and I don't have to be in that room, okay? If I know what they're talking about, the topic, I can tell you how he came across to them."

As soon as Dimitroff was hired in Atlanta, Vital didn't have to wait for the phone call. He knew where his next stop was and that he had to be ready. He was working with the Ravens at the time, recognized as one of the best scouts in the country, but Baltimore GM Ozzie Newsome understood that Vital had to go and work with a friend whom he once roomed with when they were both kids in their twenties. They were in the World League then, doing an unofficial audition for an updated *Odd Couple.* They wrestled over what was on the TV and how loud it was, jostled for position on the basketball court, and practically memorized each other's dinner orders: There would be shrimp and rice and vegetables and a huge dessert for one of them, while the other one would go for a salad, no meat, some rice, and maybe a bite of the dessert. In between their brotherly squabbles, they'd talk about moments like the one they were in now, when they'd be on the biggest stage, working together without fear of backstabbing or petty power struggles.

One of the things they never argued about now was Vital's scouting and evaluation style. Part of his strength was what he was doing before Falcons-49ers. He was watching players in action. He was looking at the San Francisco defensive backs to see how they turn their hips, even in drills. He was paying attention to cornerback Nate Clements and it was clear that he'd have something to say about him before the game began. Dimitroff knew that Vital was not going to be the one who turned in a thesis to describe a player.

"I'm not going to sit here and write a book, okay?" he says. "That's not my forte and it's not what's important, to be honest with you. Because Bill always said, the final three or four lines is what he really wanted. I know guys that can write novels and be wrong. It sounds like Shakespeare and it's dead wrong. My thing is, can you play or not? Is he going to start or not? If you can pinpoint it like that, I think it makes you exceptional.

"I always got the free pass on the novels. They wanted my opinion more than anything else. And that's how Thomas uses me here. He knows I'm going to see the player the way I need to see him. It's going to be unorthodox, but in the end it's probably going to be pretty . . . the people I've worked with will tell you, it's probably going to be pretty accurate."

People he works with now and people he's worked with in the past approached him when they noticed him on the sideline. Mike Johnson, a former Falcons assistant who worked with Vital in Baltimore, stopped by to give him a hug and say hello. There was also a visit from Falcons tight ends coach Chris Scelfo, a fellow Louisiana native who informed Vital that life should be good for the Falcons later in the afternoon.

"Tony Gonzalez is in the building today," Scelfo joked, "so I think I've done my part as a coach. I got him to the game."

They both laughed.

As players ran by, undrafted free agents and first-rounders and fifth-round finds among them, Vital broke down the art of scouting. He said he learned to focus on a player's strengths from former Browns scout Ernie Plank. Dick Haley taught him how to have confidence without overthinking the process. Haley would study a few tapes on a player, watch him practice, and see a few highlights. He would leave it at that, because he didn't want his scouts talking themselves into or out of a player by watching tape after tape. Belichick taught him to eliminate excess, hone in on what a player could be for the system, and then definitively say what he could or could not do.

"When I was a young scout, my first five years, I was guessing some, because you have no history to gauge," he says. "When you get in this for ten years or twelve years, now you have twelve drafts to compare it to. But in your first couple of years, you really don't know. You've got to be confident, and you've got to act like you know and all that, but you're guessing your ass off."

He was asked when he crossed the threshold from guessing to knowing.

"When I stopped talking to other scouts about players," he says. "A lot of times scouts will bounce it off other scouts when they see them out there. 'Hey, man, you saw this guy, what do you think?' They're cross-checking themselves. I don't even talk to other scouts about players, unless it's double-checking background information. I don't have phone conversations with scouts about players. I give all my extra time on the phone to my girls, my kids. I wouldn't want another scout to screw me up."

He looked again at the defensive backs. It was twelve thirty. More people, dressed in red and black, were filling the dome. A couple more people from personnel, Les Snead and Ran Carthon, stopped by to acknowledge him. Vital didn't lose his train of thought. He could talk players, specifically defensive backs, all day.

"I know how I feel about the guy," he says. "I have my own feelings on these players when I see them, and I'm confident in that because it's been right and it's been good to me. Trust me: If it had not been good to me, you would know and everybody else would know, too. I'd be sitting out somewhere else. So at this point in my career, I'm not worried about missing on the player. I'm going to hit most of them. I hate to say it like that, but it is what it is."

He remembers all the misses. He had two guys in his home state, Charles Tillman and Ike Taylor, whom he missed in the same year. And they played at the same school. He missed on Tillman because he thought he was too stiff. He missed on Taylor because, well, he didn't think he was too smart. He was big and fast, a former running back with limited experience at corner, but he couldn't imagine going back to his team at the time, the Patriots, and trying to sell Taylor to them. In that same draft, 2003, New England took a corner who ran much slower than Taylor, Asante Samuel.

"A lot of guys may miss on a defensive back because he's athletic. Being a good defensive back is not just about being athletic. The first thing I want to see is if the guy's natural and instinctive," he says. "If I was in the backyard picking the team, I'd want that backyard guy. Brent Grimes is that kind of guy we have here who can just play the game. You know, he's quick twitch, he's instinctive, he sees the field, he's natural at it. He doesn't really have to prepare for it. He gets out of bed, he can play.

"The guy who has to think about it, he's mechanical. You've got to overcoach him to do it, and I'm afraid of him. Because you can't coach him on that final drive. The natural instincts kick in. I'm looking for natural instincts. And of course you want mental toughness. Mental toughness is the focus. Not losing his confidence. Not getting dumb when things are not good. Having an energy about him and no one can take that away from him. Getting beat and turning around and saying, 'I couldn't care less I just got beat, come back again, my man.' He gets beat, so what? And even if they lose the game, he's going to say, 'I'm sorry it happened, man. It just happens. But I'll be back next week.'"

He stood with his arms folded as he wrapped up the conversation. He stared extra-long at number 22, the 49ers' Clements. He'd been watching him off and on for a half hour and he finally was able to say what he was thinking. The 49ers gave Clements an eight-year, $80 million contract to play in San Francisco. Clements, a big corner at just over six feet and 210 pounds, played his first six years in Buffalo.

"He's not a great corner," Vital says. "Teams aren't dumb. You just don't let great corners walk out the door. Buffalo knew he wasn't great." He watched Clements turn and chase a receiver in a drill. "See? He's not a quick-twitch guy. He's tall, so it's hard for him to change directions. If you put a double move on him, he can be exposed."

Whether Clements factored into the game or not, everyone affiliated with the Falcons understood what was at stake. Simply, people were at that point where they expected the Falcons to beat the 49ers, who were 0-3.

As one o'clock approached, Blank and Dimitroff sat side by side in a small room inside the owner's private suite. If they had opened the door, they would have seen a range of personalities, from Bernie Marcus, one of Blank's Home Depot cofounders, to the owner's wife, Stephanie, and the couple's nine-year-old fraternal twins. But the door remained closed for much of the first half, and that was a good thing.

"Daddy's not going to be a happy camper tonight," one of the twins says to Stephanie. The 49ers had taken a quick 14–0 lead.

"It's a long game, sweetheart," Stephanie replies.

Inside the small room, which is next to the replay officials' booth, Blank and Dimitroff gestured and pounded tables. After the GM's top free-agent acquisition, Dunta Robinson, was called for what appeared to be a bogus thirty-four-yard pass-interference penalty, Dimitroff yelled, "What the hell was that?" and threw his hands in the air. A few times he looked at the men in the booth and shrugged as if to say, "What are you trying to do to us?" He could be critical of his own team during games as well. He and Smith make a point of having a postgame conversation about any frustrations either of them have so issues won't become overblown later in the week or season.

In the third quarter, Blank decided that he should spend at least a couple minutes with visitors in the box. He had taken off the jacket of his expensive pinstriped suit, yet he still looked dignified in his startling white shirt with French cuffs. He is known as one of the city's most stylish residents, and although their tastes are different, Blank's love of fashion has rubbed off on his GM. Sometimes it even goes too far. Once, Blank invited Dimitroff to a weekend Hawks game. Dimitroff asked him what he should wear and the owner replied, "Well, it is a Saturday night. You probably should wear a sports coat." When he got to the game, surrounded by jeans and casual-shirt wearers, Dimitroff saw a puzzled Stephanie. "Why are you so dressed up?" she asked. All he could do was smile. He'd never thought so much about clothes in his life.

Blank sat next to Marcus for a moment and then stood for a big third-down play for the Falcons' defense. They didn't make the stop.

"No! No!" the sixty-nine-year-old owner yelled, jumping up and down in front of his ninety-six-year-old mother, Molly. It was a humorous scene and a bit unusual, but Molly gave a slight smile and continued to focus on the game. Blank left the general box and returned to the small room with Dimitroff.

The Falcons were able to score on San Francisco, but not enough to take the lead, so they trailed 14–13 with two minutes to play. Darryl Orlando Ledbetter of the *Atlanta Journal-Constitution* once joked that Smith likely doesn't know who Beyoncé or Kobe Bryant is, but you can't sneak much football information by him. The team had heard all of Smith's numbers about close games in the NFL, how 25 percent of games in the league are decided by 3 points or fewer and nearly half are decided by 8 or fewer points. His mission, he liked to explain, was to be the least-penalized team in the league and take care of the football, because the percentages told you that the game would likely be decided by a fourth-quarter drive.

Based on those stats, the Falcons were exactly where they wanted to be against the 49ers. Dimitroff's first draft pick, quarterback Matt Ryan, was leading the team down the field for a possible winning field goal. But he made a mistake. The man Vital identified before the game, Clements, leapt out of nowhere in zone coverage and intercepted Ryan's attempt. The stadium groaned. Clements certainly looked great on the play, not at all inhibited by quick-twitch deficiencies.

But the problem was that he kept running. If he'd simply slid to the turf and gave himself up, the 49ers would have had the ability to run out the clock and win the game. Clements seemed unaware of the game situation and ran for the end zone. He didn't notice Falcons receiver Roddy White running behind him, and he didn't secure the football, so after racing for thirty-nine yards Clements allowed White to poke the ball out of his hands and to the turf. It was the kind of play, defined by urgent athleticism, Dimitroff had been preaching about since he became GM. While he was college scouting director in New England, Dimitroff saw the Patriots win a play-off game in San Diego when Troy Brown made a play similar to White's and saved the season.

A play-off game in January is more dramatic than game four in October, but the excitement could be felt in the crowd of more than sixty-six thousand fans. Atlanta recovered the ball, at its own seven, and after some smart passes from Ryan to White and a key third-down conversion from Ryan to Gonzalez, kicker Matt Bryant was in position for the winning field goal. He attempted a forty-three-yarder, and at first it looked like something that Phil Niekro used to throw all those years for the Braves. But then it corrected itself and tumbled through the uprights.

Atlanta 16, San Francisco 14.

"I hate sloppy football," Dimitroff says three hours after the game. "It irritates me. I know it's a win, but I struggle with inconsistency. Our job is to limit inconsistency with our coaches, our scouts, and our players."

Inconsistency may have been a problem during the game, but Dimitroff was confident it wasn't going to last the entire season. The Falcons, at 3-1, were good and he knew it. Yes, they were going to have to fight off occasional inconsistency. But they weren't going to have to remake their offense. They weren't going to have to trade away their number one receiver because he was being a distraction. In a couple days, the whole league would know: That was a story the Patriots would have to deal with.

10.

Shelf Life

As soon as the Patriots acquired Randy Moss for a fourth-round pick on the weekend of the 2007 draft, they knew they were on a different kind of clock. It was one naturally set to an alarm, and they weren't sure when it was going to go off. It truly was just a matter of time.

They'd had previous dealings with players perceived to be controversial, so they weren't scared off by the receiver or the comments he'd made as a member of the Oakland Raiders. While there in 2006, he'd admitted to reporters that he was dropping more balls than usual. They were shocked to hear his explanation: "Maybe because I'm unhappy, and I'm not too much excited about what's going on, so my concentration and focus level tends to go down when I'm in a bad mood.

So all I can say is, if you put me in a good situation and make me happy, man, you get good results."

In one of his first meetings with his bosses in 2007, Moss wasn't as brazen. He was introspective and humble as he answered their questions, and when he spoke of his desire for a new start in New England, he began to cry.

"I'll play for the minimum," he said through tears that day. "I just want to be here."

The Patriots tore up his existing contract, gave him a team-friendly one, above the minimum, and after he set an NFL record with twenty-three touchdown receptions in '07, they signed him to a three-year, $27 million deal. He got along well with Bill Belichick, Tom Brady, and most of his teammates. He was named a team captain in 2008 and 2009. Except for the incident where he showed up late for work, he mostly stayed out of trouble and out of the news. But as he prepared for the 2010 season, the last year of his contract, getting a new deal was the one subject that seemed to preoccupy the thirty-three-year-old Moss.

As early as February, he began making public comments about how the Patriots "don't really pay" and that he understood he wouldn't be with the team after his contract expired. He emphasized that he knew it was business and he wasn't mad at anybody, but he sounded like a man who was trying to convince himself each time he said it. When it was time for mini and training camp activities on the field, he was the Moss everyone remembered: keeping practices competitive and entertaining by taunting the defense, leading to playful shouts of, "Shut up, Moss! Get your ass back to the huddle." In one practice, he spiked the ball after making a reception to incite the defense. A few of them wisely jumped on the football and said, "Hey, Moss. I didn't hear a whistle. That's a fumble, baby."

He knew how to have fun in practice, but when football activities were over he'd return to his contract obsession. He mentioned it to teammates during training camp, told a reporter he felt that he was unwanted because he didn't have a deal, and in an act that many saw as one of protest, he intentionally isolated himself at the team's Kickoff Gala, which raised money for charity. As his teammates sat at tables with fans and advertisers, Moss rejected autograph requests and sat alone, wearing his headphones and occasionally moving to the music.

He was getting closer and closer to the old Moss, the one the coaches and players in New England had seen only in short sports clips on TV and had been warned about from people who watched him in Minnesota and Oakland. After the first game of the season, a 38–24 win over the Bengals, he went to the interview room and spent nearly fifteen minutes talking about his lack of a contract, his "fair" relationship with ownership, and how it would be a "smack in [his] face" if the Patriots waited until after the season to sign him. Belichick had to be briefed on the highlights of the performance because as it was happening, the coach was smiling and talking football in his office with his youngest son, Brian. Brian was a postgraduate football player at Suffield Academy, about two hours away from Boston. He'd been a fixture at Patriots games for ten years, and it wasn't unusual for him and his brother, Stephen, to ask for and receive extensive football tutorials from their dad in his office, win or lose. As soon as Belichick heard what Moss had done, he went from thinking about teaching to maneuvering. It was clear he and his front-office staff were going to have to find a market for Moss and trade him, but another player on the roster was going to be traded first.

Laurence Maroney was traded to the Broncos a few days before the Patriots played their second game of the season, against the Jets. If Maroney, who was traded for a fourth-rounder in 2011, didn't make it in Denver, he probably wasn't going to make it anywhere. Four years after the 2006 draft, the book was ready to be titled for the Patriots' top two picks that year: *A Tale of Two Pities.* Both Maroney and Chad Jackson had squandered immense talent because of their refusal to work as hard as some of their peers in Foxboro. An undrafted free-agent running back, BenJarvus Green-Ellis, had worked his way from waivers to the practice squad to the roster and, finally, past Maroney on the depth chart. He ran and worked harder than the first-round pick. Maroney wouldn't be the featured back in Denver, but McDaniels, his new head coach and old advocate, was going to give him some opportunities. The Patriots believed that they could replace Maroney with the backs they already had on their roster, and one, Danny Woodhead, whom they signed a day before the Jets game.

Although the Patriots lost that game to their life-long rivals, there was a revelation of sorts in the 28–14 defeat. When McDaniels was the Patriots' offensive co-ordinator and learned that the team was getting Moss, he instructed his offensive coaches to make sure there were plenty of plays, for Moss and everyone else, that New England hadn't run before.

"When you've got a player like Randy on the field, you have to consider all the things that are available to you," McDaniels says. "You get a lot more Cover 2 looks when he's on the field. He helps your running game because he draws so much attention. You're getting, in general, simpler looks for the quarterback and more space for the slot receivers and running backs."

Except in 2010, that wasn't happening as much as it had in the past. Moss was able to put a move on cornerback Darrelle Revis in game two and then finish off the play with a one-handed, thirty-four-yard touchdown reception. But there were also several passes thrown his way that were forced into coverage and could be considered nothing less than low percentage. It wasn't 2007 anymore, or even 2009. Maybe the offense could be just as productive without Moss, playing a more efficient style.

Two weeks later in Miami, the Patriots scored 41 points, albeit with the help of a kickoff return for a touchdown, a blocked field goal that led to a touchdown, and a fifty-one-yard interception return for a score. The draft pick the Patriots got from the Chiefs in the Matt Cassel trade, Patrick Chung, blocked two kicks on the night and had the interception return. Patriots players talked afterward about what a great team win it was. But there was a statistical oddity on the stat sheet: no catches for Moss. It was the first time since '06 that he had gone without a reception, and based on his comments that year about being in a bad mood, maybe that wasn't a coincidence.

His shutout in Miami didn't make him happy, and he was sure to let the man calling the plays, Bill O'Brien, know about it. O'Brien, who grew up in the Boston neighborhood of Dorchester, was not a back-down type. He commanded the players' respect by knowing what he was doing and sometimes delivering his message with an edge. He and Moss were not always the perfect mix. They exchanged words that night in Miami, but the inevitable was already in motion.

While it was clear Moss was being a distraction and Belichick knew it, the head coach still had great affection for him. The irony is that if Moss had followed the path of his first three seasons in New England, Belichick might have looked at his situation differently. It wasn't *always* true that the Patriots moved on from veteran players and it wasn't *always* true that they felt receivers in their early to midthirties had no production to offer. If Moss had left Belichick with strictly a personnel decision to make during and after the 2010 season, he might have had a chance to return. But it was obvious that Moss's mind wasn't on football, at least not in New England, so three and a half years after they acquired him from Oakland, the Patriots traded Moss to his first professional home, Minnesota, for a third-round pick. He was informed of the trade by Belichick, and even after Moss was gone, the coach went out of his way to knock down media reports that Moss had been a distraction or uncoachable. Moss played fifty-four games in his New England career and produced an astounding fifty touchdowns.

It wasn't long before the Patriots saw Moss again at Gillette Stadium. The Vikings returned for a game on Halloween, and by the looks and sounds of it, Moss believed he was dressed up in the wrong uniform. He had just one catch for eight yards in Minnesota's loss, with the Patriots indeed using deep safety help to stop him, and he was moved by all the hugs, kind words, and applause he received during his return.

As a Patriot, Moss was never one for spending a lot of time speaking with reporters. In fact, that's one of the things Belichick liked about him. There would be weeks and weeks where he'd go without a single on-the-record comment. He did the same thing when he got to Minnesota, but the NFL received complaints about it from the local chapter of the Pro Football Writers Association. Moss was fined $25,000, another incident that fueled a press conference that was even more memorable than the one he gave after the season opener.

When he entered the room to meet with the media, he wore a black Red Sox cap. He then instructed everyone that this would not be the type of interview that they were all used to: "I'm going to go ahead and say this: Look, I got fined twenty-five thousand dollars for not talking to y'all. And I do answer questions throughout the week, but if the league's going to fine me twenty-five thousand dollars, I'm not going to answer any more questions for the rest of the year. If there's going to be an interview, I'm going to conduct it. So I'll answer my own questions. Ask myself the questions, and then give y'all the answers."

The next several minutes were a public love letter to the New England region, the fans, the Patriots' ownership, the team's captains and players, and Belichick, whom he called "the best coach in football history." When he mentioned the Vikings, he second-guessed a decision by head coach Brad Childress to go for a touchdown on fourth down when he could have had an easy field goal. He was also critical of the Vikings' coaching staff, who he claimed didn't incorporate any of the suggestions he made during the week on how to slow down the Patriots.

"Coach Belichick gave me an opportunity to be a part of something special and that's something I really take to heart," Moss said, conducting a one-man show that was vastly more entertaining than the standard question-and-answer sessions with postgame media crowds. "I actually salute Coach Belichick and his team for the success they've had before me, during me, and after me.

"So I'm actually stuck for words just because of the fact there's a lot of memories here. To the New England Patriots' fans, that ovation at the end of the game, that really was heartwarming. I think I actually shed a tear for that."

He ended his session with an actual salute, to Belichick and New England, and added, "I'm out." He left the room.

The next day he was fired.

Less than a month into his second stint in the Twin Cities, Moss was waived by the Vikings, who basically conceded that the third-rounder to the Patriots was a handout.

November began the firing and departure season not just for the former Patriots player but also for former Patriots coaches, who would begin to lose their grip on job security as well. In Cleveland, where the Patriots and their 6-1 record arrived on November 7, head coach Eric Mangini had spent an extra week preparing for what was essentially the Super Bowl for his coaching staff.

The Browns were 2-5 but had gone into their bye week with a surprising win in New Orleans. Everyone always said Mangini was smart, so he had to know that already having five losses by November, playing in the AFC North, was not an indicator of the play-offs.

The previous year, just a few games into his first season coaching in Cleveland, Mangini had begun to wonder if he and team owner Randy Lerner were on the same page. It seemed to him that Lerner was panicking, and after a 34–3 loss to Baltimore in 2009, Mangini already wondered if Lerner was the same man he'd had an engaging interview with shortly after leaving the Jets. Mangini had significant personnel power then and had been able to handpick the general manager, George Kokinis. But by the time the Browns hosted the Patriots in 2010, Kokinis was out and Mangini found himself answering to a new team president, Mike Holmgren, and a new GM, Tom Heckert. Those hires wouldn't have been a problem if the Browns were winning, which they weren't, but the coaching staff put an incredible amount of thought into making sure there would be a win against the Patriots.

On defense, in an attempt to simply make Brady think, the Browns switched everyone's positions: A player who normally lined up at left outside linebacker lined up on the right; the right outside linebacker went left; the strong safety became the free safety, even if it wasn't his best position. On offense, they jumped on the back of Peyton Hillis and rode along for 184 rushing yards and two scores. As the game was winding down, offensive coordinator Brian Daboll, who had left

New England angrily, went to jump and celebrate with one of his players and found himself tumbling on the ground. The Browns won 34–14 but would have trouble winning the rest of the year. The Patriots would begin a run where they seemingly couldn't lose nor be stopped on offense.

One of the many reasons for the Patriots' success on offense was Woodhead, an undrafted back out of Division 2 Chadron State. As soon as the 2008 draft ended, he got a call from Mangini, who was coaching the Jets at the time. "As the head coach, I make one of these calls a year," Mangini said that day. "We can offer you $2,500 to sign with the Jets. Do I need to call your agent?" Woodhead said the agent wasn't necessary and that he'd be there.

When he got to New York, he didn't look out of place with his talent, but he got hurt. When Mangini was fired and Rex Ryan took over, Ryan didn't have the affinity for Woodhead that Mangini did. He was cut in September to make room for receiver David Clowney, and the Patriots were able to get a player that Mangini begged Heckert to pick up. "I'll even try him at defensive back," he told the GM. "Let's just get him." He was so intrigued by Woodhead because the back basically blew the lid off the metrics that Mangini had created in his advanced Browns computer system. The system was known as the "football Google" around the office, with answers to every question imaginable about a player, team, agent, or system. When Mangini punched in various stats on Woodhead and measured them against every other player in the league, he concluded that Woodhead was a hidden star.

The Patriots got him, though, and used him as the replacement for veteran third-down back Kevin Faulk, who blew out his right knee in the loss to the Jets. Woodhead filled in for him nicely and seemed to blend in with Aaron Hernandez, Rob Gronkowski, Wes Welker, BenJarvus Green-Ellis, and Deion Branch, who was reacquired from Seattle after Moss was traded. At times during the season, it seemed like the offense was even better without the record-setting receiver. It just hadn't been the first Sunday in November.

The next week, in Denver, the Kansas City Chiefs went into a Colorado atmosphere that was even more bizarre than most people realized. And what they saw, during and after the game, was strange enough. The Chiefs arrived at Invesco Field with a 5-3 record, the best in the AFC West. Head coach Todd Haley, an unofficial nutritionist, said he knew it was going to be a good year in training camp. That's when he saw Dwayne Bowe check in at 212 pounds, compared to 242 the previous year, and Branden Albert check in at 305, down from 350. Haley would pull some players aside in camp and plainly tell them that they had no chance of success if they were too fat. Everyone knew the coach, who considers snarling Hall of Fame linebacker Jack Lambert one of his heroes, wasn't shy about sharing his opinion, which he did in Denver as well.

It was hard to imagine that the Chiefs could actually lose a game in which Matt Cassel threw for 469 yards, four touchdowns, and no interceptions, but they did. The Chiefs helped their running game in the off-season by adding rugged back Thomas Jones, whom they often told to leave the weight room because he worked so long and hard in there, as well as offensive linemen Ryan Lilja and Casey Wiegmann. But they couldn't run the ball all day against the Broncos, which allowed McDaniels's team to walk away with a surprising 49–29 win.

After the game, Haley and McDaniels approached each other for what's usually a nondescript handshake and pat on the back. But instead of shaking McDaniels's hand, Haley wagged a finger at him, apparently upset with the Broncos' late-game approach. McDaniels believed in aggressive offense at all times, so the criticism didn't bother him. Haley later publicly apologized for the incident in Denver.

But McDaniels had much more serious issues to worry about. When the Broncos traveled to England in late October to play the 49ers, the team's video director, Steve Scarnecchia, taped six minutes of the San Francisco walk-through. He told McDaniels about it and the coach, who had experienced the national wrath of Spygate in 2007, refused to watch it. Scarnecchia knew about Spygate on a personal and professional level, too. He worked in New England and so did his father, Dante, the team's respected offensive line coach.

By the time the Chiefs came to town in mid-November, Broncos executives had been made aware of the incident and the league had begun its investigation. It was determined that McDaniels had not authorized Scarnecchia to do what he did, and in a scene straight from *CSI*, the league conducted a forensic analysis of the Broncos' computers and was satisfied that no one watched Scarnecchia's work. The videographer was fired, and the Broncos and McDaniels were both fined $50,000.

All of the investigating took place in November. By the time the story went national and people had time to digest what had happened, it was nearly time for the Chiefs and Broncos to play again, this time in Kansas City. Broncos president Joe Ellis had said that the taping incident was not a fireable offense for McDaniels, but people who have been around sports long enough understand that public votes of confidence are iffy at best. Besides, there was the issue of winning. The Broncos were 3-8 going into Kansas City and had lost sixteen of their last twenty-one since McDaniels got the team off to a 6-0 start in his rookie year. The Broncos were not known as an impulsive franchise when it came to their coaches. They'd had just four in the previous twenty-nine seasons, with McDaniels following Dan Reeves, Wade Phillips, and Mike Shanahan.

The game at Arrowhead, where he saw dozens of familiar faces, was his last as a head coach. He had seen Scott Pioli, Romeo Crennel, Charlie Weis, Anthony Pleasant, and all the faces from the good ol' days. It was funny, because he wasn't that old, at thirty-four, and his time in New England wasn't that long ago. Belichick had told him that being a head coach was difficult, but even he had five years to fail or succeed during his first head-coaching job. McDaniels didn't even have two full seasons in Denver and he was out. That sure went fast.

"I went there and I made my mistakes, and I'll learn from them," he says. "And I hope that I can learn from them and be a better coach and a better person. I'll never be able to express how grateful I was for them giving me the chance, at thirty-two, to go there and be a head coach. It was awesome."

Right after he heard the news, Belichick contacted McDaniels.

"I remember he called me," McDaniels says, "and this is typical of him. He said, 'How's Laura? Make sure she's okay.' And I remember he said, 'Call your parents. Go see them. Make sure that they know that you're okay, because I know that they're going to go through this and feel terribly about it.' He told me that if I went and made sure that they saw me and they knew that I was okay, then it was going to help them. And I did. I made the trip. I went right to Ohio, spent a week with my mom and dad, and it made all the difference in the world. Because my mother and father were, you know, they were upset. And I think that made a huge difference.

"But that's him. It wasn't about, 'Hey, what happened?' Or, 'I wish you would have done this, or you should have done that.' It was personal. That's what my relationship with him is like. I can't speak for anybody else's, but he's always been that kind of influence on me. And to me it's invaluable."

The good news for McDaniels was that his friends in Kansas City and New England were having success. O'Brien, who was essentially the Patriots' offensive coordinator, was displaying his creativity and smarts with the remade offense. McDaniels and O'Brien had worked on the same staff, and they had remained in touch. The offense, incredibly, was operating at an efficiency that was on pace to be the second-best in Patriots history. New England was 10-2, with no losses since Cleveland, and racing toward the top seed in the conference.

As for the Chiefs, they weren't just trimmed down in training camp. They had a gritty mentality, too. Those who watched the Chiefs train at Missouri Western University could hear assistant head coach Maurice Carthon from anywhere on campus: "Come on, son! You've gotta catch the ball. Damn!" The other coaches on the staff who were coached by "Mo" when they played, Bernie Parmalee and Richie Anderson, often teased him and claimed he wasn't nearly as rough on these Chiefs as he was on them. "Because they'd kill themselves if I was," Carthon often replied.

"Mo's the best," Haley says. "He creates soldiers at the running back position. He's the best running backs coach in the league, and we're very close. He's got an extra instinct; there are times he'll say something and I'll think, 'Uh, that doesn't sound right to me.' And you know, it'll turn out to be right."

They received tough coaching from Weis, too. Weis was available to coach them because his career at Notre Dame had peaked in his first two years there.

The school had been so excited by Weis's quick start in South Bend that he was given a contract extension before he had completed his first year. It was a lifetime contract, and he seemed to be on the path to backing it up by accumulating more wins, nineteen, in his first two seasons than even the legendary Knute Rockne had. He got the team to two lucrative bowl games in his first two years as well, and then he hit a drought. He was Jersey-guy brash when he took the job, promising that Notre Dame would have an X's and O's advantage against most teams. But toward the end of his final season, 2009, he was saying that he'd understand if he were fired.

He was fired, and it wasn't long before he heard from Scott Pioli. Notre Dame, his alma mater, may have taken his job, but his provocative coaching style was still intact. That could be seen as early as August in the heat of Saint Joseph, Missouri. Weis sat on his motorized cart and critiqued the details of the Chiefs' route running. "I wasn't fooled by that for a second," he would say to a receiver. "Why in the hell do you think a defensive back would fall for it?"

The coaching was so good that Haley had many of the players become honorary coaches during the bye week. They wore visors, they broke down film, they coached technique. There were veteran coaches like

Brian Waters and Mike Vrabel, and there were younger coaches like Tamba Hali and Brandon Flowers.

Of course, the Chiefs weren't without their issues. There were times Haley and the man he used to share an office with in New York, Weis, didn't see the offense the same way. That was just one of the reasons Weis was looking to take a college job during the season and found one at Florida, where he would become the offensive coordinator as soon as the Chiefs' season ended. Still, the product was rarely affected. The Chiefs were the kind of team that won games they were supposed to, save for a frustrating overtime loss in Oakland in November. They were in the embryonic stages of becoming what Pioli envisioned, yet they were 8-4, and it certainly appeared that they were going the same place as the Patriots, Falcons, and nine others: the play-offs.

11.

Three and Out

Ralph Marchant recognizes the look on the face of his college roommate, Scott Pioli. He's seen them all in the past twenty-five, going on thirty, years, and none of them require an explanation. When you've known a guy since you were both teenagers, when you've won and lost big games with him, seen him be a knucklehead, seen him be a Friday-night scholar who wanted to study film when everyone else in the college crowd wanted to go drinking, laughed and cried with him, watched him humbly climb to the top of his profession, and celebrated Super Bowl victories with him, it's easy to know what he's thinking.

It's January 9, the morning of the Kansas City Chiefs' first home play-off game in seven years. Marchant, sitting on a couch in the Piolis' family room, notices that his friend is unknowingly pacing. Pioli is trying to make sure he has everything he needs before leaving the house and heading to Arrowhead for a game against a team, the Baltimore Ravens, that he knows is better than his.

"You've got that look, like you've run to the field and forgotten your helmet in the locker room," Marchant says.

Pioli laughs and agrees with him. It's the look of game day, along with the anticipation and stomach knots that come with it, and it never leaves as long as you're a part of competitive sports. At Central Connecticut in the 1980s, when Pioli and Marchant were both on the defensive line, Pioli could have an impact on the game with his play. But now his battered white-and-blue college helmet rests on a shelf in his home office, and he knows he's done all he can to help the Chiefs win in the postseason for the first time since 1993. No more drafting, trading, waiver wiring, or roster massaging. This is it.

As soon as Pioli gets into his car for the drive to the game, he cycles through his playlist and finds the artist whose words frequently dance in his head. Bruce. "Youngstown" plays, and then "The Promised Land" as Pioli drives through the neighborhoods of Kansas City, a town he has grown to love. He points to grand houses, well-kept parks, and the breathtaking Nelson-Atkins Art Museum. The University of Missouri–Kansas City is nearby, and it's where Beth Emery, wife of the Chiefs' college scouting director, is a graduate student in studio art. Scott and Dallas have fallen for Beth's oil paintings, with one hanging near their family room, and the local art scene in general. Although he would never bring it up in a press conference, Pioli has such dreams of what it would be like to win a championship for this region, and especially for the Hunts, that he sometimes allows himself to think of the perfect place in town to celebrate.

But the Chiefs are a long way from that point. They won ten games and captured the AFC West, yet they were the only division champ in the league to have a losing record, 2-4, within their division. Along with Pioli, many of the current Chiefs assistant coaches were in New England nearly a decade earlier when another dismissed team was able to surge to the Super Bowl. Charlie Weis, Romeo Crennel, Anthony Pleasant, and Otis Smith were all in New Orleans when the Patriot mystique was born in February 2002. Pioli isn't thinking about that now as a light snow falls and dusts the city roads.

"Some of our players have never played in this," he says. "I hope it doesn't freak them out."

The players will be fine. What's starting to get to Pioli is that soon he won't be able to help his team. He'll just be a guy in a black suit, white shirt, red tie, and Chiefs lapel pin, hoping for the best. As he drives toward the stadium, he stops to speak with a group of tailgating fans.

"No matter what happens," one of the fans says, "it's been a great year."

"We're not ready to go home yet," Pioli replies.

A few feet ahead, he speaks with another group and they all agree that it's really not that cold outside. The temperature won't crack 30 all day, and the wind chill will make it feel half as "warm." They wish him luck and send him off into game mode. There's no question he's there now. A yellow moving truck is blocking the area where he usually parks, and it seems as if the sun itself is sitting there in front of him with PENSKE printed on it. He's agitated that this, of all things, is preventing him from going inside and getting into his routine. When the minor traffic jam is untangled, Pioli is able to go into a small locker room that has two side-by-side dressing stalls with Chiefs-themed nameplates above them. One of them reads SCOTT PIOLI. The other one reads MIA PIOLI. Mia, wearing her bejeweled number 7 Matt Cassel jersey, will arrive later. For now, it's time to see if the Chiefs are ready to play a group of Baltimore veterans who believe they are tough and talented enough to go anywhere and beat anybody.

When both teams take the field, minutes before kick-off, they hear a wall of sound. This is why Arrowhead is called the loudest place in the NFL. It's a football crowd with rock-concert pipes. It's seventy-thousand-plus people who are truly from both sides of the tracks, Kansas and Missouri, and they cheer with a hunger that suggests they're looking for good football and perhaps something life-changing, too. Joe Posnanski found that out when he was a *Kansas City Star* columnist for thirteen years. During football season, the top ten stories on the paper's website would be dominated by anything related to football coverage: columns, game stories, sidebars, off-day stories, and notes. While Pioli had his share of "What's your name again?" episodes in New England, Posnanski says it will never happen in Kansas City.

"If the mayor was speaking one place and Scott was somewhere else doing the same thing, he'd outdraw the mayor a hundred to one," he says. "I couldn't possibly overstate how big the Chiefs are in Kansas City. There's nothing like it. The Chiefs are the one thing that brings people together. Whether it's the Kansas side and the Missouri side or the inner city and the suburbs, the Chiefs are the one thing that can unite everybody."

The fans are as loud as usual in the first quarter, but the Ravens still take the ball at their own thirty and drive all the way to the Kansas City one. They try to surprise the Chiefs with a third-down pass to tight end Todd Heap, but rookie safety Eric Berry sees the play develop, gets into position, and the Ravens have to settle for a field goal. It's a small victory, although Baltimore was able to possess the ball for nearly six minutes. The Chiefs, meanwhile, take just forty seconds to run through their first three plays before it's time to punt.

Few people in Kansas City are aware of the depths of it, but there's some tension between offensive coordinator Weis and head coach Todd Haley. They had their share of clashes during the regular season, but with Haley, that's not necessarily a story. He has fought with some of his best friends while playing pickup basketball and once got into a scrum with his brother-in-law on a basketball court, even though they were playing on the same team at the time. It's not that intense with Weis, but Haley hasn't gotten to the total trust/comfort level with him that he has with his new defensive coordinator, Crennel. It wasn't much of an issue during the regular season, when the Chiefs ran the ball more and better than any team in football. But Weis and Haley had already decided they'd be better off not working together. Before parting ways, they'd eventually have one more thing over which to disagree and debate.

After driving from their own fifteen toward midfield, the Ravens run into a 275-pound problem. Chiefs linebacker Tamba Hali is able to get to Baltimore quarterback Joe Flacco, strip-sack him, and recover the ball at the Ravens' forty-six. Two plays later, Jamaal Charles goes from running back to sprinter and bursts into the end zone for a forty-one-yard touchdown. There's a what-if moment in every game, and the Chiefs face it early in the second quarter. They have the lead, the ball, and the thought that they are going to do what the Ravens believe most teams can't against them: run. An offensive Raven doesn't come to your mind's eye when you think of the team, and players such as Ray Lewis, Haloti Ngata, Ed Reed, and Terrell Suggs like it that way. In another era, they'd be the kind of guys who'd go into bars and challenge anyone to arm-wrestle. But the Chiefs take the ball at their own fourteen and start to get into a running rhythm on the Ravens.

Charles for eleven.

Charles for eight.

Charles for nine.

As they eat up yards, the red-clad wall of sound with them for every foot, the Chiefs are inspiring everyone to think of the possibilities. If they score a touchdown and have Baltimore down 14–3, it will force the Ravens to play a game they really don't want to. An eight-yard pass from Cassel to Thomas Jones has the Chiefs at the fifty, and it's fair to say that they are controlling the game. But they lose control on the very next play, a Charles fumble, and Baltimore is able to hang on to the ball and the pace of the game. Remarkably, the Chiefs have yet another opportunity to take control just five minutes after Charles's fumble. They were able to hold the Ravens and are once more driving, going from their thirteen to near midfield again. This time, though, the mistake is a mental one: On third and three, in an area of the field where the bold Haley might authorize a fourth-down attempt if necessary, left tackle Branden Albert is called for a false start. It completely changes the game situation, pushes the Chiefs back five yards for a third and eight, and when Kansas City can't convert, it gives the Ravens life.

Flacco takes his team from its own twenty to the Chiefs' nine. He's gotten them here by following a game plan in which the idea is to get tight end Todd Heap in situations where he's matched up with linebackers. Heap was able to catch three passes for forty-six yards during the middle of the drive. Now it's nearing the end, with a third and two with fewer than thirty seconds remaining in the first half. Flacco is able to fully complete his work with a nine-yard touchdown pass to Ray Rice for a 10–7 halftime lead.

On all levels of Arrowhead, there are frustrated Chiefs. Pioli watched his old team in New England participate in seventeen of these play-off games. He understands that games in January and February generally are unforgiving when it comes to mistakes. You use the hammer when you have it, otherwise you find yourself locked in an uncomfortable game of chance. Pioli stands near the press-box elevators. His face is red, and he has so many thoughts about the missed opportunities in the first half that he doesn't have a complete sentence for what he just saw. Downstairs in the locker room, things are more verbal. Haley is upset that the Chiefs' Pro Bowl receiver, Dwayne Bowe, wasn't targeted more. He caught seventy-two balls in the regular season, fifteen of them for touchdowns, but he was completely shut out in the first half. Haley thinks some of it was the Ravens' defense, some of it was Bowe, and some of it was squarely on Weis. But as much as he disagreed with some of the things Weis was calling, Haley knew that there couldn't be any in-game switching. On offense, at least, this was Weis's game to call.

One minute into the third, the Chiefs get a break. Cassel had tried to find rookie tight end Tony Moeaki across the middle, but the ball was intercepted by defensive back Haruki Nakamura. Charles stayed with the play, forced Nakamura to fumble, and recovered for the Chiefs. So now they are driving again with a fresh set of downs from their own thirty-two. On a third and nine, Cassel finds Charles for fifteen yards. On the next play, Jones runs for ten. They've got something here, this time much deeper than before. They have a third and two at the Ravens' thirty-four. Jones runs up the middle for a yard, and the rapid headset conversations about the fourth-down play begin.

Haley is a believer in going for it on fourth down. He worked for Bill Parcells for seven years in two cities, and Parcells was as aggressive on fourth as any of his peers. Bill Belichick was an advocate of going for it on fourth down, too, so much so that he once did it from his own twenty-eight. Haley doesn't need to be sold on going for it, although he doesn't like the play that Weis is proposing. He's told that it's very likely the featured runner, Charles, will not just pick up the first but wind up in the end zone. Haley's instincts tug at him and tell him to overrule the call. But he doesn't. For a split second he thinks of calling a time-out, correctly sensing that a play like this can change the game. Still, as important as the play is, they are barely five minutes into the third, and you can't be so casual with time-outs in a game this close.

It's fourth and one from the thirty-three. The Chiefs send their jumbo reinforcements to the field, with the six-hundred-plus pounds of Jon Asamoah and Shaun Smith. This is part of the deception. Weis wants the Ravens to think about the plunge up the middle, while the Chiefs' true plan is to get Charles and his track-star speed on the edge. If the Ravens don't sniff out the play, Weis will look like a genius because no one on defense will be able to catch Charles if he gets a head start. Problem is, no one is fooled. Strong safety Dawan Landry sees that Cassel has flicked the ball to Charles, moving outside, and Landry is there instantly to blow it up. He tackles Charles for a four-yard loss. It's one of the first times all day that there's been a pause in the wall of sound.

The Ravens take the great field position and turn it into a field goal, for a 13–7 lead. After getting the ball back, the Chiefs look sloppy. Cassel is called for an intentional grounding penalty, he's then sacked by Suggs, and his eight-yard pass to rookie Dexter Mc-Cluster turns into a fumble that Baltimore recovers. The Ravens add another field goal and it's 16–7. It's still just the third quarter, but the Chiefs are crum-bling. When Cassel gets back on the field, he throws another interception, and this time there are no more defensive stands to minimize the damage. The Ravens find the end zone this time, Flacco to Anquan Boldin, and it's 23–7.

It's officially a meltdown.

Dallas Pioli sits outside one of the Arrowhead suites, draped in a stadium blanket. Despite what Scott and the tailgating fans said before the game, it is bitterly cold, and that reality begins to sink in with the increasingly lopsided score. Dallas has been around the NFL her entire life. She has seen dozens of games like this in which her father's or husband's team didn't perform as well as expected, and she has seen the brightest smiles of both men as they've cradled the Lombardi Trophy. She's an expert on the NFL that few people see; she's seen some of the all-time greats when their guards are down, when they're sincerely speaking and not giving press-conference spin, when they're in the family den truly celebrating or sulking over what happened at work. She knows that this is going to be a sulking night. She stays outside longer than most because she wants to be supportive of the team, but she's also taking a few minutes to gather her thoughts and think of supportive things to say to Scott later.

Inside the suite, Ralph Marchant is talking with his son, Louis, and two of Pioli's closest friends from high school, Matt Spencer and Paul McHugh. Dallas eventually joins them and says, "Okay, guys. What should I say to my husband?" No one has any good answers for later or for what's happening on the field. It is now a showcase between two teams playing in the quietest stadium in the league. The place has cleared, save for a few Chiefs loyalists and a couple hundred Ravens fans who have made the trip from Baltimore. The score has ballooned to 30–7. The Chiefs have produced just two first downs and twenty-five yards in the second half. Bowe hasn't caught a single ball. If anything, this is quite the humbling reminder of what Pioli and his staff have to do in the off-season.

The game is officially over, so Dallas and Mia and their weekend guests make their way to the small locker room where Pioli began his day. He has changed from his suit to jeans and a sweatshirt, preparing for a post-game tradition where he plays catch on the field with Mia. Pioli notices that everyone in the room is feeling sorry for him, and he tries to put them at ease by saying he knew all along just how much work the Chiefs had to do before they could expect to win games like these. It's clearly a defense mechanism. He's hurting, but he doesn't want the pity.

They all move outside and quickly see an emotional Jen Vrabel, who knows her husband better than anyone and is sure that this is the end of the thirty-five-year-old linebacker's career. Many of the players whom Mike Vrabel won and bonded with in New England have been cut and traded, or they've retired and moved on to cushy TV jobs. The Piolis try to reassure Jen of Mike's important contributions to the Chiefs. There are hugs and good-byes, and just before Scott and Mia head to the field, there is a voice from above. A few fans are leaning on a railing that overlooks the lot where cars and buses are parked. They recognize the general manager of the Chiefs and have something they want to say to him.

"Thank you for the season, Mr. Pioli," one of the young fans says.

Pioli looks up and gives a respectful wave. He appreciates the support, but this is not how the story unfolds when he thinks of that winning celebration that both Missourians and Kansans can enjoy. He'll play catch with Mia until she gets too tired and wants to go home. And in the morning, he'll get back to work.

On a Saturday night in Atlanta, a city that knows how to host a party, the best show in town promises to be at the Georgia Dome. The Falcons are the top seed in the NFC for the first time in thirty years, and they are a few minutes away from playing the Green Bay Packers in a divisional play-off game. As a huge American flag covers the field and sixty-nine thousand people shout their approval, Thomas Dimitroff notices that Stephanie Blank is trying to get his attention.

"Aren't you proud of this?" she says.

Dimitroff nods to the wife of the Falcons' owner and smiles at what he sees on the field. He's proud of the Falcons for putting themselves in this position, and he's proud of the fans for believing in what they've built in just three years. But he wants the same thing for the Falcons that Stephanie's husband wants for his businesses. Reliability. Consumer trust. Greatness. Dimitroff came to Atlanta with a vision of how to build a winner, and spending time with Arthur Blank, one of the most successful men in the country, has only enhanced it.

The general manager remembers the day when he was playing golf with Arthur at Augusta National. Dimitroff was wearing golf pants from a competitor of the golf retailer, PGA Tour Superstore, in which Blank has an ownership stake. When Dimitroff explained that he went to the PGA store and it didn't have the size 32 golf pants he needed, Blank was on the phone within seconds. "If our general manager had that experience, how many other people did as well?" he said that day. "Let's make sure we get more thirty-twos in there."

Blank wants to win desperately, and he'll sort through the smallest details to make it happen. So will Dimitroff. Unfortunately for them on this night, so will the quarterback of the Packers.

A few minutes into the second quarter, Aaron Rodgers finds receiver Jordy Nelson for a six-yard scoring play that ties the score at 7. Before anyone in the dome has time to have doubts, returner Eric Weems takes the Green Bay kickoff and returns it for a play-off-record 102 yards and a touchdown. Trailing 14–7 and starting from their own eight, the Packers glide through the Atlanta defense, with Rodgers completing five of six passes, and tie the score again five minutes later.

There are a couple of developing problems. One is that this is not the Falcons' game. They aren't a shoot-out team, and if they're forced to play this style the entire game they'll be in trouble. There's also the matter of Rodgers. He appears to be indefensible. He's running like Michael Vick but throwing with more accuracy. He's flashing the arm strength of a young Brett Favre but is making better decisions. He's showing the ability to escape like Fran Tarkenton used to do, but his scrambles are efficient and controlled. He is pitching the football equivalent of a perfect game, and the feeling is that if the Falcons don't have some type of score each time they touch the ball, they won't be able to beat him.

The Falcons' first mistakes are made by Pro Bowl quarterback Matt Ryan. He has helped the team drive to the Packers' fourteen, but a seven-yard sack takes the Falcons out of the red zone, and a third-and-long attempt to receiver Michael Jenkins ends with a Tramon Williams interception in the end zone. Ninety seconds later, after again completing five of six passes on the drive, Rodgers has the Packers celebrating another touchdown and a 21–14 lead.

Dimitroff shakes his head in his box, a similar reaction to most of the people in the building. They're witnessing one of the most spellbinding performances in league play-off history. But Ryan, with the help of back-to-back pass-interference calls, still has time to lead a drive that can end with at least a field goal before halftime. On a play from the Packers' twenty-six, Ryan takes a costly nine-yard sack, which forces Falcons coach Mike Smith to use his last time-out of the half. With ten seconds to play, Smith and offensive coordinator Mike Mularkey want to run something quick that will get the team slightly closer for kicker Matt Bryant. But Williams has help over the top, and he's waiting for Ryan to throw the out, the one pass Williams is sitting on. Ryan throws to the left sideline and Williams steps in front of it at the thirty, secures the football, and races seventy yards to the end zone.

It's 28–14 at halftime, which is bad news, and it's going to get even worse: The Packers will begin the third quarter with the ball.

As the third quarter begins, everyone in the dome understands the unofficial rules to the game. If the Packers score on their opening drive, it's over. It takes six and a half minutes for it to happen, and Rodgers repeats his scoring formula by completing five of six passes on the drive, but after the quarterback *runs* for a seven-yard score, it's 35–14. And the best party in Atlanta, which had so much potential at eight o'clock, flops before ten.

When it's finally over, Dimitroff stands in the interview room waiting to hear what Smith has to say about the embarrassing 48–21 loss. The GM's wife, Angeline, is sitting in one of the back rows of the room and spots him. "I'm sorry" she mouths from across the room, and leaves her seat to stand next to him. He has several family members in town, from Ohio and Canada, including his mother, Helen. The wife of a longtime coach and the mother of a pro executive, Helen had watched from a dome suite and said, "I don't know who those guys are out there. They've got the uniforms of the Falcons, but those aren't the Falcons."

Eventually Arthur Blank enters the room, and after a round of questioning from the media, Smith goes to his office to digest what he saw. He won't like it, but he'll appreciate the craftsmanship of Rodgers, who finished the night 31 of 36 for 366 yards, three passing touchdowns, and one rushing. But there was even more to the story. When Smith was an assistant coach, he would watch practice and make notes on his script when something stood out to him that he wanted to watch later. As soon as practice would end, he would hustle ahead of the other coaches so he could get back to the office to see if the film confirmed what he thought he saw. He did the same with Rodgers.

"There were five instances when we had free defenders, unblocked, who had an opportunity to get Rodgers, and all five times he was able to get away," Smith says. "I mean, five free defenders? That's a lot for a game. I think there was just one throw of his that traveled more than twenty yards in the air, the entire game. So that tells you how precise he was of moving the ball and directing the team. There were some gains after catches, but as far as twenty-plus-yard throws in the air, he had one."

Outside of Smith's office, Les Snead and Nick Polk allow themselves to get into a debate with sportswriter Pete Prisco over number one receivers in the NFL. Snead is the Falcons' player personnel director and Polk is their director of football administration. One of

Prisco's points is that the Packers truly don't have one and that Rodgers makes them all look better than they are. They go 'round and 'round before Snead admits why the topic is of any interest to him.

"The only reason I'm having this conversation with you, Peter," he says, "is that it's keeping me from stewing over what I just saw."

It's close to midnight, and soon Dimitroff will go back to a house full of friends and family members who will want to know what happened but will be too respectful to ask. Finding out what happened, talking about it, and fixing it isn't just Dimitroff's job. It's an obsession. He knows the loss is going to feel even worse on Sunday morning. A top seed loses at home. By Sunday night, the Falcons won't be the only team with that headline.

When the Patriots and New York Jets played in Foxboro on December 6, it was 27 degrees with a windchill factor of 15. Jets quarterback Mark Sanchez stepped on the field for pregame drills and mentally checked out of the game before it started.

"It's too cold for football," he said with both of his hands stuffed into the warmer around his waist. The Patriots won that game, 45–3, with Sanchez barely completing half of his thirty-three passes and throwing three interceptions.

As he often does, Bill Belichick sat in his office after that game talking football with his youngest son, Brian. From the moment he was able to pick up a football and throw it, Brian had an interest in playing and dissecting the game, just like his father. Belichick was asked how the Patriots had so much success against the Jets' defense. They had compiled 405 yards of offense and Tom Brady had thrown four touchdown passes. "You've just got to beat man coverage," Belichick answered. "That's what they play ninety-five percent of the time."

It's six and a half weeks later, January 16, and the Jets have returned to Foxboro for a divisional play-off game. Rex Ryan, the most media-savvy head coach the Jets have had since Bill Parcells a decade earlier, opened his Monday press conference with a bold statement: The game would be won by whichever head coach was better, him or Belichick. Ryan provided a lot of sound bites during that session with the media, but he left out the most significant reason for his confidence. The biggest difference between his December game plan and the one he planned to use for the play-off game?

His identical twin brother, Rob.

Rob Ryan, a former Patriots linebackers coach under Belichick, had coauthored the best game plan of the season against the high-scoring Patriots. He was the Browns' defensive coordinator on November 7, when they came out of their bye week and surprised the Patriots, 34–14. New England fell to 6-2 after that loss and then won eight consecutive games, scoring thirty-plus points in all of them. Rob Ryan couldn't help his brother in December because he had his own business to worry about in Cleveland. But when head coach Eric Mangini and his assistants were fired on January 3, it freed up Rob to talk specifics with Rex.

Cleveland had been the anti-Jets against the Patriots in November. The Browns threw a combination of two-, three-, and four-deep blitz zones at the Patriots and even went as far as coming up with completely different plans for the first and second half. Browns players must have heard it fifty times that week in practice from the coaches: "We're not necessarily trying to come up with the perfect call; we just want to make sure Brady doesn't know what's coming. We can't show a pattern or he'll kill us."

Rex Ryan had shown an obvious pattern in December: man coverage. He had a different take after listening to the brother who once took his ACT test for him so he could go fishing instead. The Browns had been able to hold the ball for thirty-eight minutes against the Patriots, and they'd intentionally lingered on defense, too. Their logic was that they didn't want to make it easy for the perceptive Brady to identify the middle, or Mike, linebacker. Rapid identification of the Mike allowed Brady to set the protection for the offensive line and break down a defense. The obvious advantage the Jets had over the Browns was that they were a much better team, so they could afford to take the essence of Cleveland's strategy and tweak it to suit their superior personnel.

Early in the play-off game, it doesn't appear that the Jets' defense is any more complex than it was in December. The Patriots have taken the ball from their own sixteen and driven to the New York twenty-eight. But Brady overthrows a screen to BenJarvus Green-Ellis—a pass he has made effortlessly hundreds of times, albeit this time it's to a back not known for catching the football—and it's intercepted by linebacker David Harris. It's Brady's first interception in an NFL-record 335 attempts. The Gillette Stadium crowd gasps at the interception, but even more surprising than the turnover is the fact that Harris is caught from behind by Alge Crumpler. The Patriots tight end is listed at 275 pounds but appears to be just as big as Jets left tackle D'Brickashaw Ferguson, listed at 307. The Jets miss a short field-goal attempt, and the Patriots begin to drive again.

This time they move from their twenty-one to the New York seven. Brady places the ball perfectly in the hands of Crumpler, a former Falcon who used to be one of Michael Vick's favorite targets. But Crumpler drops the ball and the Patriots get a field goal out of the possession. It's the best they can do for a half, and the New York defensive strategy begins to reveal itself. The Jets have effectively created traffic jams in the middle of the field and challenged the Patriots' receivers to beat man coverage on the perimeter. Often, they can't. It's a sluggish game, 7–3 Jets, with just over a minute left in the half. The Patriots have a breakdown so a fake punt is on although it's not supposed to be. It doesn't work, and the Jets take over the ball at the New England thirty-seven.

Sanchez was clearly affected by the cold night in December, but a few more degrees and no vicious Northeastern wind has made a huge difference for him in January. He puts the Jets up 14–3 at the half by making a strong fifteen-yard throw to Braylon Edwards for a touchdown.

Late in the third, the Jets still leading 14–3, Brady continues to look unsure. He has been sacked three times and is having trouble finding anyone, other than Deion Branch, who can get open on the perimeter. But the Patriots finally spring a big play over the middle when rookie Rob Gronkowski, whose ten touchdown receptions in the regular season were a team rookie record, catches a pass and gains thirty-seven yards. The play takes them from their twenty to the New York forty-three, and seven plays later Brady hits Crumpler with a ball that the big tight end holds on to for a touchdown. A successful two-point conversion makes it 14–11 going into the fourth quarter.

The Jets, beginning with Ryan, spent the week leading up to the game saying what they were going to do in New England. It started innocently enough, with the made-for-the-tabloids bravado of Ryan. It got edgier later in the week when Jets cornerback Antonio Cromartie referred to Brady as "an asshole." And after Wes Welker held a press conference in which he found creative ways to mention feet, a reference to Ryan's supposed foot fetish, Jets linebacker Bart Scott warned, "His days in a uniform are numbered." The constant talk got the attention of NFL executives, who instructed all play-off teams to be mindful of their rhetoric. You don't have to work very hard to get a New Englander's opinion on mouthy New Yorkers, so there was more local anticipation and intensity than usual for the game. But the local intensity had nothing to do with local fear. The December game had been all the proof that most fans needed that the Patriots wouldn't lose this game to the Jets. They'd gotten open at will and Sanchez sounded and looked like he wanted to be next to a fireplace.

In the fourth quarter, history is irrelevant. Sanchez, who threw eight interceptions in his previous two games in Foxboro, finds Jerricho Cotchery for a fifty-eight-yard completion to the New England thirteen. A few plays later, he connects with Santonio Holmes for a seven-yard touchdown pass that puts the Jets up 21–11.

It's beginning to become real to the sixty-eight thousand fans at the game and millions more watching across six states. A loss to the Jets? In the playoffs? Awful. No matter what happens going forward, whether the Jets win the Super Bowl or even make it there, Patriots fans are going to have to hear about this game, narrated in Jersey, Queens, and Long Island accents. That's how it is when you're within two hundred miles of your rivals who share your DNA but not your allegiances. You know how they think and vice versa, and the only consolation for your own letdowns is the knowledge that they're miserable, too. It's bad enough when they have joy, but when their joy is linked to your heartbreak, it's humiliating.

And that's the way it was on the field and in the stands after the Jets were able to walk away with a 28–21 victory. Branch called the New Yorkers classless and Scott said the New Englanders' defense couldn't stop a nosebleed. The words didn't change anything.

For the second year in a row, Belichick had to confront another play-off "first" in New England. The previous January, there was the loss to the Ravens, the first home play-off loss in Belichick's ten Patriots seasons. In January 2011, it wasn't just a loss at home, it was a loss as a number one seed in the divisional round, which had never happened to a team that had Belichick as the head or assistant coach.

Belichick was used to 14-2 teams high-fiving and patting each other on the back after these games in January. These games were the reason he and Scott Pioli had talked about being weeks behind in the scouting process, because they couldn't attend all-star games like the Senior Bowl in Mobile. They *couldn't*, past-tense. They were busy preparing for conference championships and Super Bowls. But in January 2011, Pioli, Belichick, and Dimitroff would all be in Mobile, gazing at the play-off lives of other teams, the same way other teams used to gaze at them.

The three of them have vastly different personalities, yet they were all experiencing the same feeling. It was a gnawing that wouldn't go away, equal parts anger and shame. Not once when they all worked together, not a single time, had they gone to the play-offs and come away with nothing. Hell, even the Cleveland Browns, where Belichick missed the play-offs in four of his five seasons there, were able to win in January the one time they made it to the postseason.

There are no champions of the regular season. It's the reason people praised Bill Parcells, Mike Holmgren, Jon Gruden, and Chuck Noll, although Marty Schottenheimer has a higher career winning percentage than all of them. Schottenheimer doesn't have the rings, though, while the quartet he towers over in the regular season has a combined eight.

It's what Pioli was hinting at when he had his interview in Dallas. How do you call yourself dominant at anything when you don't win a play-off game in eighteen years and win just three in the last twenty-one? He was a part of that dubious Chiefs streak now, and his challenge was to build a team that could break it. It's why Dimitroff had been so annoyed in 2009 when his team missed the play-offs. The only thing worse than missing them is losing in them. For all the praise that the counterculture GM had gotten from the mainstream, and he was on the verge of winning his second executive-of-the-year award in three years, his point was never to come to Atlanta and be known as a renaissance man who loves football. The mission was to create a contender, not a team that *still* had a link to Michael Vick: Despite Dimitroff's awards and his drafting of a new quarterback, the last time the

Falcons won a play-off game, 2004, was the height of the Vick era.

It's why Belichick undersold everything in the regular season. It's why he didn't have or crave the entertainment gene that his Jets counterpart, Ryan, possessed. Twelve wins, thirteen, or sixteen—no one cared if you didn't close the deal. Belichick and the Patriots found that out in 2007, coming so close to doing what was supposed to be impossible in a league so anchored in parity and balance. But since that night in the desert, when the Patriots were a couple minutes away from perfection, they'd missed the playoffs one year and been bounced from them in the first and divisional round the other two.

These three decision-makers all had something to prove. There wasn't even a debate about that. They felt the pressure to prove it, and so did everyone around them.

12.
The Mobile Dinner

All it takes is a simple phone call. That's been made clear to Thomas Dimitroff since his first day on the job in Atlanta. If he ever needs to use Arthur Blank's private G4 jet for business purposes, it's his, as long as it's available. So if he wants to see three different workouts in three different parts of the country and be home in time to put his son to bed, all he has to do is ask.

Dimitroff and his staff have taken Blank up on the offer many times, and they've walked away in awe of the power, luxury, and convenience after each ride. But in late January, with the entire league making its annual trip to Alabama for a week of scouting, socializing, and gossip, the Falcons decided to go SUV for the five-hour drive from Atlanta to Mobile. In the next few months, leading up to the April draft, there would be many good reasons to use the plane. Everyone knew that the general manager was determined to add explosive, urgent athletes to the roster, and sometimes finding those players meant hopping a jet in the middle of the week. For now, the search would begin with five guys on four wheels.

This trip to Alabama was already guaranteed to be more successful than the last time they all piled into a truck. This time, at least everyone was paying attention to the gas tank. The previous year, they had made the two-hour drive to Auburn to scout the university's pro day. On the way back to Georgia, they may have been wrapped up in a conversation about players, or maybe it was the good music that was pounding the speakers. Whatever the distraction was, no one noticed that the needle had gone well below E until the truck began to sputter and they had to pull to the side of the road.

What a sight: Dimitroff, Lionel Vital, Dave Caldwell, and Les Snead, the Falcons' top evaluators, stranded because they didn't evaluate the gas gauge. They were lucky, though. They were just thirty miles from home, in Newnan, Georgia, and the guy who stopped to help them was good friends with the owner of a local gas station. News traveled fast to the office, and Snead was given the bulk of the blame since he was the driver and an Auburn grad as well. The next day, he was teased by head coach Mike Smith and also found gas cards on his desk.

The trip to Mobile, with the same quartet plus director of football administration Nick Polk, had more focus, and not just with the fuel. The loss to the Packers was just two weeks earlier, and no one was over it.

"It's like that breakup you have with that girl or that guy. You wake up the next day and you still can't believe it's over," Snead says. "And as bad as I felt about it, being a longtime Atlanta person, I felt even worse for the fans. That was the best and loudest Falcons crowd I've ever been a part of."

It didn't make any of them feel better that Green Bay was not a typical sixth seed and that the Pack had gone on the road to knock off the Bears in the conference championship game. They all had opinions about what had gone wrong that night at the dome and what needed to be done to fix it.

"You need guys with edge," says Vital. "This is a mean game. You've got to have that edge, that attitude. I think it starts on defense first, because if you show me a ferocious defense, most of the time it's gonna be a team that does some damage in the play-offs."

During the season, even after victories, Dimitroff had been unhappy with aspects of the team's play. He believed the Falcons needed to take better advantage of the resources they had on offense. He was bothered by their middle-of-the-pack scoring numbers, especially since they had Matt Ryan, Tony Gonzalez, Roddy White, and Michael Turner. It almost seemed impossible that the Falcons could rank thirty-first out of thirty-two teams in explosive plays, which are plays of twenty yards or more.

Shortly after the Packers loss, Dimitroff, Blank, and Smith had met for dinner in Atlanta to discuss the season and how the Falcons could get better. Over the course of a conversation that at times became tense and animated, especially when the GM praised the talent on offense but went to the edge of questioning how it was designed, Dimitroff found himself citing Bruce Lee and Sun Tzu. "Bruce Lee was good at a lot of things, but when he wanted to knock you out he played to his strengths," he says of the martial arts icon. "He had two or three knockout moves and he used them." As for Chinese strategist and philosopher Sun Tzu, the author of *The Art of War*, Dimitroff referred to his unpredictability. "Your enemy thinks you're coming from one direction prepared to fight in a certain way and you do something totally different," he says. "It's the idea of using some element of deception to always keep an opponent on his heels."

It wasn't necessary to read philosophy or study martial arts to see where Dimitroff was going. He expected more, right now. Since October, long before the play-off loss, he had been thinking of pulling off something dramatic with his draft picks. For what he wanted to do, recent history wasn't on his side. Teams that traded multiple first-rounders to get into the top of the draft usually weren't smiling three or four years after the trades. Washington once traded the sixth and twenty-eighth overall picks for the right to move up to number four and select Heisman Trophy winner Desmond Howard. Three years later, they let him go in the expansion draft. The Saints once traded eight draft picks for another Heisman winner, Ricky Williams, and after all the stunts were over—head coach Mike Ditka wearing a dreadlocked wig; Williams appearing on the cover of a magazine in a wedding dress, signifying the commitment the Saints made to him; Williams conducting interviews wearing a helmet and visor—the Saints traded him to Miami. And although Kentucky's Dewayne Robertson didn't win the Heisman, the Jets moved up for him as if he had in 2003. They traded overall picks 13 and 20 for the right to pick Robertson fourth. Their general manager at the time, Terry Bradway, said he didn't see any players projected in the 13-to-20 range who excited him. Robertson turned out to be a bust, and several players drafted after 13, including Troy Polamalu, Dallas Clark, and Nnamdi Asomugha, turned out to be impact players.

Taking a trip to Mobile for the Senior Bowl wasn't going to solve all the concerns Dimitroff had about the Falcons, but it wasn't a stretch to say the week there could be significant. As disappointed as he was not to be preparing for the Super Bowl as the Packers and Steelers were, Dimitroff didn't believe the Falcons were two or three drafts from greatness. He and Bill Belichick both saw draft picks as capital, but there was a difference of opinion on how to spend it. Belichick liked to roll some of his picks into the future and watch them mature after a year in the bank. Dimitroff was okay with that, too, although he believed some years were for accumulating and some were for cashing out.

As the Falcons made their way to Interstate 65 toward the Gulf Coast and Mobile, everyone in the truck had a rough idea of how the five hours would unfold. The first hour or two would be used for Dimitroff to make and return phone calls. There would be a fast food stop along the way with everyone, including the pescatarian GM, walking away satisfied. The reason for that was Snead, who grew up in Eufaula, Alabama, and claimed to know where every Whole Foods and natural-foods-friendly place was in the state. He once found a "late-night hippie pizza joint with tofu subs" in the middle of Alabama as he and Dimitroff were finishing up a scouting trip. After the food stop, they would listen to music for a while, laugh, and bond. Then there would be an impromptu fifteen-minute staff meeting. Dimitroff would look at film on his iPad, and then, in the final hour, they'd all look at one another and agree: We should have flown.

Football people love the Senior Bowl and especially the week that leads up to it. They love the practices, where they get to measure just how fast and strong a player is compared to the top athletes in the country. They love to see how a player reacts when he's beaten in a drill or dominates it; how he responds to instruction from the pro coaches on-site; how he interacts with teammates who make him look either good or bad. It's a great way of getting information that has either innocently slipped through the scouting cracks or has been hidden by certain schools who don't want scouts to know everything about their players' limitations.

It's easy to latch on to a favorite player here, especially for veteran scouts. You see a player do something and it reminds you of what you saw a great one do fifteen years earlier. Dick Haley used to watch these practices and when a player jumped, Haley would shift his eyes from the height of the leap and focus instead on

the landing, because that told a more revealing athleticism story in his opinion. He'd always remind his son,
Todd, "No matter how fast and strong they are, they
still have to be able to play football. Don't lose sight
of that." Mobile is the place where you find dozens of
scouts trying to become the next Dick Haley, identifying some of the same undervalued gems that he did in
the 1970s.

Actually, that's the average scout's reward: being excited about a player, having your boss heavily consider
your opinion, and then seeing "your guy" picked by
your team on draft day. It's got to be a labor of love for
most college scouts. Some of them spend two hundred
days or more on the road, and when they go home, the
paychecks they bring with them are relatively modest
compared to the men they report to. The average area
scout makes between $40,000 and $50,000 annually,
and national scouts bring in $80,000 to $90,000. The
average GM makes $1.2 million.

In the first few nights here, some of the scouts who
hop in and out of the popular bars on Dauphin Street
are desperately trying to climb to the next professional
notch. But for many of them, it's more about football
and team-building than money. Besides, some of the
more keen football watchers believe that promotions and
pay raises will naturally come as they excel at their jobs.

One of the scouts here is Jim Nagy, who works for the Chiefs now after spending seven seasons with Scott Pioli in New England. Nagy, thirty-six, has wanted to be in football since he was a kid growing up in Michigan. The son of a high school coach, he used to take his naps on tackling dummies. When he was seven, he kept his own scouting book, filling a notebook with players the Lions drafted and ones he wanted them to draft. While attending the University of Michigan, he got an internship in the Packers' public-relations department. It turned out to be a good connection for him because when he moved to New York City in 1997, a sports-writing legend needed his help.

At that time, Dick Schaap was working with former Packer Jerry Kramer on *Distant Replay*, the final installment in their trilogy of Packer diaries. Schaap needed research help from someone who was in tune with contemporary Green Bay players, so Nagy was his man. A proud name-dropper, Schaap regaled Nagy with tales about Malcolm X, Arthur Ashe, and Robert Kennedy. Nagy helped Schaap finish the book and enjoyed the time he spent with him, but book-writing was not his passion. The next year he began working with someone who would become a sports celebrity of sorts for football fans, although he and Nagy were both unknowns at the time.

He was hired by former NFL scout Gary Horton, the founder of a think tank for draftniks called War Room, Inc. The small staff watched coaches' tape, which captures all twenty-two players at once on camera; tapped into sources from around the league; and wrote draft reports. One of Nagy's coworkers at the time was an even-younger-looking Todd McShay, who can now be seen on TV, not looking a day over twenty-five, dueling Mel Kiper during ESPN's draft coverage. "I think we're both doing exactly what we want to be doing," Nagy says. He got his NFL break in 2000 with Washington and made it to New England in 2002. When Pioli left the Patriots in January 2009, Nagy wasn't far behind him.

As he studies and takes notes on players in Mobile, he might be the most self-assured scout in town. For one, he's in his backyard. He and his wife have made south Alabama their home, so if anything happens during the week that he misses, he's got sources in the area who can fill him in. Most important, he knows what Pioli and college scouting director Phil Emery are looking for in players. He's been trained for nine years in the Patriots/Chiefs system, so when he excitedly talks about a player he's seen, there's a good chance the bosses will be excited as well.

A couple people from the week have gotten his attention.

"Well, there's Rodney Hudson. This guy is going to be a *good* pro. He's highly, highly intelligent. He was an undersized guard at Florida State, but he'll probably be a center in the pros. Really impressive guy. He was essentially an offensive line coach on the field."

The Chiefs don't need a starting quarterback, but there's a down-the-road project who the scout believes is going to surprise people.

"If I could pick a quarterback who we'll all look back in five years and say, 'Can you believe he lasted that long?' it would be Ricky Stanzi of Iowa," he says. "No one is talking about him as a high draft pick. He was the most improved player I saw all year. There's something about the guy. And I'll tell you something else: When I was watching tape here of practice, he was there, too. Watching Senior Bowl practice tape on his own."

Nagy has watched practices and tapes to back up his opinions. He admits that he used to watch too much tape because of his youth and insecurity. He'd never played the game in college, and yet he'd look around a New England draft room and see former collegians and pros like Pioli, Dimitroff, and Vital, and he'd be intimidated by the credentials that they had and he didn't. He eventually learned to maintain the intensity he brought to the job without trying to hammer people with the fact that he belonged. Pioli pulled him aside in New England and told him that he could see that he knew his stuff and respected the effort he put into his work.

When he became a Chief, Nagy realized that he was going to have to work even harder than he did in New England. Sustaining a championship roster is hard work, but building a roster from the bottom up is even harder. There were things the scouts in New England took for granted that scouts in Kansas City couldn't. The Patriots' scouts already knew the system, so they didn't need the two-week scouting seminar that Emery conducted when he arrived in Kansas City. He talked out the grading scale and then put on film so he could specifically point out acceptable examples of athletic ability, change of direction, explosive strength, etc., until he was convinced everyone got it.

As for who "everyone" was, Pioli had predictably chased all the slackers out of the department. Sometimes he intentionally put his employees in situations that might frustrate them, just so he could see how they'd respond to it. It was his go-to move, and even his friends weren't exempt. He had known Jay Muraco for nearly a decade when Muraco, then working for the Eagles, called him in 2000 and asked if Pioli had anything with the Patriots. Pioli told him that he did, but the move would be lateral, and the best he could offer Muraco was a 30 to 40 percent pay cut from what he was already making. Pioli wanted to see if Muraco truly could accept a job doing the same work, for less pay, and not have a bad attitude while doing it. Muraco called him back the next morning and accepted the deal. After a while, after proving himself, Muraco was given a raise.

"He purposely grinds guys," Nagy says, "to test their mettle."

Pioli even did that when Dimitroff was the Patriots' director of college scouting. He gave him a modest salary for the position, and when his friend proved himself, his salary doubled. It was going to be the same story for anyone working for him with the Chiefs.

If they stepped back and thought about it, Kansas City employees would see that turning the Chiefs into champs, in terms of degree of difficulty, would be the most ambitious challenge of Pioli's career. In New England, he had an advantage that no one could match: On draft day, he had one of the top draft evaluators and strategists on his side in Bill Belichick; on Sundays, he had one of the most accomplished head coaches in pro football history on his side in Bill Belichick; and while Belichick got credit for the team's success, he also was mentioned first when things didn't work, therefore getting blame for his own mistakes as well as the mistakes of others working for him. No other team in football had anyone with that combination of power and pedigree, and Pioli was smart enough to know that it couldn't be re-created. He couldn't exactly re-create the how of his Patriots days, but he was constantly in search of players, coaches, and scouts capable of getting to the same finish.

On a pleasant January night, many of the NFL's coaches and general managers have left Dauphin Street and ventured a couple miles away to Ruth's Chris Steak House. On one side of the restaurant, Cowboys owner Jerry Jones is entertaining a group at his table. Across the room is Saints head coach Sean Payton. At a table not far from the front door is Chiefs defensive coordinator Romeo Crennel, who is having dinner with his son and a couple friends. Not far away, but out of the crowd's view, old friends Pioli and Dimitroff take their seats in a booth and order a bottle of red wine.

When the two have dinner, the conversation never follows a predictable pattern, but it does reinforce why their friendship works. They balance verbal jabs with thoughtful conversations about their families and jobs. They reminisce. They challenge each other, each refusing to say anything that he doesn't believe, even if it's what the other one wants to hear.

As Pioli raises his glass for a toast, he mentions how blessed they are. They have four executive-of-the-year awards between them. They both can remember take-home pay that was far lower than what the area scouts make now, even if you factor in inflation. There were no expensive bottles of wine back then, just bottles of Pabst Blue Ribbon. A reference to the 1990s reminds them of the days when Dimitroff was working on the Browns grounds crew and doing some part-time scouting, ironically, for the Chiefs.

"You'd lime the field and you'd have grass chips in your hair. And I swore you didn't know what deodorant was," Pioli says. "You'd come and funk up my office. You'd smell like tree bark."

"Nah. I think it was tea tree," Dimitroff says. "Or those crystal deodorant rocks."

They both laugh.

"Just so you know," Dimitroff says, "and this is the honest truth: I think the Chiefs still owe me per diem from way back then. They told me they were going to pay me, and sometimes they did. It was so haphazard."

Getting more precise financial records and slashing unnecessary spending is something Pioli has been working on in Kansas City for two years. He's even more diligent about the budget because he wants to make sure no one is taking advantage of the fact that team owner

Clark Hunt is five hundred miles away in Dallas. He shoots back to Dimitroff's claim, "I'm surprised they didn't pay you. They paid everyone else money."

As close as they are, Pioli and Dimitroff don't get many moments like this. They talk all the time, but there are few moments to sit down, face-to-face, and talk shop while teasing each other along the way.

"I love Senior Bowl week," Pioli says. "It's the first time that these kids are out of their element. And you see how they behave in a noncontrolled environment, or at least a foreign environment. You get to see their personalities relatively early because by a month from now, you know these kids are going to be dialed in and trained. Some of them are already."

Dimitroff nods in agreement. Mobile is the first look for evaluators and agents. Once the agents get a sense of what the decision-makers are saying about their clients, they have a little more than a month to correct, or hide, the holes in their clients' games. That could be off the field, as Pioli referred to, or on it.

"For me, as you know, I'm enthralled with movement and athleticism," Dimitroff says. "I mean, you have to like power and such, but I do, I really love to see movement. I love to see recovery. And I love urgent athleticism. And I get a chance to see it all on the field here. It's an equal playing surface. Not just one guy playing against a down-the-line guy from another team. But talent meeting equal talent."

They both remember being in Mobile as young scouts and the first-time excitement of seeing the legends of the game, like Bill Walsh, here. Years later, they both worked for and won championships with a legend in New England, so the fact that the restaurant is filled with influential NFL people doesn't affect them the way it did when they were in their twenties. But the awe of their twenties has been replaced by appreciation in their forties.

They point out some of the arguments they've had over the years. In New England, Dimitroff would often tell Pioli to back off the scouts a bit. Pioli would tell him that one day he would run a department and he'd see that certain tough-love management styles are necessary.

"I can't tell you how many times I've gone back to my office the past three years, wheeled back in my chair, and said, 'Holy Pioli. That was the most Pioli-esque moment I've had so far,'" Dimitroff says.

There is laughter and more wine. A waiter comes by and says, "Can I get you anything else, Mr. Pioli?"

Pioli is surprised. He spent years in Boston, walking through Logan Airport and Fenway Park, and was scarcely recognized. A waiter in Alabama knows who he is? What gives?

"I watch ESPN, sir," the waiter says. "And I know you, too. How are you, Mr. Dimitroff?"

Even if the kid, a student at the University of South Alabama, is working for a tip, he's charismatic enough where it doesn't matter. He even pronounces "Dimitroff" flawlessly, not making the common mistake of putting "meat" where "mitt" should be. You can imagine him going to Jerry Jones's table and applauding him on the brilliance of his previous draft picks and the new Cowboys Stadium. He makes sure they have everything they need and then leaves.

Pioli and Dimitroff mention how much their lives have changed in Kansas City and Atlanta. They do things now in their jobs that they never would have dreamed of doing with the Patriots.

"And honestly," Dimitroff says, "the differences are not as related to scouting and team-building as much as they are to football business relationships that we have. Some of the marketing relationships and decisions we make. Whether it's training camp or accessibility . . ."

"Or being in a commercial on a bus," Pioli interrupts.

Dimitroff, head coach Mike Smith, owner Arthur Blank, and many other Falcons were in an NFL commercial in which they were head-bopping on a bus as music played. Except Dimitroff never bopped. Once.

He's been ragged on about it since the commercial first aired. Dimitroff smiles and continues.

"I think it's a by-product of this league changing a little bit, too. And you and I understanding as we're evolving, as much as we're football traditionalists and historians and very mindful and appreciative of it, we also understand that this is entertainment and there are things that we have to do . . ."

"I will never say that it's entertainment," Pioli says.

"I know you won't. I will."

The word itself in a football context seems to be heretical to him.

"As soon as I succumb to that word, I'm out," he says. "It's a part of it, but it's not what it is. Is it a part of it? Yeah. It's always been a part of entertainment, that's why I watch, you know, it entertained me in the truest definition of the word, but . . ."

"And this is probably the fundamental difference between my personality and yours," Dimitroff says. He adds, laughing, "You're the guy who has called me Eurotrash. The idea of the pomp and circumstance and the shining lights . . ."

"Drives me crazy," Pioli says. "You see it all with the fireworks in some of these stadiums."

"That would be us," Dimitroff replies, knowing that's exactly what the Falcons did, and more, before

their play-off loss to the Packers. "And again, I'm a re-
alist because I know that's where it's going."

"I can understand that's where it's going, but I'm
not buying."

Dimitroff, who has zinged Pioli in the past by calling
him a blue-collar guy with blue blood, tweaks him again.

"You can make your multimillions and not buy until
you get out, or whatever."

"Oh," Pioli says. "You're gonna put that out there?"

The flattering waiter returns and wants to know if
he can get them anything. Pioli asks if it's okay if they
hang out awhile, and he says it's fine. They continue the
discussion. They would likely have it anyway, but it's
even more topical now. The NFL is just over a month
away from a work stoppage, and there are lots of strong
opinions about what that will mean for the league. And
who's at fault. And if the essence of what made the
league what it is will be choked away in legalese.

"We have all . . . I'm not going to say compromised,
because it's not compromising," Pioli says. "We understand it and we're evolving. But I know deep down
inside, you don't love all of it, either. You understand,
but you would love it to be more of football in its purest
sense. However, that's not what it is anymore."

"Well, I mostly agree with you. I'll differ only on
this: My energy store is, like everyone's, it's limited.

And I can't use my energy fighting the inevitable. So it's like, all right, if this is the way it's going, what's the best way to manage and accept this and not waste my energy and angst on something that you know isn't going to change? This is the way it's going. It's not going backward."

Pioli's positions very much echo the sentiments that he and Belichick had while both were in New England. Dimitroff, even while working with them, frequently disagreed. He knew he would do things differently if he ever got a chance to run an organization, and they would be things that Pioli and Belichick wouldn't endorse. For example, Dimitroff never understood why the Patriots did not allow all of their scouts in the room during the entire draft, and he was always puzzled why the scouts weren't given all-access passes so they could celebrate with everyone else on the field when the team was winning Super Bowls. He's teased about the corporate perks he has in Atlanta: access to Blank's G4 jet, golfing trips to Hilton Head and Augusta National, and an ownership group—and a draft room—that is open to celebrity advisers and limited partners such as Hank Aaron, who grew up playing football and baseball just two miles away from the restaurant.

"There's something we did in New England and I do now and it's limit the number of people in the draft room," Pioli says. "I need to be able to focus. I need silence. I need, even if it's just not people talking, I need limited activity."

"You'd be interested to see the difference in our place," Dimitroff says with a smile. "And that goes back to the conversation we had way back. Remember what I always used to say to you, at least early on?"

Pioli nods. "You'd say, 'You should let the scouts in.'"

"And then finally I let it go and it was a nonissue. So now I have a place in our draft where our scouts sit. They're very mindful and they all know if it gets unruly they won't be in there. But we also have things that you would never allow in your draft room."

"Like what?"

Dimitroff explains the layout of the enormous Atlanta draft room, with several tables for scouts and rows of seats for some of the advisers and partners, if they're interested. In theory, the Falcons could have Aaron in the draft room, sitting next to Andrew Young, the civil rights leader and former Atlanta mayor. Pioli shakes his head.

"This is how I see it differently," he says. "This goes back to the entertainment conversation. Draft day is not entertainment in that room, okay? I understand that it's going to be on ESPN and the NFL Network. I get all that. But again, there's degrees of compromise here. So we've got to have that. Last year I spent thirty million dollars guaranteed on one pick. I've gotta have a clear head to make that decision. This is not entertainment. Do Fortune 500 companies have people coming into their boardrooms? I don't know, maybe I'm taking myself too seriously."

"Respectfully, Scott, if my mistakes are because we have seven limited partners and a couple business associates in there, then my personal opinion is I'm not the right person for the job. I'm not being flip or derogatory toward your comment. We all operate in a different way."

Pioli agrees. "My way's not the right way. Your way's not the right way. It's finding out what's the right way for the leader or the leadership group. What's the right way for the people? I'm very passionate about this, but not in the sense of where I'm saying, 'I can't believe you, Thomas.' I say it because I can't concentrate and be as effective and/or thoughtful with distractions. You can."

The statement makes Dimitroff pause. The April draft will represent a turning point for both of them, for different reasons. The Falcons have the more mature roster, so the GM believes he can be more aggressive with his draft picks. The Chiefs are still in rebuilding mode, despite their division title, and this will be Pioli's second draft with the system in place and

Phil Emery alongside as college scouting director. It's a chance to come up with another strong class like they did in 2010, when first-round pick Eric Berry made the Pro Bowl. Pioli had just three months to prepare for his first Kansas City draft.

"To your point," Dimitroff says, "I might be spending more time trying to manage the room than focusing on the next pick. Because in the three years that we've had drafts, there have been some unruly occurrences that have been pretty agitating to me. You're right. It's our game day."

"With millions upon millions of dollars at stake. And the franchise's future."

They're heading toward a place they've been many times. Last men standing. There are fewer and fewer sounds of knives and forks lightly tapping against plates. The conversations in other parts of the restaurant aren't as anonymous as they were forty minutes earlier. They could have this conversation for a while and continue to make strong arguments. Pioli gets the final word before they settle and give the kid waiter the tip of his life: "You know, we've got to be careful about how much of football loses its soul. Because we got to where we are because we kept the football soul."

It's a topic that they will certainly reprise many times in their careers. They are virtually brothers, but some things they just don't see the same way. There are many times in Atlanta when Dimitroff will listen to the requests of the marketing side, weigh how much time they will take and measure what their impact on the team will be, and then decide to do them. It was one of the things that stood out to Blank during his interview: He had a football mind for building teams, yet he was also able to see all the things that make an organization successful. Pioli can see it, too, even if he sometimes sees it and grimaces.

As they go to leave the restaurant, it turns out they're not shutting the place down after all. Jones spots Pioli and goes over to give him a hug. "I'm proud of you," the Cowboys' owner says. Crennel still is there, too, and they chat with him.

When they step outside, the mission is clear again. They will always have dinner conversations that will go unexpected places. But this is late January, just a few weeks away from draft meetings and the Combine, and they are two GMs whose teams were bounced from the play-offs. They didn't win anything in Kansas City and Atlanta that they'd be willing to brag about. There's plenty of work to do.

13.
Chief Assembly

The agreement they always have is that they will share the music, right down the middle. As they drive the streets of Kansas City on a Sunday afternoon, the day before Valentine's Day, they listen to a naturally eclectic playlist. One song is Scott Pioli's, the very next one belongs to his seven-year-old daughter, Mia. It's Springsteen to Swift, the Stones to Usher, and then one that they can both claim, Michael Jackson.

They've had a rare day with no office time for Pioli, and soon they will head across town to sit down for burgers. But first Pioli pulls the car in front of one of the city's restored architectural marvels and shares a glimpse of a dream. He's parked in front of Union Station, a true beauty. Its ceilings, ninety-five feet high, seem to be adjoined to the sky. It has thirty-five-hundred-pound chandeliers, which is one thousand pounds heavier than the combined weight of the Chiefs' starters on the offensive and defensive lines. It's a structure that *looks* important, built to host bustle and big events.

One day, Pioli says, this will be the place where Kansas City celebrates a Super Bowl title for the Chiefs. He can envision a main stage in front of the station and thousands and thousands of fans, from Missouri and Kansas, occupying spots around the stage and on the hill that overlooks it.

Pioli doesn't make a habit of sharing this vision when he's on the job. The message might be twisted. People might think he's trying to say that the Chiefs are on the doorstep of winning the Super Bowl. But what he really wants is to be a part of a winner in this region, for an owner whose father literally spoke "Super Bowl" into existence. It doesn't seem right to him that Clark Hunt doesn't even have memories of the last time the Chiefs won a championship. Neither does Pioli. He and Hunt were even younger than Mia when the Chiefs upset the Vikings in January 1970. The closest Hunt has gotten to that Sunday in New Orleans is the home videos he's been shown. The game was such a part of another era that it started at two thirty in the afternoon central time. These days, that's the time slot for hour three of a marathon pregame show.

The only way to make the celebration happen is to work at it, adding the right players to the roster, and that process will continue tomorrow. That's when Pioli, Phil Emery, and all the scouts will head to the office for an entire week of draft meetings. It's when they'll begin determining how the draft board should be stacked and which players should be pushed up or down. Pioli will be more than prepared for that. Tomorrow. For now, he's placing a call to local resident and longtime family friend May Tveit.

"You've got to help us out here, Ms. May," he says as he wheels away from Union Station. "We're in the mood for a good burger, and we know you know the place."

May is cleaning her house. She was focused on that until Pioli mentioned burgers, and now she has a taste for one. She goes over a few possibilities before she gives the final answer.

"You've got to go to Westport Flea Market," she says.

Pioli and Mia are just a few miles away from the one-of-a-kind Kansas City establishment: a burger joint in the middle of a flea market. You can get discount items, you can sing karaoke, you can play cards, and you can get a ten-ounce burger that uses top-notch beef from a local butcher shop, McGonigle's. As Pioli and his daughter walk in, not too many heads turn. It's not that kind of place. Some people are watching TV and others are digging into those burgers. When it's time for Pioli to pick up his order from the chef's station, the cook does a double take.

"You look familiar," he says. "You a cop?"

Pioli laughs.

"You *are* a cop, aren't you?" he says.

Pioli swears that he's not and says that he works for the Chiefs.

"Oh! You're Scott Pioli! Good to see ya, man. Welcome."

Father and daughter are no strangers to quirky burger joints or exploring new places in a city. They did that all the time in New England, and Pioli even got Mia to come with him on Thanksgiving mornings to serve food to the homeless. He realizes that she's much more privileged than he ever was, so he and Dallas are conscious of raising a child who is grounded despite the high-profile position her father has. They're doing just fine so far. Mia politely asks for a dollar so she can operate one of those claw machines that grasps at stuffed animals. She goes to a waitress, hands over a bill, and asks for four quarters. She whiffs a couple times, with the claws proving to be impossibly slippery, and laughs, and her father laughs with her. It's almost time to leave.

"I just want to say it's nice to meet you, Mr. Pioli," one of the waitresses says. "Thanks for coming in."

"Thanks for saying that," Pioli says. "You can call me Scott. Mr. Pioli is in New York."

Their afternoon is over, and they can head home and honestly tell Dallas that they had a blast at a flea market. After he and Dallas and Mia have hung out for a couple hours and Mia has gone off to bed, Pioli goes into his home office and begins to focus on the next day. He can't help coming home to work: The Chiefs' IT staff has made it so his desktop is plugged in to all systems at the team's facility, so whatever he can do at the office he can do at home. He knows the next day is going to be busy. Not only will he be breaking down players with Emery and the scouts, he'll be trying to finalize a deal that will make Jim Zorn the Chiefs' new quarterbacks coach.

Pioli will use his elaborate highlighting system to help him better process and organize all the information he'll be getting tomorrow and for the next couple months.

"I learned the system in college," he says. "I'm a visual guy. It's how I actually started getting good grades. It keeps me structured, puts clarity and boundaries to things, and it eliminates noise."

He has no illusions of who the Chiefs are as he prepares for his third draft with them.

"We're just not good enough," he says. "At the end of the year, at the end of this season, when we couldn't sneak up on teams and we played good teams, we felt it. What do we need? There aren't many positions we can look at and say we don't need the help there. We've got holes today, but we also have holes that are a year away. I've seen a great roster. We are so far away from a great roster. So far away.

"You know, we couldn't get anyone open to catch a pass in the play-offs."

It's going to take some part of great for Union Station to be transformed into that Chiefs carnival that he dreams of. Tomorrow, he and his staff will begin closing the gap.

Pioli arrives at work just before seven on Monday morning. He has a few things he wants to take care of before the draft meetings start, and one of them is trying to reach Nathan Whitaker, the agent for Zorn, so they can begin to negotiate a contract. He also needs to contact Tripp MacCracken, the Chiefs' director of football administration, an experienced negotiator who can help shepherd the Zorn deal. Throughout the day, Pioli's plan is to be a presence in the meetings, stay in touch with MacCracken, and keep Hunt and head coach Todd Haley in the loop.

"I've never seen somebody who works this hard," Hunt says. "And at times in my life I've thought I've worked hard. But being around Scott I've realized that

I was slacking off. The guy is constantly working on something, and this is not somebody who is trying to break into the business and show that he belongs."

Just before heading into the meetings, Pioli receives a call from Whitaker and they begin to talk numbers. Haley is a huge Zorn fan and he believes the hire is important for the continued development of Matt Cassel. Haley has been an offensive coach his entire career, but he doesn't consider himself a quarterback guru; he considers Zorn to be one of the best. There's a reasoned, conversational tone between Pioli and Whitaker, and based on the sound of things it seems as if they're well on their way to getting something done by the end of the day. The Chiefs have to be careful, though, because Zorn is also being pursued by the Titans and Jaguars.

Pioli walks into a draft room that seems prepped for the long day. There's a whiteboard with the Chiefs' depth chart, appropriately written with an easy-to-erase marker, and there's a board for every team in the league. There are magnetic strips with the names of every college player they'll discuss now and going forward. Between all the scouts and assistant general manager Joel Collier, there are dozens of binders and notebooks on a large conference table. There's also plenty of coffee, tea, and water. Before he officially begins the meetings, Pioli reaches into a box and hands out nine personalized "AFC West Champs" game balls for the scouts, which leads to their applause.

When it comes to their reports during these meetings, the scouts are expected to read a general summary of what they've observed from the player in person and on tape, as well as what they've gleaned from head coaches, strength coaches, teammates, and other sources. (The best scouts have as many sources as investigative reporters.) Each scout's report is always expected to include answers to the following six questions:

What will this player's role be as a Chief? Will the role change from year one to year two? How many downs can he be expected to play? Which current player on the roster will he beat out? What's his value on special teams? Does he have positional versatility?

After they give their reports, some type of discussion will follow. At times it will be breezy. At others, especially when there's some inconsistency between the report and the grade, it will be tense.

Pioli and Emery will sit near each other, and Collier will be at the other end of the table. Emery will lead the discussions.

The first time Emery became a college director, in Atlanta in 2004, he got a phone call from one of his mentors, Mark Hatley, reminding him that one of the

keys to a successful department is listening to everyone's opinion. Emery listens, closely, and if there's
something that doesn't seem right he'll bring it up. He
worked at the Naval Academy for seven years, so he's
not a career military man, although he does sound like
one: His voice is clear and commanding, and you'll have
to work a little if you want to talk over it. He's wearing a long-sleeved shirt, blue jeans, and black cowboy
boots. He's got an iPad in front of him with his notes
as well as reports from the scouts. His recall is impressive. Not only does he remember players he scouted in
Chicago and Atlanta before coming here, he can also
pinpoint conversations that were had about the player
at the time. You get the feeling the iPad isn't always
necessary due to his ability to give historical playbacks
from memory. He's ready for business.

As he listens to a scout's report on a running back
and then looks at the grades the back has been given,
Emery has a problem. A grade of 5 in a category is
above average. A grade of 7 is a notch below excellent.

"I look at the strength and explosion grades,"
Emery says, "and then I turn around and look at
the power-run grades. I'm confused. No one put his
power-run grade above five, but we had two scouts
give him a seven in strength and explosion. So we're
not connected there."

Emery doesn't believe an above-average back on power runs can also be exceptional in strength and explosion. He's either one or the other.

"Are we talking pound-for-pound strength or overall strength?" one of the scouts asks.

"I'm talking about true overall strength," Emery answers. "How does he get to be a five power runner? I mean, if he's that explosive?"

"Well, because he's not that big," the scout says.

"That's getting back to my point," Emery counters. "I don't see him being able to anchor. But we have two sevens on him when it comes to strength and explosion. And then I look down at the power run and you guys are saying, 'Well, it's because he's small.' Well, then for the NFL projected, I don't know how he's a seven. That's a very good grade. That's flashes of brilliance for the next level in that category, but we have no higher than a five in power run.

"With all these little guys, why do we say they're playmakers when they have these low yards-per-carry averages? They get to the line of scrimmage and they can't break tackles. So that their averages, even though they have some big plays, their averages are relatively low."

Pioli observes this exchange without saying anything. He knows exactly what this is because he's been through it hundreds of times in his career: It's a thinking exercise, not a bigfooting tactic. Emery has no interest in having the scouts simply change their grades so they can placate him. Rather, he's hoping that they can explain or carefully consider their logic. If they can't make a case for their grades, they'll change them on their own.

Emery pauses. He wants to be sure no one is taking this personally. It's never personal, although it's easy to feel like it is when your grade is being questioned in front of the group. But all the scouts know that Emery's diligence has nothing to do with trying to make himself look good at someone else's expense. What he's trying to encourage is depth, consistency, and thoroughness when it comes to reports and grades. He has worked for Pioli and Dimitroff, two men who cringe at inconsistencies. They expect this area of the draft forest to be completely cleared by the time they begin strategizing with their picks.

"I'm just bringing it up because that's your grade," Emery says. "I'm not just saying it. Because I've got a four on him. You've got a five, but you've got a seven over here. And basically we're looking at the same quantity. And I'm talking about it from a perspective of being on the same page as a staff so that we're all looking at things the same way so that we can have conversation. That's all."

When another small-back discussion comes up later, Pioli has an idea that he says he wants to see executed after the draft. He tells one of the scouts to supervise a research project done on undersized backs.

"What are the common physical traits? Whether it's yards after contact or something else. Off the top of my mind, a number of these undersized guys are making it because yards after contact is a pretty important thing for them," Pioli says. "That's a Darren Sproles thing and that's a Maurice Jones-Drew thing, too.

"But I want to know who made it. Why did they make it? Or why you think they made it. I think it would be a great thing for us as we go into training camp. As we do the project, it's also important to understand what type of offense they played in college, especially with all the spread crap out there right now."

They move on to other areas. At one point, Pioli applauds scout Terry Delp for consistently including a player's special-teams value in his reports and reminds others that they need to do the same. When they get to offensive linemen, Emery says of one prospect, "At what point should I start watching where he's not getting slung around?"

The offensive-line conversation is an important one. The Chiefs clearly need an upgrade at center, where they currently have Casey Wiegmann, who'll be thirty-eight when training camp begins. Pioli puts the discussion of college centers on hold briefly and asks a few scouts to tell him how they see Wiegmann. They all rave about his durability and toughness and willingness to compete, yet all agree that his days as a starter are over.

Of the pure centers discussed, there is a silent disagreement with the report on Florida's Mike Pouncey and agreement on the take of Cincinnati's Jason Kelce. Pioli is high on both players, but he doesn't feel compelled to share that during the conversation. Kelce reminds him of Patriots center Dan Koppen, whom the Patriots drafted in the fifth round in 2003. Pouncey, in his mind, is someone who can captain an offensive line and set an aggressive tone for a decade. He listens as the discussion about both players takes place.

"You know, really, when I think of him, he's not as good as his brother," a scout says of Pouncey. "Of course, his brother was an All-Pro as a rookie."

Emery asks the scout what he thinks the difference is between Maurkice Pouncey of the Steelers and his twin brother.

"I think his brother is more savvy," the scout says. "He's got more awareness. Part of that could be that this guy played center for one full year, whereas his brother played for three years. Hell, I guess he could be seventy percent of what his brother is and still wind up with a good career."

On Kelce, Emery calls himself out on his initial analysis of him. But he followed the advice that Hatley gave him when he first got into scouting: Go back to the tape.

"I did four more games. And then I watched some tape of the Bears," Emery says. "The guy reminds me of Olin Kreutz. I mean, it's not pretty. You know, his body type and all that stuff. He's kind of a throwback guy. He's mean. Nasty. Aggressive. Strong smaller guy with good hips."

Pioli is expressionless as Emery is describing Kelce. But during the rundown he has one thought: The guy sounds like a perfect Chief.

They decide to take a break and eat subs. Pioli goes back to his office and begins working the phones again. He's making progress with Whitaker, and he just needs MacCracken to double-check with the league to make sure the creative deal he's structuring for Zorn is legal. In the meantime, he leaves a message for Haley and lets him know the latest. Between phone calls, he's looking at spreadsheets that show where the Chiefs are spending money. The sheets are looking good. This is part of general-managing, too, and the way Pioli approaches it and other things often gets the owner's attention.

"One thing I would say about Scott that has been a complete surprise, because I don't think this is the kind of thing you can get in an interview, but I've never had an employee who is more attuned to looking after my and my family's interests than Scott is," Hunt says. "If Scott had a hundred decisions to make, none of which I would ever know about, that could either benefit him or benefit the organization, I'm confident that one hundred out of one hundred, he would make the decision that benefits the organization. And that's a special quality."

It's the combination of geography and history that makes Pioli protective of the Hunts' interests. They're in Dallas, away from the day-to-day Chiefs activity, so he often sees what they can't. They might be surprised at how far he goes to make sure supplies aren't being wasted. During the season, he has an employee check the meeting rooms after the players have left. There are always discarded pens in there, and Pioli has them picked up and placed in a shoebox for reuse. The only sign of extravagance is the brand of the shoebox: Gucci. He's always been meticulous about spending and operating efficiently, but it's even more of a focus now that he's here. When he returns to the draft room, he will look across the table at a scout who can explain, better than most, how Pioli has changed over the past few years. He clearly did his job well in New England and had a purpose in what he was doing. But the purpose seems sharper now.

Jay Muraco has known Pioli for nearly twenty years. Muraco, who grew up just outside of Cleveland in Brecksville, has seen the evolution of Pioli. It started when Pioli was in Muraco's hometown as a Brown, and it continued with the Patriots and now Chiefs.

"He wasn't always as direct as he is now," Muraco, who scouts the Northeast for the Chiefs, says. "I've never been a morning guy, so I would do the same amount of work as everyone else but not get there as early. I remember years ago I came in and Scott said, 'Hey, man. Something was said about what time you came in.' I asked who said it and he just said, 'Something was said.' Now? He would just say, 'Get your ass in here.' "

With Pioli's rise, Muraco has consciously drawn a line between how he is with him at work and how he is when they're just hanging out. "We're so close," Muraco says. "I'm mindful of joking around with him too much here and doing something that will compromise his authority. So I don't think I bust on him nearly as much as I used to. At least not at work."

It's time to go back to the draft room, and it's easy to see why Dimitroff thought Emery and Pioli would be such a good fit. Emery is a good listener and a get-to-the-point type. He wants to be sure a tackle truly has position flexibility when a scout says that he does.

"This stuff has to be real now," Emery says. "When it gets down to brass tacks, a lot of guys, we find a lot of these tackles don't really have the true flexibility that we kind of hope that they have. I want it to be you really believe this. Not just being hopeful."

There's more immediacy to these meetings than the ones they had in December. Then, the idea was to go over several names, whether they were draftable or not. Now, less than two weeks before the scouting Combine in Indianapolis, the players discussed in depth are the ones who will be on the front board when the Chiefs start drafting in April. There's more big-picture urgency, too. Everyone is aware that the fancy footballs they were given at the beginning of the day are nice items for office shelves and family dens, but the goal is to get one of those footballs from a Super Bowl. When Emery and the scouts speak of another running back, 2009 Heisman Trophy winner Mark Ingram of Alabama, they're all in agreement about who he is and where he could help them go.

"He'll be a starting running back for many teams in the league," one of the scouts says. "For the Chiefs,

Ingram is a three-down starter who is a younger, more athletic version of Thomas Jones. He's not as fast as Jamaal Charles but is a more complete back that can stay healthy and on the field for three downs."

"Can he make people miss in the hole?" Emery asks.

"I don't think he's a shake guy," the scout says. "He's your classic Steady Eddie. He's just going to do the same thing. He's closer to Thomas than he is to Jamaal, if you want to compare the two."

"And I know he got hurt this year toward the end of the season. Was he back to being as good as he was in '09?"

"I thought so," the scout replies.

"So you see him as a replacement for Thomas?"

"Yes."

"And a complement for Charles?"

"Absolutely. I mean, if we're going to continue to have a dual group back there like we did this year, I think he'd be the perfect replacement."

Emery obviously knows the answers to many of these questions before he asks them, and even in February, two months before the draft, he knows the Chiefs are unlikely to spend a first-round pick on a running back. But he wants them all thinking in a certain way, and they all know what way that is with his next question.

"If I'm not saying this straight, just ask for clarity: Is he a guy that can help us win championships? Or is he a guy that is *the reason* for winning championships?"

"I would say he'd be one of the reasons we could win a championship," the scout says without hesitation. "Just because I think he's a salt guy. You know, he's the guy that's going to finish off the game. He's never going to put the ball on the ground. You can just see the confidence in him especially at the end of the game to protect the football."

The exchange is proof of how far Pioli has brought the Chiefs' scouting staff since he took over in 2009. The group is detailed and conscientious now, from top to bottom. Still, there can only be so many debates and analyses in a day, even for football careerists, before they begin to wear down. They'll be back tomorrow to repeat the process. As for Pioli, he's had a productive day. He has absorbed good information from the meetings and redirected them when necessary. He's also closed a deal for a new quarterbacks coach. Sometimes you truly become a better team one day at a time.

14.

Picking and Dealing

Two weeks before the draft, Bill Belichick sits at his desk in his Foxboro office and goes over possibilities and strategies. He's relaxed, and just in case you can't see that, you can hear it. He's dialed into the Margaritaville station on satellite radio, with the familiar bass line of "Get Up, Stand Up" resonating off the walls.

If there's a day when he considers walking away from pro football and throwing himself into another passion, that day won't come in April. He loves the draft too much, layer by layer and pick by pick. He's reached an anniversary of sorts this year: It was exactly twenty years ago when he arrived in Cleveland with a grading and scouting idea that has now grown into a grading and scouting *system*, with general managers in the Midwest and Southeast running some version of it. He refuses to take all the credit, saying that it was Mike Lombardi in Cleveland who helped till the land and it was Scott Pioli in New England who helped cultivate it into what it is today.

What he's got now, in the NFL, is something collegiate-sounding. He's got a program. It's part of the reason that two weeks from now, the Patriots will pick seventeenth and twenty-eighth in the first round, and then pivot for pick 33, the first choice in the second round. Belichick is the rare coach who is operating with the long view, so he's not always in a hurry to see the player right now; he'll wait a year or even two years, which is the story with the seventeenth pick, acquired in 2009. Pick 33, which originally belonged to Carolina, was his reward for patience. The Patriots had picks 89 and 90 a year ago; the Panthers wanted 89, and they were willing to pay with their 2011 second-rounder. The result sounds like some Internet scam: Give us the eighty-ninth choice right now and you, my friend, could have a selection as high as 33 one year from now. And all you have to do is . . . wait for it.

It's almost one year to the day of that deal, one of many that have shaped how Belichick goes about his draft business. He may have a grading system when it comes to the draft, but he swears that there is no draft formula, unless you consider "do your homework" to be a formula.

"You've obviously got your own feelings about players, but you've really got to know what the league thinks, too," he says. "Whether it's by numbers, like which positions have depth, or by players, like identifying who the risers are and what players are in free-fall. All of that information affects your decisions. Especially if you know a team or teams are after a certain player. It doesn't even matter which team it is. You just know there's a certain guy teams are trying to climb to get. Well, if you're in position for that player and you don't really want him, then, you know, you have a market."

On the flip side, sometimes you want a player and you perceive the rest of the league wants him, too. It can lead to a case of overdrafting, or picking a player too high, which Belichick admits the Patriots did in 2009.

"Sebastian Vollmer is a good example," he says of the Patriots' starting right tackle, one of the team's four second-rounders in '09. "There's no way he was really a second-round pick. Based on film or really based on the player he was at the end of the '08 season. You know, East-West game and all that. You took him betting on improvement and upside. We knew that there was an undertow of Vollmer. And it was just the question of, 'When's this guy going to go?'

"He should have been a fourth- or fifth-round pick, by the film, by his performance. But you saw him as an ascending player and he had rare size, and there were a lot of things that you had to fix and all that. But it was clear the league liked him. Now, the question is always, 'How much do they like him and where are they willing to buy?' I'm sure for some teams it was the fourth round. For some teams it was the third round. But we just said, 'Look, we really want this guy. This is too high to pick him, but if we wait we might not get him, so we're just going to step up and take him.'

"And sometimes when you do that you're right and sometimes when you do that you're wrong and everybody looks at you like, 'Damn, you could have had him in the fourth.'"

The upcoming draft will be Belichick's seventeenth as a head coach, his twelfth with the Patriots. Over the years, his teams have had a sampling of enough first-round positions to qualify them for a draft lotto: 2, 6, 9, 9, 10, 13, 14, 21, 24, and, of course, 32. His penchant for draft-day deals has put his teams in draft slots that belie their success. After their last Super Bowl appearance, in February 2008, they held the seventh overall pick and after a trade down picked tenth. They had the best record in football last season, 14-2, yet they have multiple picks woven into the early rounds of the

2011 draft, which will allow them to be the team most capable of steering it in their favor.

Belichick remembers all the drafts, through and through, without notes or media guides. He remembers the time, in 2003, when he started to panic. The Patriots held pick 14, the Bears were on the clock, and just one of New England's desired defensive linemen was on the board. Belichick had a feeling that the Bears would take a defensive lineman, too, and he didn't think it would be his guy, Ty Warren. But he wasn't sure.

He called Bears GM Jerry Angelo, an old friend, and asked if he wanted to move the pick. He was offering a sixth-rounder to move up one spot. Angelo asked what he was coming up to get.

"A defensive lineman," he said.

"Well, we're taking a defensive lineman, too."

"I know you are," Belichick said. "But if we're not coming to get your guy, it's basically a free sixth."

They danced for a few seconds, trying to see who would actually mention a name first. Finally, Belichick said, "We want Ty Warren." And Angelo said, "We want Michael Haynes." They made the deal anyway.

Belichick has seen enough drafts unfold that he has been able to pick up a general pattern of what each round represents.

"The first-rounders are the guys, obviously, with the fewest questions. In the second round, a lot of times you find players with first-round talent but not first-round performance or production, if you will," he says. "Then in the third round, you see guys who are maybe better football players than a lot of guys in the second round, but not as maybe overall talented, in terms of measurements. So I think there's a certain bust factor, if you will, in the second round. That's just in general."

He's been around long enough to have specific examples from his own teams.

"In last year's draft, Brandon Spikes was a good football player who didn't run well and didn't test particularly well, but he's probably a better football player than a lot of guys that were taken in the second round ahead of him who tested well, who had more upside but produced less on the field than he did," Belichick says, referring to his young inside linebacker. "I'd say that's fairly common. In the second round, you're more likely to say, 'Let's get somebody fast. Let's get a Bethel Johnson or a Mike Wallace.' Okay, well, one of those guys works out and one of them doesn't. Neither one of them was any big deal in college.

"You want that speed. Or if you want that kind of upside, you want that kind of potential, then that's where you've got to take it, because it's not going to be there in the third round, generally speaking. Those players, if you don't take them somebody else is going to take them. I'm not saying a guy who just goes out and works out. I'm saying a guy who's got a lot of stuff going for him as a player but not enough to really buy early.

"You know, Ben Watson. Thirty-second pick. He's practically a second-round pick. Now, if he had played to his ability in college he would have gone in the middle of the first round. But he didn't, so you hope you can generate that out of him. Then you have an All-Pro tight end. But in the end, he played in the pros about like he played in college."

Watson was drafted in 2004 because of his size and speed. He played six seasons with the Patriots, with his best production coming in a forty-nine-catch third season. His signature play featured a different kind of catch, though. He ran from the goal line, crossed the field, and then ran the entire length of the field to catch cornerback Champ Bailey and prevent him from scoring on a hundred-yard-plus interception return. The Patriots lost that play-off game in Denver, but people still talk about that play. Watson left New England after the 2009 season and currently plays for the Browns.

Even now, still a week away from the final positioning of the Patriots' board and fifteen days from the start of the draft itself, Belichick senses emerging plans and information that will help him in the draft room. He thinks he's got a handle on who this year's tumbler is: Clemson defensive end Da'Quan Bowers, who has scared off a lot of teams with his microfracture knee surgery. He notices that many teams have visited with quarterbacks and seem prepared to draft them early, a move that will help the Patriots because it will help push down more good players that they want. He also envisions a pack of players, likely selected in the 15 to 40 range, who have similar value.

"I think some teams are going to look up at that board in the first round, see where they've ranked their players, and say, 'Okay, well, here's our guy. He's still there. Let's go get him.' Whereas to me the reality of it is that guy's packed in with a bunch of other guys and it's just a question of how the league ranks them," he says. "This year it's all jumbled, so when you say, 'That's our number one guy . . . three guys have gone ahead of him, he's still there.' Well, that's because he's probably still there on ten other boards, too.

"It's the dynamics of each year as the whole thing gets put together and there's no real—I don't think there's any real formula to it. You've just got to do your homework and then as things happen during the draft be able to put it together."

Anyone who has ever worked with Belichick understands how much of an emphasis he places on being
prepared. They also have been told, time and again,
that what he wants to know about players is how they
will help the Patriots. That's all that matters. So if
Vollmer is drafted in the second round and the talking
heads on TV say it's a reach, it's irrelevant. His mission is always to help the Patriots, and sometimes the
swings have connected and sometimes they've become
Bethel Johnson and Chad Jackson.

What you do is gather all the information that you
can, listen to a number of opinions, and then do what
you believe is right. One thousand miles away, in
Atlanta, that's what one of the men who used to work
for him has been doing for the last month.

Only a few people know what Thomas Dimitroff has
been thinking about in the last three and a half weeks.
He wants to move out of the Falcons' first-round pick,
number 27, and get the team in position to draft either
Julio Jones of Alabama or A. J. Green, the kid from
just down the road at Georgia. Both players are wide
receivers and top-ten talents, so the jump from 27 to,
say, 4 or 6 will be a pricey one.

Talent is not an issue.

When asked to compare Jones and Green, Lionel
Vital quickly gets to the point.

"Green is Randy Moss," he says. "Jones is Terrell Owens."

When Les Snead is asked, his answer differs slightly.

"When you turn on the film, Green reminds you of a better-route-running, just-as-fast Randy Moss," he says. "He plays fast and has that great body control. With Julio, I think you're looking at a better Michael Irvin. He's just a strong human being. Both of those guys are going early. They're both starting receivers in this league."

Dimitroff doesn't need convincing. He's already made several exploratory phone calls. He initially thought of playing a bit of draft leapfrog, where he would call a team like Washington, which holds pick 16. He would then take 16 and make another move to the top ten. But it's the equivalent of buying two one-way tickets when a round-trip flight is the cheaper and more efficient way to go. So he's made calls to teams residing at the top of the draft, calling Denver at 2, and he's worked his way down to San Francisco at 7.

Two friends of his in the business, Tom Heckert and Trent Baalke, are representatives of picks 6 and 7. Heckert and the Browns have pick 6 and Baalke and the 49ers are right after them at 7. Dimitroff is trying to discern what it will take to move up twenty or twenty-one spots, and the answer to the question won't come for a while. Throughout the process, he's up-front with Heckert, who wants to know if he's talked with Baalke, and he's honest with Baalke, who wants to know if he's talked with Heckert.

"It's important to have candid conversations with people you can trust," Dimitroff says. "It saves a lot of time because you're able to talk compensation without going through the feeling-out process."

But there is a process, and it's in-house. Arthur Blank supports Dimitroff's idea, but in the spirit of collaborative business, Blank wants him to talk it over with people outside of personnel. It's yet another example of how different Atlanta is from New England. Belichick would be taken aback if team owner Robert Kraft asked him to share his trading plans with multiple people in the organization. It might even be a deal breaker. Belichick knows what he wants, and he has many assistants, from linebackers coach Matt Patricia to veteran offensive line coach Dante Scarnecchia, whom he can go to for advice. With that said, sometimes he tells them what he's up to and sometimes he doesn't. Blank's suggestion to Dimitroff doesn't come from lack of confidence or disrespect; it comes from the Home Depot. In the business that made him billions, Blank had gotten used to an organizational structure in which everyone, including himself and Bernie Marcus, was available to be challenged if an idea seemed to be too bold or even reckless. It didn't mean that those working under them had veto power, but there was always the possibility that a raised point would at least act as a speed bump.

After working with Blank for three years, Dimitroff understands him. The two are so friendly that when they tried, without an agent, to renegotiate Dimitroff's contract a couple months earlier, they abruptly stopped. They had gone for Italian food one night, and when they talked about the parameters of a deal at dinner, it didn't feel right. They decided that they wanted a new contract to be done, but they didn't want to bring negotiating into their relationship. That led to the potentially odd situation of Dimitroff's agent trying to make a deal with Rich McKay, the Falcons' president, whom Dimitroff succeeded as general manager. It quickly became a nonissue, as Dimitroff's original contract, which was well below the $1.2 million average annual salary for GMs, swelled to one of the best deals among league executives.

Blank didn't know Dimitroff before he hired him; he's gotten to know him better since working with him, but perhaps this proposed deal the GM wants to do is most revealing about who he is. The fact is, no one in the organization or community is pressuring him to do a deal. They're comfortable with him. He's brought a steadiness to Atlanta that the Falcons have never seen, with their thirty-three wins in his three seasons representing the best forty-eight-game stretch in franchise history. In town, corporations are willing to pay top dollar for him to speak. He and Angeline belong to a church, Peachtree Presbyterian, where the pastor sometimes mentions him by name during sermons. He has great relationships with local and national media members, who praise him for his accessibility and thoughtfulness.

It's comfortable. But that's not his goal. If he wanted to be a general manager who collects checks and carefully protects the job he has, he'd never even dream of dealing for Jones or Green. What's the point? Why make yourself a target when no one else is making you a target? Because of all his other interests, which take him from bike paths to snow-covered mountains, people sometimes overlook a humble confidence that comes from being born into a football family. His father was never about retreating. He attacked. Sometimes the elder Tom Dimitroff did that too much, like the time in Canada when he felt a player was being too mouthy and too disrespectful, so he just popped him. Right in the kisser. His youngest child subscribed to a newer school and had a different temperament, but he wasn't afraid to fully dive into something seen as unconventional and, in the eyes of some, foolish.

Dimitroff is not insulted by Blank's insistence that he listen to more voices before trading into the top ten, but he is nervous that too many people with knowledge of the plan will cause a media leak. It doesn't happen. Soon, all sides of football operations are tuned in to what could be happening on draft day. The people in the know include Vital, Snead, and college scouting director Dave Caldwell; pro scouts Ran Carthon and DeJuan Polk, whose early research shows that the Falcons will be left with a player such as Wisconsin tackle Gabe Carimi if they stay at 27; and members of Mike Smith's coaching staff, including offensive coordinator Mike Mularkey and receivers coach Terry Robiskie.

Even as the Falcons continue to think in terms of acquiring either player, stories of Jones's competitiveness are popping up in, of all places, Kansas City. The Chiefs had the receiver in for a visit, and he and head coach Todd Haley began going in depth on a couple subjects. Haley has coached two Hall of Fame–caliber receivers in Terrell Owens and Larry Fitzgerald, and one just a notch below that level in Keyshawn Johnson. Haley quickly fell for Jones, and what may have sealed it was a challenge.

"We started talking about Ping-Pong and how I love to play," Haley says. "I have a table at my house. When he found that out, he wanted to skip lunch and drive to the house instead so we could see who was the best. He just had that confidence about him. I remember Keyshawn was like that: Tell him that the game was in the parking lot and he'd be there."

A couple months earlier in Indianapolis, Jones blew away league evaluators when he decided to run, even though doctors had discovered a small fracture in his foot. He had planned to sit out, but the competitive atmosphere got the best of him and he turned in a torrid workout, which included a sub-4.4-second performance in the forty-yard dash.

The more the Falcons study him and hear about him, the more they like him. Their scouting department has given him the same grade, 8.0, that they had on Matt Ryan in the spring of 2008. The only thing left for the organization to do is go see him, one-on-one, in Alabama.

There are times to take an SUV for a quick trip to a neighboring state, and this is not one of them. Dimitroff, Smith, Mularkey, Robiskie, Snead, Vital, and Caldwell are able to make themselves comfortable, easily, on the owner's G4 jet for the short trip to Tuscaloosa. The plane says a lot about Blank. While it has top-of-the-line finishes and was smartly designed by Blank's wife, Stephanie, who has a passion for interior design, there is no Falcons logo to be found on the aircraft. When Dimitroff once asked Blank the reason for that, he replied that it was important to be stylish but not ostentatious. He just didn't believe that a Falcons logo on the plane was in good taste.

The lack of an emblem certainly doesn't affect the ride for the Falcons' party. They were in Atlanta one moment and standing in the lobby of the Hotel Capstone the next. When they see Jones, it's hard to remember that they are visiting with a receiver. He's built as if he moonlights as a bronze sculpture. He's six feet two inches and every bit of 220 pounds, his muscles perpetually flexed, seemingly just as capable of punishing as being punished. On this day, briefly, he's also annoyed.

He has met with many teams already, and all of them have a more realistic shot of drafting him than the Falcons. He has a look on his face that seems to ask the obvious question: How in hell do you expect to move from the late twenties to the single digits? With your draft picks and someone else's?

The meeting with Jones quickly turns pleasant. Atlanta's former college director, Phil Emery, described Jones as a "joy to be around" and someone who had "moxie" and Jones displays those qualities for the Falcons. At one point Mularkey asks him about a negative play he saw on film. Jones acknowledges the play and then promises the offensive coordinator, "Listen, I will *kill* that guy."

He handles himself well when ribbed and tested by Robiskie, who has seen it all in thirty years of coaching and has a son, Brian, playing receiver in the NFL. The younger Robiskie is a member of the Browns, one of the teams Jones has heard is in the market for him. But as the coaches have their conversations with Jones, Dimitroff's mind has wandered and he's decided that there's no way Jones will be playing in Cleveland or anywhere else but Atlanta. He thinks about the times during the regular season when defenses would get creative and tilt their coverages to Roddy White. He imagines the challenges of a team having to deal with White and Jones and Tony Gonzalez.

"This is no disrespect to Mike Jenkins, because he's a damn good receiver," Dimitroff says later. "But I've always been intrigued with the prospect of having a one and one-A with Roddy and someone like Julio."

It's what he thought about in October when he stood in his office and stared at what were just numbers and names on a board. He thought about it many times during the season, and even after with the scouting trips to Mobile and Indianapolis. But just as Blank believes that you get what you pay for, and therefore gets the finest material for his suits and high-quality finishes around his home, the same is true to a degree in the NFL. There's a heavy price to move up, yet there's no guarantee that the player will be as great as you project.

When Dimitroff talks to Heckert again, he's got an idea of what the move will cost: He'll obviously have to exchange 27 for 6, but he'll have to include next year's first-round pick, a second and fourth in 2011, and a fourth in 2012. He weighs the player vs. the pain of the compensation. He can live without the fours. The exchange of 27 for 6 is the obvious cost of doing business. But the 1 and 2 will sting. He says *will* sting because he's going to do it.

Leading up to the draft, he goes back and forth with Heckert: Will you do the deal even if a player unexpectedly slips to you at 6? Will you do the deal if a player unexpectedly comes off the board? Each time the answer is yes. The Atlanta Falcons and Dimitroff are going to make a bold play for the top of the draft, a move that won't be endorsed by one of the voices in the business that Dimitroff respects the most.

15.
War Room

On Thursday afternoon, several hours before the start of the NFL draft, the phone lights up in Bill Belichick's Foxboro office. It would be tough to argue that the incessant ringing bothers him. Since becoming the coach of the Patriots in 2000, Belichick has made a draft-day deal with all but eight teams in the league. The Jets are among the eight who have never called, and if they ever do, Belichick will likely think Sol Rosenberg and Frank Rizzo, two of the telephone prankster characters from the Jerky Boys, have something to do with it.

The current call is from Atlanta, and it's not the usual trade inquiry. Thomas Dimitroff is on the line, and he wants to exchange ideas about many things, including the dramatic trade he has on the table with Cleveland.

In the past six weeks or so, Dimitroff's most singular thought has been moving to the top of the draft and taking Alabama receiver Julio Jones. He's visualized Jones as a Falcon so often that when he visualized on Wednesday night, he briefly panicked. He wondered if the organization had sent any Falcons gear to New York for Jones to wear when his name is announced at Radio City Music Hall. He was relieved to learn that all of those details are handled by the league. For the next three days and seven rounds, all he has to worry about is picking football players.

After some general draft conversation, Dimitroff and Belichick get into the specifics of the Falcons-Browns trade.

"Thomas, I'm just telling you as a friend," Belichick says, "I wouldn't do it."

Belichick has a couple good reasons for his analysis and he's willing to share. He often says that the primary job of a receiver is to simply get open and catch the ball, and he doesn't like what he sees from Jones in either department. He thinks the receiver struggles to get open on intermediate routes, doesn't play as fast as his superb timed speed suggests, and too often displays inconsistent hands. There's also the issue of value. When Belichick began studying the 2011 draft, he saw great depth at the receiver position. Why go all-out for someone like Jones when you can likely have a Jonathan Baldwin, who, as far as Belichick can see, is just as good if not better than Jones? If Belichick wanted even more insight on Jones, he could always ask the receiver's head coach, Nick Saban, the two-time national championship winner who was Belichick's first defensive coordinator in Cleveland. But Belichick has seen enough on his own without going to Saban for an additional report.

Dimitroff is not shocked by the comments. Not only does he respect Belichick's opinion, but some of his own opinions exist because of what Belichick has taught him over the years. When he first got to the Patriots in 2002, he took a more scientific approach to studying hands and separation after hearing Belichick describe what a good receiver should be able to do. But, in this case, what it comes down to is a basic, subjective disagreement.

From his film study and interviews, Dimitroff concluded that a lot of Jones's drops came from his competitiveness and his belief that he could make a play each time he touched the ball. Sometimes he simply got ahead of himself. There's also the chance that Lionel Vital's pithy breakdown of Jones is so accurate that the Falcons will have to learn to live with some surprising incompletions. After all, Vital said that Jones is Terrell Owens, and for all his greatness, Owens has often been criticized for his drops.

As for the criticism that is surely coming his way in a few hours, Dimitroff also learned from Belichick how to approach it. He watched and listened when Belichick chose to go with Tom Brady over Drew Bledsoe in 2001; released Lawyer Milloy less than a week before the start of the 2003 season; "reached" for a future All-Pro guard named Logan Mankins in the first round in 2005; and even allowed one of the icons of the 2001 championship season, Adam Vinatieri, to make it to free agency and eventually become a Colt in 2006. Belichick's standard line for all occasions is the same: "I did what I thought was best for the team."

Dimitroff believes that he's doing the same thing. Based on where the Falcons are at this stage of their development, accumulating picks is not what they need. What they need, their general manager thinks, is to cobble some picks together, move up from 27 to 6, and get an impact player. He's thought about that for more than a month. He's cross-checked it with the Falcons, starting with Arthur Blank and working his way down the organizational chart. He's mentioned it to two friends, Belichick and Scott Pioli, and his record with them is 1-1. Pioli, who was told of the plan before Dimitroff's conversation with Belichick, said he would do it; Belichick said no way.

Even if Pioli and Belichick told him different things, at least Dimitroff knows that those two understand what kind of step he's taking and the ramifications of it. If he's wrong, no one will write about the democratic nature of the process and how the entire Atlanta organization was on board with the move. If this goes bad, he's the star of the movie, and depending on just how bad it is, it could cost him his job or at least his reputation as a sound GM. If he succeeds, even the ticket-takers and their cousins will claim a role in helping the deal go forward. It's the way it is, and he's content with it.

Dimitroff, Belichick, and Pioli will enter the draft with different team needs and different ideas on how to fill them. All three of them have been thinking about the best way to go forward for weeks. They all had winning seasons in 2010, but it didn't feel that way. Since being turned away from the play-offs on consecutive January weekends, one coach and two GMs have spent long hours scouting and planning. They've been thinking of what they're going to do in their respective draft rooms, how their decisions in rooms with neutral-colored walls can get them back to playing the last game of the season on a neutral field on Super Bowl Sunday. Soon, finally, it will be time for all of them to turn their thoughts to action.

As the first round begins, no one in New England, Kansas City, or Atlanta is surprised by the first five picks. At number six, the huge Atlanta draft room, twice the size of New England's and Kansas City's and filled with twice as many people, erupts into high-fives and smiles when the much-discussed deal is announced. There are two TVs in the room, one tuned to ESPN and the other to the NFL Network, and the volume happens to be up on the ESPN TV when analyst and former NFL coach Jon Gruden gives his thoughts on the trade. The very first thing he mentions is . . . the inconsistent hands of Julio Jones. ESPN has taken sports visual media to another level with its unlimited resources, so there is a well-produced montage for millions and millions to see that Jones, apparently, can't catch. There are dismissive waves at the TV from the Falcons' draft room and instead a focus on what has been accomplished. The bank of phones at the head table, where Dimitroff, Blank, and head coach Mike Smith sit, begins to ring.

It's Kansas City.

"Hey, man," Pioli says to Dimitroff. "I'm sitting here with Clark and we both say that took some big ones. Congrats." Clark Hunt, the Chiefs' chairman of the board, has a line for Blank that Pioli relays. "Hey, Thomas. Clark wants to know if you've told Arthur how much this move is going to cost him."

They all laugh as the draft continues. It is now making up for the surprises it lacked in the top five. One of the top three players on the Chiefs' board, Missouri defensive end Aldon Smith, goes seventh to the 49ers. Smith is instinctive and powerful, and in his first full year of college ball he produced an impressive eleven and a half sacks. The Chiefs didn't expect him to go in the top ten, but with so many teams talking about getting to the quarterback in a quarterbacks' league, the selection isn't outrageous.

Quarterbacks and pass rushers, in fact, have now accounted for ten of the first fourteen selections in the draft. At number fifteen, with Miami on the clock, the Chiefs have a stake in the player who will go here, too. Pioli is willing to trade up six spots from number 21 so the Chiefs can draft Florida's Mike Pouncey. They see him as a day one starter in the league, a center with smarts, toughness, and the type of talent that can transform an entire line. They spent a lot of time talking about the position in their draft meetings, and they were going to take at least one center, maybe even two, in this draft. But as much as they love Pouncey and as pressing as their need at center is, they can't agree to what they believe to be a fair deal with the Dolphins and their general manager, Jeff Ireland. So the Dolphins take the in-state kid, and the Chiefs and Patriots excitedly look at the remaining players on the board. The run on quarterbacks, four in the top twelve, has led to the availability of some excellent players.

Belichick sees an opportunity to grab one of the two first-round tackles that he has been extremely high on during the draft process. Dallas took one of them, Southern Cal's Tyron Smith, at number 9. "I think you'll have a hard time pointing to three or four players in this draft who are better than he is," Belichick says of Smith.

One of the hardest things to do, before or during a draft, is to predict where Belichick will go with his first pick. Most of the pre-draft speculation had the Patriots taking an edge rusher, either a big defensive end or a linebacker in the 260-to-265-pound range with the bulk to hold up against the run and the speed to get to the quarterback. If Belichick wants to go that route, he has two good options available. One is Adrian Clayborn, a defensive end who played at Iowa for Kirk Ferentz, a member of Belichick's first coaching staff in Cleveland. The other is 280-pound defensive end Cameron Jordan of Cal. But that's not the side of the ball Belichick is looking for.

He was able to draft tackle Sebastian Vollmer in 2009 and watch him excel and become an immediate starter. That may not be the case for Nate Solder of Colorado, since longtime left tackle Matt Light could be re-signed and resume his starting position on Tom Brady's blind side, but it's only a matter of time before Solder will become a star. Phil Emery said he had never seen a man of Solder's size, six feet eight inches, show such athleticism and ability to recover after being pushed. What the Patriots were going to have to work on was that Solder *could* get pushed. What they, and Brady, were going to love is that he rarely, if ever, fell down.

There is always an expectation that the Patriots will trade out of first-round picks, but the expectation is unfounded when New England has multiple picks in round one. In those instances, the Patriots have never traded out of the "lead" pick. Their history is that they use the first pick and then trade the second one, usually for a future selection.

After the Patriots take Solder at 17 and introduce him by phone to the man who will be paying him, owner Robert Kraft, they wait to see how the rest of the board falls before they are scheduled to make their next pick, at 28. As Pioli alluded to during his dinner with Dimitroff in Mobile, the Patriots' draft room is an exclusive and mostly quiet place. There are no jokesters or loud storytellers. Those who want food can take a walk downstairs to the first-floor cafeteria, but this is not the place to bring your plate of chicken wings with blue cheese dip on the side. If Belichick needs additional information from a scout, he'll have someone call him in. Otherwise, most Patriots scouts are in the same position as most football fans in America: on the outside looking in, waiting to see what will happen next. In the meantime, Pioli and the Chiefs are feeling good about what they're seeing. There are several players on the board whom they would happily welcome to Kansas City. When their phones ring at a center table, occupied by Pioli, Clark Hunt, Daniel Hunt, head coach Todd Haley, and assistant GM Joel Collier, they are ready to deal if something makes sense. Cleveland is offering the pick it got from the Falcons, number 27, along with its third-round choice, number 70, for 21.

The deal is too good to ignore. It's an opportunity to grab a player with a chance to be an immediate contributor in exchange for moving back six slots, and they already see six players they like. The Chiefs agree to it and then go into the same waiting mode as the Patriots, whom they now sit directly in front of. They are in different states of mind, though. The Chiefs are waiting to make a choice. The Patriots have one eye on the board and one dozen on the phones. If he doesn't get a deal he wants, Belichick knows he will take Virginia corner Ras-I Dowling at 28. He'd rather have someone call, though, because he's confident he can get Dowling tomorrow, in round two. It'll be a mostly quiet wait in the Patriots' library atmosphere, but there will be some chatter as long as the player ESPN keeps showing, 2009 Heisman winner Mark Ingram, stays on the board, tempting some team to get him.

Since A. J. Green and Jones went at four and six, respectively, no receiver has been taken off the board. The Chiefs were ready to pick Baldwin, the six-foot-five-inch receiver Belichick mentioned to Dimitroff, at number 27, which happened to be Atlanta's original pick. But Baltimore and Chicago thought they agreed to a trade, with the Bears moving up by swapping first-rounders with the Ravens, 29 for 26, and giving the Ravens a fourth-round selection as well. The Bears failed to properly contact the league to confirm the trade, and so the Ravens, unaware that they were on the clock and not the Bears, sat as their allotted time expired. When that happens and the team has no card to submit in New York, the next team in line can skip ahead. That's how the Chiefs got Baldwin, to the delight of Haley, at number 26. The Ravens, quickly realizing what happened, had their card ready for pick 27 so they couldn't be skipped again and denied their target, cornerback Jimmy Smith. The mix-up between the Ravens and Bears has all the draft rooms talking, with the consensus being that the Bears were solely responsible for the screwup.

The Chiefs are thrilled to get Baldwin, at 27 or 26. Haley has gotten the most out of receivers, of all personality types. He used to push Larry Fitzgerald so hard in Arizona that Fitzgerald playfully offered him hundred-dollar bills before team meetings so his mistakes wouldn't be pointed out in front of his teammates. He helped receivers think about the nuances of the position, like turning to look back for the ball while still maintaining leverage. When he looked at Baldwin, he saw some of the traits and growth potential in him that he saw and brought out in others. And if the team had someone like Baldwin against the Ravens in the play-offs, it wouldn't have been so easy for Baltimore to take Kansas City's Pro Bowl receiver, Dwayne Bowe, out of the game.

At 28, the Patriots get their wish: a trade partner. It's New Orleans on the phone, and it's relative Mardi Gras in the usually serene Patriots draft room. The Saints want Ingram, the only running back the Chiefs had unanimously praised in their draft meetings on Valentine's Day. It really was a love story that day, as one scout gushed, "He's a coach's dream because the message is not diluted in any way. He is the guy who believes the team is way more important than the individual award. He's a grounded guy that never bought into the hype of his Heisman. He's respectful and prompt. He treats everyone like they are the most important person in the world. He does everything the way a pro should." He sounded like someone the Patriots would like, and they do like him. But they like the deal even more. The Saints are offering next year's first and this year's second, at number 56. Belichick accepts the offer.

All three friends have completed their work in round one. They'll stare over the boards once more, go to bed, and come back tomorrow to do it all again.

On Friday morning, the hottest draft topic in America is the Atlanta Falcons. Their trade for Julio Jones produced easy debate fodder for local and national columnists, bloggers, talking heads, talk-show hosts, and anyone who wanted to say it in 140 characters or fewer in a tweet. The question was simple: Did Dimitroff give up too much or not? Those on his side said he was bold. Otherwise, he was a fool.

He spends most of a gorgeous, sun-splashed Georgia morning and early afternoon inside. He does interview after interview in which he wants to hammer a couple of major points: He didn't make this decision on a whim, and neither he nor anyone else in the organization is trying to send the message that Jones is the one player who will take the Falcons to the Super Bowl. By the time Dimitroff finishes his interviews, Jones has arrived at Falcons headquarters in Flowery Branch.

One hour before they will go into their draft room for the beginning of the second round, Dimitroff, Blank, and Smith are on a dais with the newest Falcon, the enthusiastic and personable Jones. They have finished a press conference, which Jones handled like a pro, and now it's time to take pictures. There's one with all of them together, one with Blank and Jones, and another with Dimitroff, at five-nine, with the six-two Jones. Showing that he's read up on the team, Jones looks at the camera and also manages to say, through a smile, to Dimitroff, "Come on, boss. Rise up with your height."

The top draft pick already seems comfortable with where he was taken in the draft and all the expectations that come with the selection. And now he's even quoting the key line from the team's marketing campaign? To tease the GM? Not bad.

If it isn't clear just how much the Falcons surrendered on day one to get Jones, the empty seats in the back of the draft room on day two say it all.

Atlanta makes a row of seats available to limited partners, advisers, and some of their friends on draft day. In New England and Kansas City, this would be considered downright treasonous. But no one is here on day two. In fact, limited partner Warrick Dunn was spotted at the airport in the morning, wearing jeans, sandals, a polo, and sunglasses, hustling out of town with his golf clubs in tow. That's what happens when you pick sixth and your next selection is not until number 91. On paper, the eighty-five-selection gap between picks doesn't begin to capture the amount of waiting in the draft room. There is a lot of time to talk, a lot of time to watch, and a lot of time to make other plans. During one lull, team owner Arthur Blank told Dimitroff that he was taking his son to dinner and that he'd be back in a little while.

As he watches the draft unfold, Dimitroff sometimes goes to the phones and dials Kansas City, for no other reason than to gossip with Pioli about what's happening. They're like two buddies who are watching the same movie in different cities, with occasional calls to say, "Did you see that?" There aren't many reasons to do that in round two, although a few Atlanta scouts are surprised that Belichick used his second-round pick on Dowling rather than trade it. A couple scouts had side bets and placed odds on the likelihood of a trade. They were amazed at the ease with which Belichick not only made trades in the current draft but stacked them for later as well. The Patriots did receive calls on the first pick of round two but weren't tempted to move on any offer.

Vital walks around the room with a sheet of paper, keeping personal notes on what teams are doing. Through the fifties, he says he likes what Tampa has done so far, drafting two defensive ends, including

Da'Quan Bowers, the first-round talent who slipped to the second round because of concerns about his knee. He's not sure what Cleveland has in mind for Jabaal Sheard, a defensive end they took at 37. "He's playing with one arm," Vital says. "They drafted him like he's going to come in and start at defensive end for them. Not gonna happen." He says the Raiders took a center at 48, Stefen Wisniewski, whom the Falcons had rated as a fourth- or fifth-rounder. The Chiefs and Patriots had back-to-back picks, at 55 and 56, with the Chiefs getting their likely starting center, Florida State's Rodney Hudson, and the Patriots adding Cal's Shane Vereen, giving them a dimension at running back that they don't have anywhere on the roster: a back with track-star speed.

Of all the players on the board with character issues, with the most extreme examples landing in the undraftable skull-and-crossbones column, Vital shakes his head as if this is a classic example of overthinking.

"Character is not a problem if you have a strong organization," he says. "If you have a soft organization, it's a problem. What happened at your aunt and uncle's house when those bad kids came over? They straightened them out, didn't they? Because they didn't take any junk. But in a soft house, those bad kids will run the house."

Falcons head coach Mike Smith had been laughing and joking with Blank and Dimitroff, but now a TV report has obviously sapped his energy: The NFL lockout, which had been lifted by the federal courts a couple days earlier, is now back on. Team president Rich McKay walks into the room and confirms the report and adds more details. The effect on Smith is obvious. When he entered the facility earlier in the day, he was still allowed to speak to his players, go over film with them, and talk with them extensively about off-season workouts. Now he can't. Smith is essentially checked out for the night. He's a teacher without students. He seems withdrawn.

With sixteen picks to go before the Falcons' selection, Dimitroff leaves the room to watch film with Vital, Les Snead, and Dave Caldwell. They return when they're twelve picks away. Dimitroff provided a clue about what he was thinking earlier when he called to scold Pioli for pick 70, which Kansas City used to take linebacker Justin Houston of Georgia. "You told me you weren't going to pick him," Dimitroff says. "We wanted him." Pioli knows he's halfway joking. If Kansas City hadn't taken the pass-rushing Houston, some other team would have, long before Dimitroff and the Falcons got a chance. There's still lots of waiting. The rows for limited partners and advisers have one person, the son of limited partner Jay Williams. A couple scouts leave the room and return with plates piled with food. The scene seems like a skit for a Scott Pioli roast. It would send him over the edge.

After Kansas City's pick at 70, the Patriots are a couple slots away from back-to-back picks. With the first one, number 73, they add another running back in Stevan Ridley. The eyebrow-raiser came with number 74, Arkansas quarterback Ryan Mallett. The quarter-back's talent alone should have made him a top-fifteen selection. But there are lots of stories about Mallett's character, with lots of whispers about marijuana use, at least, and perhaps other drugs. For the Patriots, Mal-lett was a risk worth taking. To Vital's point, if the house is strong, Mallett will fall in line and be either a backup to Tom Brady or a down-the-road replacement for him. If not, the team will move on.

After the Chiefs take Houston, they continue to work on their defense by selecting Florida State defensive end Allen Bailey. The Patriots are scheduled to pick right after Atlanta, at pick 92, but Belichick gives the Falcons' scouts something else to talk about: He trades the pick, toward the back end of the third round, to the Raiders for a second-rounder in 2012 and a seventh in 2011. "How does he do it?" one of the scouts says with a laugh. It's finally time for the Falcons to help their team, and they're looking for a thumper at linebacker who can also help them on special teams. The man they have in mind is another linebacker from Georgia, Akeem Dent. Once again, they have ESPN and the NFL Network on, and once again they have the volume turned up to Gruden, who is talking about their pick.

"The only question," Gruden says, "is can he play on third down?"

"We don't give a shit!" Dimitroff says back to the TV.

The draft room bursts into laughter.

They're done for the night, with their one pick, so they're now focused on eating chicken wings and chips and watching two TVs. One of them is tuned in to the Memphis Grizzlies and San Antonio Spurs in an NBA play-off game. The other one still has the NFL Network, where they get even more entertainment from Charles Davis.

"If Bill Belichick had made that Julio Jones trade, we'd all be saying, 'Look how brilliant that is,'" the analyst says. "But it's Thomas Dimitroff. Look, he's a two-time executive of the year. He knows what he's doing."

They all applaud and go wild. Then, as if on cue, one of them says, "Okay. Now for the rest of the story: Charles Davis is the analyst for our preseason games."

It's time for more laughs. It's approaching midnight and anything and everything seems funny now. The only person who, noticeably, isn't enjoying himself is Smith. He sits and talks for a while and then leaves before anyone else, still bummed about the lockout. After a full day of interviews in which he found himself playing defense, a press conference, some phone time with Pioli, and a marathon wait between picks—about twenty-seven hours in real time—Dimitroff heads home. He can't even say, "This is my plan for tomorrow . . . ," because it is tomorrow. His wife and son have left town for the week because they know how chaotic the draft can be. By the time Dimitroff mentally replays the day and finally clears his head, it'll be close to starting time for round three.

One of the biggest differences between fans and executives going into the final day of the draft is that the executives still see a draft board filled with good players. The fans, naturally, are drawn to the early rounds. But there are fewer and fewer familiar names in rounds four through seven, and although the impact players are there on occasion, you've got to dig to find them.

On a sunny Saturday morning in Kansas City, Scott Pioli looks forward to the challenge. The general manager is wearing a blue dress shirt, brown slacks, and a light-colored blazer.

"Does this match?" he says with a laugh.

He's on his way to his office and then to a place that he pointedly calls the draft room for round four. He's always been bothered by the common and casual use of "war room" to describe what's happening among pro football personnel types. He won't acknowledge the term if one of his scouts uses it. "This is our livelihood, but it's not war," he says. "When I call a kid and his parents, I'm usually calling with good news. When parents of soldiers get phone calls, it's usually not a call they want to take. I just don't like the analogy."

Before the league officially starts the clock, Pioli will have a pep talk for everyone in the room. He didn't think the names were pulled off the board quickly enough the day before and thought the overall operation was a step behind, so he wants to make sure everyone is fresh and motivated to finish the draft strong.

He still sees several good players on the board, and he wants to make sure he's got a clear head and an in-tune room when the Chiefs are in position to get them.

"He is like a fish in water in the draft room," Clark Hunt says. "That's his element. And not that he's better at calling other teams and making trades than anybody else, but he's very thoughtful and very analytical about how he's doing that. He has the whole thing in his head, and therefore, when we're talking about X, Y, Z player in the fourth round, it's not some isolated, 'Okay, this is the best available player and we're just going to have to do this.' There's a master plan that's associated with that player and where he'll fit in the team. You actually look out over the next four or five years. So, I think he's the best at that."

Maybe Pioli gave the speech before the start of round four because he knew how busy he'd be today. There is no time for a warm-up or a throat-clearing. As soon as everyone sits down, the Chiefs' phones are quickly ringing, and one of the first calls is from in state. The Rams are on the phone, looking to offer their fourth-rounder, 112, for two Chiefs picks, 118 and 223. Pioli is thinking of rejecting the offer, but he wants to wait a minute before definitely saying no. He wonders if it's really worth it to go up six spots here when he's confident he can get the player he wants anyway.

He turns down the Saint Louis deal, and the Rams, with new offensive coordinator Josh McDaniels, pick up a weapon with Hawaii receiver Greg Salas. The Chiefs use 118 on Colorado cornerback Jalil Brown, a team captain, always a plus for Pioli.

Chiefs assistant head coach Mo Carthon is in the draft room. He's an old-school, no-nonsense coach who played for and coached with Bill Parcells and Bill Belichick with the Giants, Jets, and Patriots. Carthon's son, Ran, is a pro scout with the Falcons and often draws laughs by imitating his father's phrases. "And the way he is with other people," Ran says, "his older brother is like that with him. It's hilarious." Carthon tries calling a number that he thinks is Brown's and doesn't reach him. He finds him on an alternate number. Carthon gets on the phone and says, "Jalil, what's going on? What's up with this number I have for you? You ready to be a KC Chief or what?"

Haley and Hunt follow Carthon to the phone, and after they hang up, Haley turns to Pioli.

"I'm excited about this guy," Haley says.

"Oh, yeah," Pioli replies. "He's got a chance to be a good player."

If he plays as well as Pioli and Haley think, Brown will be another reliable player in a secondary that has added Eric Berry, Javier Arenas, and Kendrick Lewis in the last year. The unit also has one of the top corners in the league in Brandon Flowers.

The Chiefs are now looking to deal up. It never hurts to have good passers in an increasingly pass-happy league, and the Chiefs want Iowa quarterback Ricky Stanzi, but their next pick is not until 135. That's a ways off, and who knows what Buffalo is going to do quarterback-wise at 133? The Chiefs want to move up into the 120s, so they call Baltimore and Ozzie Newsome, sitting at 123. They offer 135 and one of the two seventh-rounders they have in 2012. Newsome says he'll think about it, and he calls back with a counter. Pioli repeats

514 · WAR ROOM

what he says out loud so someone can write it down: "Instead of the seventh this year . . . they'd like our fifth next year . . ." Pioli is shaking his head no as he's talking but still tells Newsome that he'll call him back.

He calls back in ninety seconds.

"Hey, Oz," he says. "We're gonna pass."

They thought they had a deal done with Houston, picking at 127. Pioli even called to New York and told the Chiefs' man on the scene, "Write this name down: Ricky Stanzi, Iowa." But when they called back to confirm while Houston was on the clock, the Texans bailed and picked Virginia Tech corner Rashad Carmichael.

"Can you tear up that card?" Pioli says to the guys in New York. "Well, can you keep it hidden?"

This is all great news for scout Jim Nagy, who saw his guy Rodney Hudson picked yesterday and has been campaigning for Stanzi all year. No, the Chiefs haven't been able to swing a deal to get him, but he's inching closer to them naturally. The Colts call and offer next year's fourth for 135. Pioli doesn't like it. "Too many good players left on this board," he says. The calls keep coming. This time it's Dallas: They want 135 and are willing to give up 143 and 176. But the Chiefs can see Stanzi approaching, and as long as Buffalo doesn't take him, they should have their guy.

The Bills take running back Johnny White from North Carolina.

Nagy beams as he pulls the name off the board.

At pick 138, two selections before the Chiefs are scheduled to be on the clock again, the Patriots pull off a stunner. They take the most talented tackle on the board, by far, in six-foot-five-inch, 360-pound Marcus Cannon from Texas Christian University. Cannon is on the board because a couple months earlier, at the scouting Combine, doctors discovered that he had non-Hodgkin's lymphoma. Before the diagnosis, he was expected to be taken long before the fifth. Belichick checked with the Patriots' doctors and was told that he shouldn't be afraid of the diagnosis. Besides, Belichick, a Red Sox fan, didn't have to look very far for an example of a pro athlete who had beaten cancer: Jon Lester, an All-Star pitcher, found out he had cancer in 2006 and won the deciding game of the World Series in 2007.

At pick 140, the Chiefs grab another of Nagy's guys, Oregon State linebacker Gabe Miller. Miller is raw, having played tight end for part of his career. Nagy got nervous when Miller went through his individual workout and turned in a phenomenal performance. It was so good that it was something the scouts talked about around the office. When Miller visited Kansas

City, he noticed a *Total Hockey* book on the desk of Haley, a Western Pennsylvanian who is partial to the Pittsburgh Penguins. Miller is a hockey fan, too, and he and Haley connected with inside hockey talk.

"You ready to come out here and talk some hockey?" Haley says as he welcomes Miller to the NFL. "That's what did it, Gabe. Your hockey background."

Phil Emery doesn't crack a smile with the announcement of pick 145, but he easily could. His old team, the Falcons, took running back Jacquizz Rodgers, who is listed at five feet six inches. Rodgers was one of the running backs Emery had in mind when he had the animated discussion with two other scouts during the Chiefs' draft meetings in February. Dimitroff was going to find out if he had a true change-of-pace back to complement big Michael Turner or if he had someone who could help Parcells retell one of his favorite draft jokes. Whenever a team took multiple undersized guys, Parcells would quip, "You can fit your entire draft class in a VW."

As the draft moves on, the Hunts break to the cafeteria for Chinese food that has been especially catered for the draft. They see coaches Romeo Crennel and Anthony Pleasant, speaking with one of yesterday's third-rounders, Justin Houston, the linebacker from Georgia. Clark introduces himself and says he looks forward to seeing Houston play.

"And I'm going to make sure I give you a reason to notice me on the field," Houston says. "I'm excited to play."

Back in the draft room, Pioli is swinging a wooden Louisville Slugger with his name inscribed on it. It's likely a gift from one of his best friends, Mark Shapiro, the president of the Cleveland Indians. The bat is helping him think. He's been fortunate in that he's gotten what he's wanted so far with Brown, Stanzi, and Miller. Now, as he holds his bat, he's thinking about a player who would be a hard-nosed catcher if he played Major League Baseball: Jason Kelce, the center who reminds Pioli of Dan Koppen. He thinks Kelce will be there for the Chiefs in the sixth round, at pick 199.

As Pioli looks at the board and talks with Haley, someone shouts out, "Kelce just went." Pioli stops in midsentence. "Huh? He did? Who took him?" He's told Philadelphia. "I'll have to give them a call in the next couple days," he says. "That's a good pick."

The new target for 199, the same spot the Patriots selected Tom Brady, is nose tackle Jerrell Powe from Ole Miss. Pioli tells someone to call David Price, the team's athletic trainer, so they can get a quick medical report on Powe. Price enters the room a couple minutes later and appears to be winded. "You wanna have a seat?" Pioli cracks. "That trip up the stairs really knocked you out." Pioli and Haley illustrate to the doctor what a nose tackle does with a hand punch, and they want to be assured that Powe doesn't have any medical concerns that would prevent him from doing that. They are satisfied that Powe checks out and then wait to see if he falls to them.

Powe was so popular on the Ole Miss campus and in town that he was called the mayor there. Pioli often became incensed when scouts dismissed a player as a character problem or not bright without first doing the research. The Chiefs' scouts were thorough in their breakdown of Powe, who at times struggled in the classroom because of attention deficit disorder. The Chiefs found that he was a determined student, despite the disorder, and had the respect of everyone around him because of the way he competed in the classroom.

When the Chiefs draft Powe, they tell him they want him to compete against something else: calories.

"Keep yourself in shape," Haley warns him. "You can eat yourself out of the league before you ever get into it. It's easy to gain weight, Jerrell. It's hard to lose it. Let's get you up here playing some real football. Away from all those spread offenses where all the linemen are moving sideways."

Pioli is heading toward the end of his day. There is still a seventh-round selection for the Chiefs, and the

GM consults with Haley and Carthon. He asks Carthon what fullback he liked most and he says it's Shane Bannon of Yale.

The day has gone smoothly, perfectly even. But two minutes before going on the clock in the seventh, the phones go dead.

"We're sorry, all circuits are busy . . ." is all they hear.

Emily Claver, Pioli's administrative assistant, walks into the room and notices the stressed faces. She looks at the phones, which are all tested and programmed by the league, and says, "Let's see. I'll try the line that's marked 'Backup Line' and see what happens."

She presses the button that is clearly marked, yet no one had seen it. It's a perfect connection. They all stare. Claver smiles and goes back to her office. Silly boys.

"You have a name yet?" asks the Chiefs' man in New York.

"Yeah, relax," Pioli says, and the room laughs.

It's the end of the day, and you can tell they all believe it's been a good one. They have spent months at this, scouting and debating and paring the prospects. Now, even if it's just for a couple hours, they can exhale. They're even in the mood to annoy Pioli. He had mentioned earlier in the day that certain songs bother him because they have the ability to crawl into your head and not go away. So when he left the room, Joel Collier, the assistant general manager, finds a live version of one of the songs Pioli was referring to, "Celebration" by Kool & The Gang. When Pioli reenters five minutes later, the song is playing. Five minutes after that, he's whistling it.

Some of the scouts ask what others are doing for dinner, and some set up trips to the airport in the morning. After Pioli changes from his business attire and digests the day, he heads home to see his wife and daughter. Well after his daughter has gone to bed, he goes to his laptop and calls up a *Kansas City Star* story that insinuates that Powe is a character problem. He's more hurt for Powe than he is angry, knowing that it's one of those generalizations that he'd never let his scouts get away with.

On Sunday morning, with the three-day draft flurry over, it's back to the normal thoughts. It's back to plotting and scouting and scheming against thirty-one other teams in the league, who have the same salary cap and restrictions that you do. Two of those thirty-one decision-makers happen to be two of your best friends. You know how they think, you know how adaptable they are, you know their families, and you love them. Genuinely love them.

But in this business, at some point, your love is forced to be conditional. You want to root for your friends to reach the very top of their profession, but if that happens, it means you haven't done it. Once upon a time, in Cleveland and New England, it wasn't an issue. They were all on the same team then. Now they all support one another and try to win championships independent of one another.

Who knows where it will go from here? Maybe one January Pioli's Chiefs and Belichick's Patriots can meet in the conference championship game, with the winner taking the Lamar Hunt trophy and earning the right to play Dimitroff's Falcons in the Super Bowl.

That's just part of the story, though. The other part is seeing what can happen when an idea is expanded and permitted to grow. It was the idea of creating a way of doing things that drew Belichick to Cleveland, and then Pioli after him, and then Dimitroff after that. They didn't know that a mature idea would take them on a ride through NFL history, winning game after game, week after week, and compiling titles. They built many teams, some better than others, three of them the absolute best, and one of them nearly perfect. They built a lifelong bond, too, one that transcends the rings and trophies that they've spent their lives working for.

Epilogue

On July 22, two days before the end of the NFL's four-and-a-half-month lockout, dozens of people on both sides of the multibillion-dollar dispute arrived in Newton, Massachusetts. It was one of the hottest days in the history of the Boston area, with the temperature in some parts of the region climbing to 103 degrees. It was one of the rare lockout days when everyone was humbled, and talking heads were replaced by bowed ones.

It seemed as if the entire league, accompanied by an incredible cross-section of celebrities, was in town to honor the life of Myra Hiatt Kraft, wife of Patriots owner Robert Kraft. On July 20, Myra, who had been married to Robert for forty-eight years, died of cancer. She was sixty-eight years old. The daughter of a local philanthropist, Myra was the conscience of the Patriots and one of the most beloved figures in New England.

Her funeral service proved that she was capable of bringing people together, side by side in some cases, and smoothing over any perceived gaps between them. On one side of Temple Emanuel, NFL commissioner Roger Goodell sat near his negotiating adversary, DeMaurice Smith, the executive director of the NFL Players Association. In another section of the temple, many players who had left New England with sour tastes in their mouths, such as Richard Seymour, Drew Bledsoe, and Willie McGinest, returned to pay their respects and were often nearby Bill Belichick, the man who either traded them or allowed them to leave as free agents. Local politicians, including the mayor of Boston and the governor of Massachusetts, were among the mourners as well as those known for being critical of politicians, such as syndicated radio host Rush Limbaugh and real estate giant Donald Trump.

Long before the lockout was nearing its conclusion, Robert Kraft had been praised behind the scenes, by both sides, for his determination to get a deal done. Those working closely with him knew what was happening in his personal life, how he would negotiate with purpose and passion but sometimes leave sessions early so he could spend time with his wife. He had the respect of Smith, who felt that Kraft was much more interested in arriving at a deal than walking away with a "win." Most people with knowledge of the proposed collective bargaining agreement's details credited Kraft with engineering a proposal that would preserve the 2011 season and give the league ten years of labor peace.

As important as the end of the lockout was to fans, players, owners, and anyone associated with the game, the details seemed inconsequential now as Kraft walked down the center aisle of the temple, escorted by his four sons, his daughters-in-law, and his grandchildren. His gait was slightly unsteady, and his face was ashen. Years earlier, in a Boston café, he had caught the attention of his future wife by winking at her, a spark in his eyes. She had seen that playful and knowing wink many times in the subsequent years as her husband made savvy business deals, including a multifaceted one, almost two decades earlier, that eventually landed him the Patriots in 1994. But as he walked down the aisle, trailing his wife's coffin, his eyes were glazed and sad; he was clearly heartbroken. His family spoke eloquently about the sense of social justice that Myra brought to her family and everyone who met her. Jonathan, the eldest son and Patriots team president, recalled carrying his mother, a petite woman, away from trouble in South Africa in the early 1980s because she was loudly questioning a police officer on the practice of apartheid. "My mother," Jonathan said during his tribute, "she lived her life looking at the world through empathetic eyes."

After the emotional service, it was hard to imagine either side being in the mood to negotiate as intensely as they had over the previous 129 days. After a weekend of looking over what Kraft and his fellow owners had proposed, Smith and the players officially agreed to the deal on Monday, July 25. What it meant was that teams would soon be able to welcome back their players under contract and make bids for those who weren't. The Patriots, Chiefs, and Falcons all had surprising forays into the trade and free-agent markets.

The Patriots drew the most attention, causing eyes to bulge and jaws to drop, with a couple of transactions. They traded for Washington Redskins defensive tackle Albert Haynesworth, known throughout football for being highly paid (he made $35 million in twenty games with the Redskins), high risk (he had a sexual assault case hovering as this book went to print), and often underachieving. When playing to his potential, Haynesworth was considered an All-Pro talent, but second-year Washington head coach Mike Shanahan was so eager to get the defensive lineman out of the organization that the price tag for the Patriots was just a fifth-round pick in 2013.

Belichick could see the obvious risks in acquiring the player, but he also weighed the substantial payoff of getting an in-shape and focused Haynesworth. The 335-pound lineman arrived in town during a time of transition for the Patriots defense. Belichick always preferred a defense, whether with a four- or three-man line, with two-gapping principles. In essence, it was a disciplined defense that required interior linemen to stay square at the point of attack and control the gaps on either side of them. The new approach in Foxboro allowed the interior linemen to attack and go upfield. Belichick always wanted his system to be adaptable to the times, and the new defensive approach appeared to be the antidote to the Patriots' third-down defense in 2010, which was ranked near the bottom of the league.

On the other side of the ball, the Patriots added a veteran receiver who entered the 2011 season with 751 career receptions, the twenty-eighth best number in league history. The cost of acquiring him was also low, fifth- and sixth-round picks. Those were the black-and-white details of the acquisition; the full-color story came with the name of the player: Chad Ochocinco (né Johnson), who had gained popularity more for his entertaining antics, such as racing a horse and riding a bull, than his play on the field. In other words, he was known for things that the Patriots usually frowned on. Ochocinco seemed to accept that he would have to conform to what was perceived to be the Patriot Way, which was bad news for his millions of Twitter followers; they could no longer expect to receive updates that would even hint at anything insightful during practice, in the locker room, or in the meeting rooms. Belichick may have intentionally mispronounced Twitter when asked about the social media platform by reporters, but he knew the power of it, and he made a point of telling players to be cautious, and preferably bland, when communicating with the public.

The Chiefs and Falcons didn't acquire controversial players, nor did they tweak their systems. What they did was spend money. A lot of it. The Chiefs began free agency by signing former Arizona Cardinal Steve Breaston, a good complementary receiver who Chiefs head coach Todd Haley knew from his days as the Cardinals' offensive coordinator. Breaston got $9 million in guaranteed money, or $26 million less than Chiefs linebacker Tamba Hali, a gifted pass rusher. The Hali deal assured the Chiefs of having two of their defensive anchors, Hali and safety Eric Berry, locked into long-term deals through the middle of the decade.

In Atlanta, Thomas Dimitroff was able to find a pass rusher. Former Vikings defensive end Ray Edwards was signed to a deal that called for $11 million in guarantees. In Minnesota, Edwards didn't always believe that former head coach Brad Childress treated his players like men; in Atlanta, he was almost assured of finding the opposite in the straightforward and fair Mike Smith. Under Dimitroff and Smith, the Falcons had run a 4-3 defense since 2008. It meant that they didn't usually find themselves looking for the same defensive players as the Patriots. But when free agency began and they found themselves discussing adding Edwards, apparently he had also gotten the attention of New England. Ultimately, the Patriots decided that he wasn't a match for them, and the Falcons were in position to happily sign him to a contract.

Despite the chaos of the lengthy lockout, each team went into the 2011 season believing that it was better than the year before, when all three won their divisions and two were top seeds. Each team had begun to take on distinct identities that were respectful yet different from one another.

The Patriots, the philosophical home base for the other two, seemed to be the most in transition. They were going to install that new defense, and they were going to do it with Belichick once again as the unofficial defensive coordinator. There was also the guesswork of the locker room, with the same question being asked week to week: Is this Patriot leadership group strong enough to straighten out a guy like Haynesworth, as previous groups were able to deal with Corey Dillon and Randy Moss?

The Falcons entered the season with a quiet confidence. Whereas Scott Pioli believed that the Chiefs needed to fortify several positions between 2010 and 2011, Dimitroff thought the Falcons needed to add some subtle pieces and get over some psychological hurdles (like finally beating a team like the Philadelphia Eagles). Dimitroff and Pioli, ironically, were still mindful of their Patriots training when it came to acquiring players, so they weren't necessarily above acquiring high-risk players, just cautious of it, but they did not believe Haynesworth or Ochocinco, the former a high-risk player and the latter a high-attention one, were good fits for their locker rooms.

The major differences between the Falcons and Chiefs were defensive schemes, 4-3 vs. 3-4, and the collective maturity of the roster. The Patriots were different from the other two simply because of the three Super Bowl titles, which gave Belichick much more confidence, not to mention latitude with the public, to try unconventional things. Ultimately, though, the three team leaders, birthed from the same system, had one goal in common, a goal not achieved since February 2005: to stand on a podium holding the Lombardi Trophy.

Acknowledgments

As far back as 2004, when my first book was pub-lished, I've thought of writing about the process of team-building and drafting. There was a chapter in that book, *Patriot Reign,* that touched on the process, but it's always gnawed at me for that reason: It *touched* on the process. There are several steps that scouts and evaluators go through before they think of which names to call on draft day, and I wanted to explore that jour-ney more thoroughly.

In a sense, I think many of us do. The popularity of the NFL draft and fantasy football has made ama-teur team-builders of us all, leading to as much sec-ond-guessing for the people who put teams together as those who play in the games. I'm not ashamed to admit that analyzing how teams are built has been a nerdy obsession of mine for as long as I can remember. A couple years ago, I had the thought of "doing something" on the draft with the New England Patriots as the centerpiece. What you're holding today is possible thanks to dozens of people who helped me bring that undefined thought into focus.

It was quite a blessing to be able to focus at all. In the early stages of reporting and researching, there was a surprising phone call from my wife, Oni. She was a few months pregnant and had gone for what we expected to be a routine appointment. Instead, she was told that she was being placed on immediate bed rest. It was a frightening time, although neither of us admitted just how frightened we were until after our son was born in December 2010, one month early but with no complications. I don't know how she was able to do it, but Oni made everything seem normal while being a constant supporter of this project. I often told my editor, Mauro DiPreta, that my wife was just as exacting as he was when it came to staying on a writing schedule. There are many reasons it's been a privilege to live in New England the last seventeen years, but number one is that this is the region where I met Oni, an incredible mother, my inspiration, and my best friend.

My literary family, agent Basil Kane and editor DiPreta, went to another level in the last couple years.

I've always had good professional relationships with both of them, but we've grown to the point where we're friends and the titles are secondary. Kane is always there with fatherly advice ("Make sure you stay in shape . . . and hug the kids for me"), and DiPreta has the rare ability to be brutally honest and critical while also encouraging. I'm lucky to have them both on my side. Thanks also to Aja Pollock and Jen Schulkind, who saved me more times than I can count.

There would be no book if the three principal characters, Bill Belichick, Thomas Dimitroff, and Scott Pioli, weren't so secure. It's uncommon in the increasingly spin-conscious world of pro sports to allow an author access without receiving some assurances in return. All three agreed to share insights about their organizations and themselves without ever asking to be in control of, or asking to see, what was written. They were generous enough to endure my lurking as well as my questions and requests for more than a year, although I may have gone too far when I peppered Pioli with questions a couple days before day one of the draft. "Do you realize I have a draft to get ready for?" he said. "When I get fired, maybe you'll be kind enough to let my family live in your attic." Teasing aside, all three men provided quite an education on my favorite sport, and I'm thankful for that.

The teams for which they work were extremely helpful, too. Arthur Blank and Clark Hunt were accommodating and generous with their time. Robert Kraft and his entire family have maintained the same level of professionalism over the years. I've attended many games in Foxboro, Massachusetts, and seen the passion of Patriots fans. It was fun to witness a similar level of devotion in Kansas City at Arrowhead Stadium and in Atlanta at the Georgia Dome. The achievements of Belichick, Dimitroff, and Pioli wouldn't be as meaningful without their observant and critical fans.

Each organization has several people in it, or affiliated with it, who contributed to this project and helped me connect some loose ends. I'd rather not put them all in a cluster, so I'll break them down region by region:

Atlanta: Helen Dimitroff, Angeline Bautista-Dimitroff, Stephanie Blank, Kim Schreckengost, Mike Smith, Lionel Vital, Reggie Roberts, Laura Moore, Les Snead, Darryl Orlando Ledbetter, DeJuan Polk, Ran Carthon, Nick Polk, Dave Caldwell, Marvin Allen, Steve Sabo, Dean Stamoulis, Brian Cearns.

Kansas City: Dallas Pioli, Emily Claver, Daniel Hunt, Ryan Petkoff, Todd Haley, Phil Emery, Jay Muraco, Romeo Crennel, Anthony Pleasant, Otis

Smith, Maurice Carthon, Jim Nagy, Joel Collier, Brad Gee, Pam Kramer, Joe Posnanski, Pete Moris, Field Yates, Ralph Marchant, Tripp MacCracken.

New England: Berj Najarian, Stacey James, Tedy Bruschi, Troy Brown, Vince Wilfork, Bianca Wilfork, Rosevelt Colvin, Ellis Hobbs, Josh McDaniels, Eric Mangini, Lenny Clarke.

Special thanks also to Ted Crews of the Saint Louis Rams, who went far above and beyond the call of duty to set up an interview with head coach Steve Spagnuolo. Roland Williams, who was a member of the Raiders when they lost the Tuck Rule game to the Patriots in 2002, was kind enough to recall each key moment of the game, even though it still bothers him to this day. Mike Lombardi, Belichick's director of player personnel in Cleveland, answered numerous questions about the conception and development of the draft system the Patriots, Chiefs, and Falcons use today. Neil Swidey, a terrific author, encouraged me even as he was at work on his own book. He sent frequent texts, sometimes to help me out of ruts and sometimes just to say hello. My bosses and colleagues at WEEI radio have been positive and helpful, from telling me to write more books (easier said than done, right?) to giving me the time to complete these projects. Alice Darling Secretarial Services in Cambridge, Massachusetts, put me at ease with flawless transcription work.

As usual, my extended family was supportive and understanding when I disappeared for long stretches of time as I tried to complete this book. Thanks and love to the Holley, Soberanis, Igartua-Preston, Johnson, Shakur, Robinson, Green, Cravanas, and Sales families.